P9-DEQ-909

THE
GREAT DEPRESSION

THE
GREAT DEPRESSION

Edited by

DAVID A. SHANNON

Associate Professor of History
University of Wisconsin

A SPECTRUM BOOK

PRENTICE-HALL, INC.

©—1960, by
PRENTICE-HALL, INC.
Englewood Cliffs, N. J.

ALL RIGHTS RESERVED. NO PART OF THIS BOOK
MAY BE REPRODUCED IN ANY FORM, BY
MIMEOGRAPH OR ANY OTHER MEANS, WITH-
OUT PERMISSION IN WRITING FROM THE
PUBLISHERS.

Library of Congress
Catalog Card No.: 60-8764

First printing ...... February, 1960
Second printing ...... August, 1960

PRINTED IN THE UNITED STATES OF AMERICA
36352-C

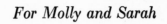

For Molly and Sarah

Introduction

The subject of this book is the impact of the Great Depression of 1929 and thereafter upon the American people. It does not concentrate upon economics, nor politics, nor social and intellectual matters, although there is something here of all these. Its emphasis is the effects of the depression upon its victims, and much of the material allows the reader to see the events of the 1930's through the eyes of these victims.

As a psychologist might put it, the Great Depression was a traumatic experience. It was all the more traumatic because the immediately preceding years had been quite comfortable ones on the whole and the American mood had been unusually optimistic. During the 1920's business and political leaders spoke of the New Era. The map to the New Eldorado had been found, they said with smug satisfaction. An ever-expanding economy, full employment, and the elimination of poverty were permanent features, many believed, of the New Era. Everyone could be rich. One had only to save his money and invest it in stocks of the industrial corporations that were transforming American society.

Some segments of the population did not share in the prosperity of the 1920's. Most farmers had a difficult time after 1920, as did workers in some industries, such as coal and textiles. And many of the nation's intellectuals, who were generally prosperous enough in their Bohemian quarters in Greenwich Village or the Left Bank of Paris, criticized American civilization as shallow and commercial. But the farmers, the coal miners, the textile mill hands, and even the intellectuals failed to alter the general spirit of optimism, complacency, and comfort. The "best people" believed in the munificence of the New Era.

And then came the crash of October 1929. Optimism faded quickly. The spokesmen of the New Era issued reassuring public statements, but to most people the statements had a hollow tone. The Wall Street panic triggered a general economic collapse. Within only a few months unemployment became a serious problem. Forlorn, down-and-out men shuffled hopelessly through bread lines. Banks began to fail at an alarming rate. Farm prices dropped to disastrous lows. City after city became unable to cope with its relief problems.

The most disheartening aspect of the early depression was that there was no sign of a recovery. Earlier depressions had spent their force in a few months, the direction of the economy had reversed itself, and there had been a slow climb back to normal conditions. But in the Great Depression things became steadily worse for three and one-half years.

In 1931 and 1932 talk of social revolution became common. Surely, thought thousands of people, the dispossessed and the hungry will revolt against the government and the economic system that had brought them to their desperate situation. But no revolution came. At least, there was no revolution such as many anticipated, with rioting, blood in the gutters, and violent overthrow of government. Instead, a majority of the electorate switched its allegiance from the party of Herbert Hoover to the party of Franklin Delano Roosevelt.

Roosevelt and his party succeeded in partially alleviating the personal distress of the Great Depression and in effecting a partial economic recovery. But after a little more than four years of New Deal there came another downward movement of the business cycle, the "recession," or the "depression within a depression." About mid-1938 the economy began to improve again, but the Great Depression remained. Not until 1940, after the outbreak of war in Europe, did the physical volume of American industrial production equal the record of 1929, and even in 1940 about seven and one-half million workers were unemployed, roughly fourteen per cent of the civilian labor force. The Great Depression actually did not end until defense spending and war stimulated the economy in 1941.

For about twelve years, then, the American people suffered from the Great Depression. Such an experience inevitably wrought many changes in American society—in politics, in economics, in social values, in formal culture. An historian may legitimately focus on any of these aspects. I have chosen to put the emphasis of this book upon what might be called the human terms of the depression, upon how the Great Depression affected individuals and families, because an appreciation of the hardships suffered is basic to an understanding of any other aspect of the period.

There is now a whole generation that has no personal memory of the Great Depression whatsoever. Many people old enough to have lived through the 1930's remember some features of the period only dimly because of man's fortunate tendency to blur his image of long-past unpleasantness. Yet even those who were unborn during the depression have been affected by it in a myriad of ways, some of them obvious and direct, others of them indirect and subtle. The present is only the cutting edge of the recent past, and if one would understand the United States today he must know the Great Depression.

David A. Shannon

Contents

IV   NOMADS OF THE DEPRESSION | 55

V   THE MIDDLE CLASSES: BANK FAILURES
AND UNEMPLOYMENT | 72

THE
GREAT DEPRESSION

I

CRASH!

IF EVER ONE DAY was a watershed in American history it was "Black Thursday," October 24, 1929, when the bottom dropped out of the stock market. That afternoon a group of New York bankers succeeded in temporarily halting the plunge, but five days later Wall Street was in a panic again. Thereafter the prices of stocks and bonds, ironically called "securities," skidded downward almost steadily for three and one-half years.

The Wall Street debacle directly and immediately affected only a relatively small part of the American population, but a new and dismal era had begun. Despite the assurances—or incantations—of business and political leaders that the stock market crash did not reflect upon the health of the economy in general, it was not long before almost every indicator of the nation's economic welfare showed trouble. Unemployment among workers dependent upon wages for their own and their families' livelihood, perhaps the most serious and difficult problem of all the Great Depression's numerous headaches, began soon to increase alarmingly.

After several months of depression America was indeed a place turned topsy-turvy. Even the surface appearances of the cities changed. Former bond salesman were on the sidewalks trying to sell apples. Former clerks roamed the business districts in an attempt to make a living by shining shoes. Unemployed and homeless men welcomed arrests for vagrancy and the warmth and food to be had in jail. Over a hundred thousand American workers applied for jobs in the Soviet Union. Shanty towns appeared in and around the industrial cities, and the inhabitants of these housing developments born of desperation bitterly named them for the President of the United States.

The following selections, most of them from contemporary newspapers, illustrate the confusion and some of the desperation of the times.

1

1 · BLACK THURSDAY

From The New York Times, *October 25, 1929*

WORST STOCK CRASH STEMMED BY BANKS

12,894,650-SHARE DAY SWAMPS MARKET
LEADERS CONFER, FIND CONDITIONS SOUND

THE MOST DISASTROUS DECLINE in the biggest and broadest stock market of history rocked the financial district yesterday. In the very midst of the collapse five of the country's most influential bankers hurried to the office of J. P. Morgan & Co., and after a brief conference gave out word that they believe the foundations of the market to be sound, that the market smash has been caused by technical rather than fundamental considerations, and that many sound stocks are selling too low.

Suddenly the market turned about on buying orders thrown into the pivotal issues, and before the final quotations were tapped out, four hours and eight minutes after the 3 o'clock bell, most stocks had regained a measurable part of their losses.

The break was one of the widest in the market's history, although the losses at the close were not particularly large, many having been recouped by the afternoon rally.

It carried down with it speculators, big and little, in every part of the country, wiping out thousands of accounts. It is probable that if the stockholders of the country's foremost corporations had not been calmed by the attitude of leading bankers and the subsequent rally, the business of the country would have been seriously affected. Doubtless business will feel the effects of the drastic stock shake-out, and this is expected to hit the luxuries most severely. . . .

The total losses cannot be accurately calculated, because of the large number of markets and the thousands of securities not listed on any exchange. However, they were staggering, running into billions of dollars. Fear struck the big speculators and little ones, big investors and little ones. Thousands of them threw their holdings into the whirling Stock Exchange pit for what they would bring. Losses were tremendous and thousands of prosperous brokerage and bank accounts, sound and healthy a week ago, were completely wrecked in the strange debacle, due to a combination of circumstances, but accelerated into a crash by fear. . . .

Under these circumstances of late tickers and spreads of 10, 20, and at times 30 points between the tape prices and those on the floor of the Exchange, the entire financial district was thrown into hopeless confusion and excitement. Wild-eyed speculators crowded the brokerage offices, awed by the disaster which had overtaken many of them. They followed the market literally "in the dark," getting but meager reports via the financial news tickers which printed the Exchange floor prices at ten-minute intervals.

Rumors, most of them wild and false, spread throughout the Wall Street district and thence throughout the country. One of the reports was that eleven speculators had committed suicide. A peaceful workman atop a Wall Street building looked down and saw a big crowd watching him, for the rumor had spread that he was going to jump off. Reports that the Chicago and Buffalo Exchanges had closed spread throughout the district, as did rumors that the New York Stock Exchange and the New York Curb Exchange were going to suspend trading. These rumors and reports were all found, on investigation, to be untrue. . . .

FINANCIERS EASE TENSION

Wall Street gave credit yesterday to its banking leaders for arresting the decline on the New York Stock Exchange at a time when the stock market was being overwhelmed by selling orders. The conference at which the steps were taken that reversed the market's trend was hurriedly called at the offices of J. P. Morgan & Co.

The five bankers who met at the headquarters of the famous banking house at noon yesterday and again at 4:30 P.M., following the meeting of the board of the Federal Reserve Bank of New York were:

CHARLES E. MITCHELL, chairman of the National City Bank.
ALBERT H. WIGGIN, chairman of the Chase National Bank.
WILLIAM POTTER, president of the Guaranty Trust Company.
SEWARD PROSSER, chairman of the Bankers Trust Company.
THOMAS W. LAMONT, senior partner of the Morgan firm.

Exclusive of the vast wealth of the house of Morgan this group of bankers represented more than $6,000,000,000 of massed banking resources. . . .

"There has been a little distress selling on the Stock Exchange," Mr. Lamont said, "and we have held a meeting of the heads of several financial institutions to discuss the situation.

"We have found that there are no houses in difficulty and reports from brokers indicate that margins are being maintained satisfactorily." . . .

"It is the consensus of the group," he said, "that many of the quotations on the Stock Exchange do not fairly represent the situation." . . .

The Stock Exchange firm of Merrill, Lynch & Co., in a message advising customers to keep accounts well margined without waiting for a direct request, said that investors "with available funds should take advantage of this break to buy good securities."

Other houses sent similar messages to their customers.

2 · TRAGIC TUESDAY

From The New York Times, *October 30, 1929.*

STOCKS COLLAPSE IN 16,410,030-SHARE DAY, BUT RALLY AT CLOSE CHEERS BROKERS

BANKERS OPTIMISTIC, TO CONTINUE AID

STOCK PRICES VIRTUALLY COLLAPSED yesterday, swept downward with gigantic losses in the most disastrous trading day in the stock market's history. Billions of dollars in open market values were wiped out as prices crumbled under the pressure of liquidation of securities which had to be sold at any price.

There was an impressive rally just at the close, which brought many leading stocks back from 4 to 14 points from their lowest points of the day. . . .

Efforts to estimate yesterday's market losses in dollars are futile because of the vast number of securities quoted over the counter and on out-of-town exchanges on which no calculations are possible. However, it was estimated that 880 issues, on the New York Stock Exchange, lost between $8,000,000,000 and $9,000,000,000 yesterday. Added to that loss is to be reckoned the depreciation on issues on the Curb Market, in the over the counter market and on other exchanges. . . .

Banking support, which would have been impressive and successful under ordinary circumstances, was swept violently aside, as block after block of stock, tremendous in proportions, deluged the market. Bid prices placed by bankers, industrial leaders and brokers trying to halt the decline were crashed through violently, their orders were filled, and quotations plunged downward in a day of disorganization, confusion and financial impotence. . . .

CROWDS AT TICKERS SEE FORTUNES WANE

Groups of men, with here and there a woman, stood about inverted glass bowls all over the city yesterday watching spools of ticker tape unwind and as the tenuous paper with its cryptic numerals grew longer at their feet their fortunes shrunk. Others sat stolidly on tilted chairs in the customers' rooms of brokerage houses and watched a motion picture of waning wealth as the day's quotations moved silently across a screen.

It was among such groups as these, feeling the pulse of a feverish financial world whose heart is the Stock Exchange, that drama and perhaps tragedy were to be found . . . the crowds about the ticker tape, like friends around the bedside of a stricken friend, reflected in their faces the story the tape was telling. There were no smiles. There were no tears either. Just the cameraderie of fellow-sufferers. Everybody wanted to tell his neighbor how much he had lost. Nobody wanted to listen. It was too repetitious a tale. . . .

3 • WHISTLING IN THE DARK

The following account by Broadus Mitchell, a distinguished economic historian, is from Depression Decade: From New Era through New Deal, 1929-1941, (*New York: Rinehart & Co., Inc., 1947*), *pp. 31-32. Reprinted by permission of the author.*

PUBLIC STATEMENTS AT THE NEW YEAR on the business outlook for 1930 damaged more reputations of forecasters than they bolstered. In the midst of the stock market debacle two months earlier, prominent persons whose word was apt to be taken—bankers, industrialists, economists, government officials—had declared their confidence in stocks, not to mention underlying business soundness. At the beginning of the year more perspective might be looked for. The optimism expressed, however, was hardly representative, for most of those with serious misgivings about the future did not offer their opinions or find them published. Secretary of the Treasury Andrew W. Mellon committed himself blithely: "I see nothing . . . in the present situation that is either menacing or warrants pessimism. . . . I have every confidence that there will be a revival of activity in the spring and that during the coming year the country will make steady progress."

The White House reported the President as considering "that business could look forward to the coming year with greater assurance." Willis H. Booth, president of the Merchants' Association of New York, saw "no fundamental reason why business should not find itself again on the upgrade early in 1930."

The Guaranty Trust Company of New York expressed qualified hope: "Although there is no failure to appreciate the importance of the collapse of stock prices as an influence on general business or to ignore the historical fact that such a collapse has almost invariably been followed by a major business recession, emphasis has . . . been placed on certain fundamental differences between the conditions that exist at present and those that have usually been witnessed at similar times in the past." . . .

Secretary of Commerce Robert P. Lamont contented himself with listing the gains that the year 1929 as a whole had registered over 1928, and with predicting prosperity and progress "for the long run." He did not say how long the run was to be.

6 CRASH!

4 · THE COURSE OF UNEMPLOYMENT

An economist in this selection briefly traces the ebb and flow of the unemployment problem from 1929 until 1940. From Paul Webbink, "Unemployment in the United States, 1930-1940," Papers and Proceedings of the American Economic Association, XXX (Feb., 1941), pp. 250-251. Reprinted by permission of the American Economic Association.

WITHIN A FEW MONTHS after the stock market collapse of October, 1929, unemployment had been catapulted from its status of a vague worry to be considered some future day into the position of one of the country's foremost preoccupations. Unemployment increased steadily, with only a few temporary setbacks, from the fall of 1929 to the spring of 1933. Even a cursory reference to the several existing estimates of unemployment will amply show the rapidity with which unemployment established itself as an economic factor of the first order of importance.

For March, 1930, the estimates range from nearly 3,250,000 to more than 4,000,000. A year later these had doubled to between 7,500,000 and almost 8,000,000. By March, 1932, a further increase of roughly 50 per cent had occurred, bringing the estimates to between 11,250,000 and nearly 12,500,000. Then came the peak early in 1933. By March, 1933, according to the independent estimates of Dr. [W. S.] Woytinsky, non-agricultural employment had fallen more than 8,050,000 over the spring of 1930, while the supply of persons who might normally be considered to be seekers of gainful work had during the same time increased by 1,200,000. Adding to these an estimated 1,850,000 "additional" workers brought on the labor market through the unemployment of usual bread-winners, and the approximately 3,200,000 persons whom Woytinsky estimates as already unemployed in April, 1930, a total of 14,300,000 is reached. Other estimates for March, 1933, range from Robert Nathan's 13,577,000 to the National Industrial Conference Board's 14,586,000, the American Federation of Labor's 15,389,000, and more than 16,000,-000 on the part of the Congress of Industrial Organizations.

The spring and summer months of 1933 brought the "NRA boom" and a sudden fall of 3,000,000 or 4,000,000 in the number of unemployed. This still left unemployment at a level of 10,000,000 or 11,000,000 but a gradual diminution occurred during the next four years, and by September, 1936, the volume of unemployment was set by various estimators at between 5,378,000 and 8,145,000. A sharp increase resulted from the renewed depression of the winter 1937-38, reaching, according to Woytinsky, a total somewhat over 9,000,000 in March, 1938, or, according to others, a level of 10,000,000 or 11,000,000. That a decided drop in unemployment has taken place during the subsequent two and a half years is recognized by all of the estimates. . . .

5 • AND THE "LUCKY" WHO KEPT THEIR JOBS

Even the employed had their difficulties with reduced rates of pay and shortened work weeks. This selection by Don D. Lescohier is from the third volume of John R. Commons, History of Labor in the United States, 1896-1932 *(New York: The Macmillan Co., 1935), pp. 92-96. Reprinted by permission of the publishers.*

THE FIRST IMPACT OF THE DEPRESSION of the 'thirties did not affect the wages structure. It cut the earnings of millions through unemployment and part-time work before it affected wage rates. It was not until the last quarter of 1930 that appreciable downward changes in manufacturing wages occurred. The drop was about one cent an hour from the 1929 average of 59 cents an hour.

The next year, 1931, saw a slow but progressive decline in hourly earnings, which dropped about three cents before the end of the year. Weekly earnings, on account of unemployment, dropped much faster. While the average weekly earnings of 1929 in the industries reporting to the National Industrial Conference Board were above $28.50; and for 1930, $25.74; they were but $22.64 for 1931. The rapidly expanding depression cut hours from an average above 48 per week in 1929 to 44 in 1930, and a little over 40 in 1931. They were only 38 in the last four months of 1931.

In 1921 wage cuts were advocated early in the depression to liquidate labor costs. In 1930-31 they were opposed both by the government and by leading employers, in the hope that the maintenance of wage earners' incomes would furnish a market for products and help business recovery. In 1921 they were inaugurated long before business had reached a dangerous position; in 1931 they became common only after a large number of businesses had taken heavy losses. Realization of the reluctance of a large number of employers to cut wages caused wage earners and the public to accept them calmly when they did come, perhaps too calmly. It is not strange that the ultimate necessity of cutting wages aroused doubts whether high wages would in themselves guarantee a market for industry. Apparently the theory had been accepted too readily and too much importance given to the purchasing power of labor. For when the purchasing power of millions of farmers and investors holding delinquent securities was seriously reduced wage earners' purchases could hardly sustain the market. As things were in the world of 1930-34, high wages *alone* could not guarantee prosperity. But it was equally clear that they were an essential factor of prosperity.

The downward trend of wages in 1931 and 1932 proceeded very irregularly. Wages fell at different times and in different amounts in the various localities, industries, and plants. For one thing employers felt the burden of proof for wage cuts rested definitely upon them. They had not forgotten the living wage argument of the war and early post-war years. They sensed the importance of maintaining purchasing power and realized the opposition of the public to the cutting of wages. The President took a very firm position in opposition to wage cuts. In a series of conferences with different industrial groups in the fall of 1929 he pressed upon them the importance of maintaining wage scales. In his public speeches throughout 1930 he took a similar position.

In the fall of 1929 nearly four times as many employers reported increases in wages to the Bureau of Labor Statistics as reported wage reductions. During 1930, the facts were reversed. Wage increases were reported by only 125 concerns, while 900 reported wage decreases. Nearly all of these cuts were below 10 per cent. The United States Steel made its first cut of 10 to 15 per cent of salaries in August 1931 and a month later announced a 10 per cent cut for 220,000 wage earners. The rest of the steel industry quickly followed.

The cuts in steel played an important part in precipitating an epidemic of wage cuts in the fall of 1931. During the first six months of the year few general reductions were made by the larger industries, although some of them were nibbling at piece rates and hiring rates, precedent to the large bites which shook the morale of labor in the year. But cuts were reported by 3586 concerns with 654,687 employees before the year ended. In 1932 the size of the cuts increased, reaching an average of 17.6 per cent by October 1932. In the last six months of 1932 the number of cuts was declining but the size of the cuts was increasing. Concerns which had delayed making cuts made more drastic ones than those of 1931. It was also true that the prestige of the high wage theory had waned; labor had come to expect cuts; and widespread unemployment had made labor helpless to resist cuts. Wage cuts had been received by most of the wage earners by the end of 1932.

The attack on public salaries, heretofore local and scattered, became a widespread movement early in 1932. On January 13, 1932, Governor Pollard of Virginia proposed a 10 per cent cut in the salaries of all state officials, including teachers and public school officials. The next day Governor Emmerson of Illinois called a special session to consider reduction in state and municipal salaries, and Governor Roosevelt of New York announced that he would forward to the legislature of New York a proposal of the Mayors' Conference that municipalities postpone all salary increases. Four bills to reduce federal expenses were introduced into Congress, and the cut was finally enacted in June 1932, during which month there was also another epidemic of wage-cutting in private industry. . . .

In Ohio [a representative state for which good statistics are available] the total amount paid to wage earners in 1929 was $1,492,141,261; in 1932 but $606,713,713; a reduction of nearly 60 per cent. During the eight years 1923-30 wage earners' incomes never fell below 1193 millions of dollars, and averaged above 1300 millions. In 1931 they dropped to approximately 878 millions and in 1932 to the 606 millions. Office employees' incomes dropped nearly 100 millions or over a third 1929-32 and the earnings of salespeople (not traveling) were almost cut in half. The salaries of superintendents and managers dropped a third. Their actual cuts may have averaged as high as those of wage earners but they suffered far less from unemployment. In 1929 their salaries constituted 6.5 per cent of the total wage and salary payments of reporting industries; in 1932, 9.4 per cent; a change largely due to carrying the managerial staff through the depression. In manufactures the shrinkage was even greater. There was a decline of 270 millions or 25 per cent in wage earners' incomes in Ohio from 1929 to 1930; another loss of 235 millions (21 per cent) in 1931; and of 188 millions more (17 per cent) in 1932—a total shrinkage of 693 millions or 69 per cent in wage earners' incomes, 1929-32. Office workers in manufactures (Ohio) were not affected much in 1930. Their total incomes shrank only $130,000, less than 1 per cent. Salaries of executives dropped more; over 3 per cent. Salespeople's incomes were cut almost in half. They suffered more seriously in 1930 than any of the other groups. But they took most of their deflation in that one year. The other groups lost heavily during the succeeding years. . . .

The Ohio figures are the only ones available giving a picture of the changes in average annual earnings for a large industrial area during the depression years. In Ohio manufactures, wage earners received average annual incomes of $1598 in 1920 and of $1252 during the depression of 1921. In 1929 their annual incomes were $1499; in 1930, $1365; in 1931, $1185; and in 1932, $960; an average decline approximating $180 a year for three years in succession. These are very close to the average incomes received by wage earners in all the Ohio industries (combined) in the respective years.

The widespread and drastic wage cuts of 1931-33, the prevalence of but part-time work for those who had jobs at all, and the extremely low living standards of the millions of families who subsisted on relief during the depression period, combined to accustom American wage earners from 1931 onward to much lower standards of living than they had enjoyed from 1900 onward. There was no time between 1890 and 1930 when living standards of wage earners were demoralized like they were between 1931 and 1934, except from 1893 to 1896. It will be pointed out that standards of living in the 1930's even for relief families, were higher than were standards for comparable groups between 1893 and 1896. That is true. The nation had registered some progress between 1890 and 1930, and not all of the new items added to the American standard of living were eliminated, even for the unemployed, during the depression of the 'thirties. But the reductions both in incomes and living standards were serious.

6 · SELLING APPLES
AND SHINING SHOES

The next five readings indicate the changed values of the American people and the "new look" the early depression put upon the face of America. Selection 6 describes some of the new ways the unemployed earned a living—or tried to. From The New York Times, *June 5, 1932.*

DARWIN'S THEORY THAT MAN can adapt himself to almost any new environment is being illustrated, in this day of economic change, by thousands of New Yorkers who have discovered new ways to live and new ways to earn a living since their formerly placid lives were thrown into chaos by unemployment or kindred exigencies. Occupations and duties which once were scorned have suddenly attained unprecedented popularity.

Two years ago citizens shied at jury duty. John Doe and Richard Roe, summoned to serve on a jury, thought of all sorts of excuses. . . . They called upon their ward leaders and their lawyers for aid in getting exemption, and when their efforts were rewarded they sighed with relief. But now things are different.

The Hall of Jurors in the Criminal Courts Building is jammed and packed on court days. Absences of talesmen are infrequent. Why? Jurors get $4 for every day they serve. . . .

Once the average New Yorker got his shine in an established bootblack "parlor" paying 10 cents, with a nickel tip. But now, in the Times Square and Grand Central zones, the sidewalks are lined with neophyte "shine boys," drawn from almost all walks of life. They charge a nickel, and although a nickel tip is welcomed it is not expected.

In one block, on West Forty-third Street, a recent count showed nineteen shoe-shiners. They ranged in age from a 16-year-old, who should have been in school, to a man of more than 70, who said he had been employed in a fruit store until six months ago. Some sit quietly on their little wooden boxes and wait patiently for the infrequent customers. Others show true initiative and ballyhoo their trade, pointing accusingly at every pair of unshined shoes that passes. . . .

Shining shoes, said one, is more profitable than selling apples—and he's tried them both.

"You see, when you get a shine kit it's a permanent investment," he said, "and it doesn't cost as much as a box of apples anyway. . . ."

According to the Police Department, there are approximately 7,000 of these "shine boys" making a living on New York streets at present. Three years ago they were so rare as to be almost non-existent, and were almost entirely boys under 17.

To the streets, too, has turned an army of new salesmen, peddling everything from large rubber balls to cheap neckties. Within the past two years the number of these hawkers has doubled. . . . Fourteenth Street is still the Mecca of this type of salesmen; thirty-eight were recently counted between Sixth Avenue and Union Square and at one point there was a cluster of five.

Unemployment has brought back the newsboy in increasing numbers. He avoids the busy corners, where news stands are frequent, and hawks his papers in the side streets with surprising success. His best client is the man who is "too tired to walk down to the corner for a paper."

Selling Sunday papers has become a science. Youngsters have found that it is extremely profitable to invade apartment houses between 11 and 12 o'clock Sunday morning, knock on each apartment door, and offer the Sunday editions. Their profits are usually between $1.50 and $2.

The condition of business, with the resulting necessity of watching the market-basket expenditures, has proved a boon for the small New Jersey truck farmer. Between 5 and 6 o'clock in the morning the ferries are clogged with horses and carts and vegetables. And while he is not yet shouting his wares on Park Avenue, he has invaded many a neighborhood in which a vegetable hawker had not been seen in years. His goods may or may not be cheaper than the corner grocer's, but there is some psychology about buying vegetables from a cart that is dear to the thrifty housewife. The number of vegetable hawkers has increased by 40 per cent within the last two years, according to the estimate of the City Licensing Bureau. . . .

7 • AMERICANS
SEEK RUSSIAN JOBS

From Business Week, *October 7, 1931, pp. 32-33.*

AMTORG GETS 100,000 BIDS
FOR RUSSIA'S 6,000 SKILLED JOBS

NEW YORKERS DOMINATE the flow of Americans who have decided, at least for the time being, to cast their lot with the Russians. Pennsylvania, New Jersey, and Illinois show heavy quotas of recruits under the new call for "6,000 skilled workers," and Michigan, Ohio, California, and Massachusetts are well represented.

More than 100,000 applications have been received at the Amtorg's New York office for the 6,000 jobs. One morning's grist of applications last week totaled 280. All but 10 states were represented. Both Alaska and Panama furnished an applicant, and 18 Canadians wanted to "try their luck in Russia."

Industrial states naturally supply the largest number of applicants, but others are represented. Iowa, Texas, and Idaho each offered some kind of skilled worker.

Because of the general knowledge that Russia is "industrializing," applicants usually are skilled workers at machine construction, on the railroads, in steel mills, automobile factories, or the building industries. A glance at the qualifications of some of the 280 applicants on this "typical" morning showed that experts in all lines were after work, even if it meant going to Russia and accepting pay in roubles. There were 2 barbers, 1 funeral director, 2 plumbers, 5 painters, 2 cooks, 36 "clerical" workers, 1 service station operator, 9 carpenters, 1 aviator, 58 engineers, 14 electricians, 5 salesmen, 2 printers, 2 chemists, 1 shoemaker, 1 librarian, 2 teachers, 1 cleaner & dyer, 11 automobile mechanics, 1 dentist.

About 85% of the applicants are citizens of the United States, though only 40% are native born. The 60% foreign born are largely from Eastern Europe. A few negroes have applied but the number is small because the majority are unskilled laborers.

Women form only a small percentage of the applicants, though many wives have decided to accompany their husbands on the new venture. The majority of workers who apply are married and have children.

Three principal reasons are advanced for wanting the position: (1) Unemployment; (2) disgust with conditions here; (3) interest in the Soviet experiment. Foreign-born workers practically all state that they intend to remain in the U.S.S.R. Of the engineers, only 10% to 20% plan to stay.

8 · JAILS ARE BETTER THAN SUBWAYS

From The New York Times, *October 7, 1932.*

FIFTY-FOUR MEN WERE ARRESTED yesterday morning for sleeping or idling in the arcade connecting with the subway through 45 West Forty-second Street, but most of them considered their unexpected meeting with a raiding party of ten policemen as a stroke of luck because it brought them free meals yesterday and shelter last night from the sudden change in the weather.

All the prisoners, among whom was one who said that he had waiting for him in England an inheritance of £6,000, or about $20,000 at the present rate of exchange, sat patiently in the West Side Court yesterday afternoon, waiting for the official fingerprint men to determine whether they were professional vagrants or unemployed men who were down on their luck.

The work of fingerprinting and making necessary comparisons with police records required so much time that Magistrate Renaud postponed the men's trials on charges of disorderly conduct until this afternoon. This insured them sleeping quarters for the night and more free meals today.

The prisoner who told of his fortune in England said he was Adolph Richard Hugo, 42 years old, an electrical overseer, who came to the country in 1923. He said that for four years he has been trying to get money enough to go to England to claim an inheritance that was provided by an uncle, John Pike, manager of a diamond mine in South Africa. He produced a letter which ostensibly came from an English barrister, Henry Vincombe of Mutley, Devon, notifying him of the legacy. Hugo said his wife and two daughters are in needy circumstances in England and the British Consul here has been unable to help him return to them because he has taken out first citizenship papers.

9 · THE PRESIDENT'S MONUMENTS

From The New York Times, *September 22, 1932.*

ACTING CAPTAIN GEORGE BURNELL of the Arsenal station and a squad of patrolmen staged a polite raid last night on the residents of a new suburban development. The policemen, with apologies and good feelings on both sides, arrested for vagrancy twenty-five inhabitants of Hoover Valley, the shantytown that sprang up in the bed of the old lower reservoir of Central Park near the Obelisk.

The raid was staged on the orders of Deputy Park Commissioner John Hart, who explained that the Park Department, much as it regretted it, intended to raze the settlement this morning.

"We don't want to do it, but we can't help it," Mr. Hart said, adding that although the men had maintained good order, had built comfortable shacks and furnished them as commodiously as they could, there were no water nor sanitary facilities near the settlement.

Friendly relations between the police and the inhabitants having already been established during the last four weeks while the men were building permanent shacks, some of them of brick, for the Winter, the men went along with the policemen without quarrel. . . .

Hoover Valley—the name is officially recognized by Park Department heads—sprang up during the Summer months but it was only during the last four weeks that the men who made their homes in the southern end of the lower reservoir built more permanent structures. Seventeen shacks, all of them equipped with chairs, beds and bedding and a few with carpets, were erected.

The manor of the colony, a brick structure 20 feet high in front of a boulder, having a roof of inlaid tile, was built by unemployed bricklayers who dubbed it Rockside Inn. The other colonists call it Custer's Last Stand. Another shack, built of fruit and egg crates, with a tattered American flag flying atop of it, bears a sign, "Radio City." That has the only radio in the "jungle" and all residents are welcome to lounge inside. Twelve shacks, some of them less pretentious, are being built in back of the seventeen, which were set out in a row called "Depression Street."

Police and Park Department officials said they believed that almost all the men are New Yorkers, and that none of them are hoboes. They repair in the morning to comfort stations to shave and make themselves look presentable and keep their shacks as clean as they can, it was explained, but because of sanitary conditions must leave before the Board of Health takes action.

10 · HOMELESS WOMEN
SLEEP IN CHICAGO PARKS

From The New York Times, *September 20, 1931.*

CHICAGO, SEPT. 19 (AP).—Several hundred homeless unemployed women sleep nightly in Chicago's parks, Mrs. Elizabeth A. Conkey, Commissioner of Public Welfare, reported today.

She learned of the situation, she said, when women of good character appealed for shelter and protection, having nowhere to sleep but in the parks, where they feared that they would be molested.

"We are informed that no fewer than 200 women are sleeping in Grant and Lincoln Parks, on the lake front, to say nothing of those in the other parks," said Mrs. Conkey. "I made a personal investigation, driving from park to park, at night, and verified the reports."

The commissioner said the approach of Winter made the problem more serious, with only one free women's lodging house existing, accommodating 100.

II

The Farmer
in the Depression

THE ECONOMIC DRY ROT of the 1930's afflicted the countryside as well as the cities. Farm owner-operators, renters, and sharecroppers all suffered from the miserably low prices they received for their products, and it made little difference whether one were an Alabama cotton grower, an Iowa corn and hog farmer, a Wisconsin dairy producer, or a California citrus rancher. In the worst years of the Great Depression all of them considered themselves fortunate if they could sell their product for enough to meet their costs of production.

It is difficult to say whether the unemployed urban worker or the farmer suffered the more from the depression. Both were poverty stricken, although the farmer continued to work as hard and as long as he ever did. The farmer typically lost much or all of his capital, which the urban worker usually had never had. The farmer could usually raise some food for his own family's needs and the city man could not, but the relief facilities of urban governments were generally superior to those in rural areas. The farmer's depression lasted longer, since he had not shared in the prosperity of the 1920's. During the lean years families in both groups thought it could improve itself by moving into the other; some down-and-out farmers abandoned the country in a search for industrial jobs, and many unemployed city dwellers went back to the land in an attempt to eke out a living. Certainly, to make a judgment about which group was the harder hit involves a bitter arithmetic.

The following selections help toward an understanding of the farmer's economic difficulties.

11 • FROM OWNER-OPERATOR
TO RENTER

This article by Bernhard Ostrolenk, "The Farmer's Plight: A Far-Reaching Crisis," from The New York Times, *Sept. 25, 1932, describes in easily understood language the economic handicaps under which the farm owner worked and how he frequently became a renter on the land he had once owned. Reprinted by permission of the publishers.*

THE MOST SUPERFICIAL STUDY of the statistics reveals that while industry reached a new peak of prosperity between 1920 and 1929, the farmer met with one financial setback after another; that he was becoming poorer and poorer; that the disaster of 1920 was followed by an even greater financial catastrophe in 1930. That story can be told simply and graphically by considering the case of Ole Swanson—a case that is not unlike that of hundreds of thousands of other farmers.

By 1912, Ole, then 35 years old and a renter, had accumulated some $2,000 in cash, two teams of horses, a reasonable supply of implements, a few brood sows and some cattle. He decided to buy his deceased father's farm of 160 acres in Southern Minnesota for $20,000. He paid $2,000 in cash, gave an $8,000 second mortgage to the estate and a $10,000 first mortgage to an insurance company.

Between 1912 and 1920, because of exceptional thrift and competence, Ole was able to pay off the entire second mortgage of $8,000, besides improving his barns, adding more cattle to his herd, increasing his equipment, building a porch to his home and making other improvements, as well as buying furniture, rugs and books, and giving his children an adequate education.

But between 1920 and 1928 Ole found that his expenses, because of the industrial prosperity, were increasing. He had to pay more and more for labor and for goods. On the other hand, because of the drop in agricultural prices, his income was constantly falling. So, in those years, he was unable to amortize his remaining $10,000 mortgage, and, moreover, found that his standard of living was rapidly declining. By 1925 his net income for his labor had fallen to less than $400 annually. His 18-year-old daughter, who had become employed in town as a typist, with no experience whatever and without invested capital, was earning $15 a week, or nearly $800 a year, almost twice what Ole was earning for his labor during that period.

In 1929 Ole was unable to meet a total interest of $600 and taxes of $300 and was compelled to give the insurance company, holding his mortgage, a chattel mortgage for the interest debt. In 1930 he was compelled to give an even larger chattel mortgage.

In 1931 his gross income was insufficient to meet either taxes or interest, and the insurance company, now having failed to get interest for three years, foreclosed the mortgage in the Spring of 1932. Ole, at the age of 55, was again a renter on his father's farm—the farm upon which he had been born and on which he had labored for a quarter of a century; having lost his entire equity of $10,000, he was left carrying a burdensome chattel mortgage.

Ole's career exemplifies the trend of American agriculture today. Not all the farmers have been foreclosed, but all are carrying heavy burdens. A mortgage of $10,000 on a 160-acre farm means that the farmer must pay $3.60 interest per acre. His taxes amount to about $1.90 per acre, making a total funded debt of $5.50 per acre. But with oats selling at 10 cents a bushel, the forty bushels he may be able to raise per acre, if lucky, will give him less gross return than he needs for those purposes alone. Certainly there is nothing left for out-of-pocket expenses, such as binder twine and tool repair, labor, seed and interest on the equity which he himself has in the farm. . . .

Ole, now a renter, has estimated that his gross income at present price levels will be about $800 for 1932. Instead of paying interest and taxes of $900, as he was expected to do last year before his foreclosure, he will now pay as rent to the insurance company that held his mortgage only one-third of his sales, or about $265.

Yet the average farmer is reluctant to surrender his status of independent farm owner even under such conditions. Though he becomes progressively poorer, he clings to the land as long as he can.

And just as he is unwilling to relinquish his farm, so the mortgage holders become unwilling owners. They bought the mortgages to receive interest, not to go into farming directly or indirectly. In fact, the transfer from mortgage holders to farm owners is involving them in heavy losses. The insurance company that will collect $265 from Ole Swanson will have to pay the taxes of $300 on the farm it has taken over from him, and, of course, will receive nothing for its $10,000 mortgage investment. . . .

[Yet] Farmers are rapidly changing now from owner-operators to renters . . . in our greatest agricultural regions the independent owner-operator had always been represented as the typical farmer. It is in these regions—in Minnesota, the Dakotas, Iowa, Nebraska—the regions known throughout the world as having the most fertile soil and the most progressive methods—that farm tenancy has increased most sharply in recent years. These regions of corn and grain and alfalfa, of hogs and beef and cheese and butter, are joining the cotton regions of the South in being farmed by renters and owned by absentee landlords. . . .

12 · SHIRT SLEEVES TO
SHIRT SLEEVES IN THE CORN BELT

This article by a conservative lawyer from Mason City, Iowa, describes the impact of the Great Depression upon a rich agricultural community and the decline of farm fortunes. Remley J. Glass, "Gentlemen, the Corn Belt!" Harper's, CLXVII (July, 1933), pp. 200-206. Reprinted by permission.

MY HOME COUNTY may well be considered a fair example of Iowa and the Corn Belt. It is one of the ninety-nine counties of Iowa and similar to those throughout the Middle West. Its condition and problems are typical of the entire Corn Belt. Organized before the Civil War, its early citizenry was purely American pioneer stock which successfully withstood the attacks of Indians and the vicissitudes of border existence. To this nucleus have been added a considerable group of Irish immigrants who are centered in two or three southern townships, and a larger proportion of Scandinavians who constitute the majority in five or six northern townships. The manufacturing industries in our county seat have brought groups of laborers from the south of Europe, while Mexico likewise has furnished its full quota. Two railroads first came through this county in the late sixties, and other lines were built to tap its agricultural and manufacturing resources as late as the beginning of the present century.

The wheat and corn of pioneer farming gave place in part to hogs, beef cattle, and dairy herds, and the development of sugar beets added to its prosperity. The county seat, with the establishment of large manufacturing industries, assumed an almost metropolitan air with comfortable homes and a contented people. Railroads radiating from the town made it the trading and jobbing center of a considerable area. A conservative prosperity was ours.

In the early days of the century Iowa, along with the rest of the Middle West, enjoyed a gradual, conservative increase in the values of farm products and farm real estate. Men who had homesteaded their farms from the government, paying $2.50 or $3.00 per acre, saw the price of land gradually increase to around $100 per acre, and thereby built up comfortable fortunes. Early investors at $7 to $15 per acre profited by that same increase. Even though sales of farm lands were rare in those days, the new values seemed definitely established.

This increase in values, though Henry George would have condemned it as "unearned increment," did not come like the Biblical manna in the

Wilderness; it was the result of pioneer effort in the upbuilding and improvement of those farms and of the States in which the efforts were put forth.

The boom period of the last years of the World War and the extreme inflationary period of 1919 and 1920 were like the Mississippi Bubble and the Tulip Craze in Holland in their effect upon the general public. Farm prices shot sky high almost over night. The town barber and the small-town merchant bought and sold options until every town square was a real estate exchange. Bankers and lawyers, doctors and ministers left their offices and clients and drove pell mell over the country to procure options and contracts upon this farm and that, paying a few hundred dollars down and expecting to sell the rights before the following March brought settlement day. Not to be in the game marked one as an old fogy, while paper profits were pyramided and Cadillac cars and pleasure trips to the cities took the place of Fords and Sunday afternoon picnics. Everyone then maintained that there was only a little land as fertile as the fields of Iowa, Illinois, and Minnesota, and everyone sought to get his part before it was all gone. Like gold, it was limited in extent and of great potential value. Prices skyrocketed from $100 to $250 and $400 per acre without regard to the producing power of land.

During this period insurance companies were bidding against one another for the privilege of making loans on Iowa farms at $90 or $100 or $150 per acre. Prices of products were soaring. Everyone was on the highroad, not only to comfort, but to wealth and luxury. Second, third, and fourth mortgages were considered just as good as government bonds. Money was easy, and every bank was ready and anxious to loan money to any Tom, Dick, or Harry on the possibility that he would make enough in these trades to repay the loans almost before the day was over. Every country bank and every county-seat town was a replica in miniature of a brisk day on the board of trade.

Settlements were made on March 1, 1920, but, alas, from then on the painful awakening from this financial carousal brought long continuing headaches to the investors, the holders of second mortgages, and the bankers who had financed these endeavors.

The next decade was marked by a gradual decrease in the price of farm commodities, a shrinkage in farm values, and increasing attempts by the holders to collect second and third mortgages given during boom times. However, the foreclosure of a first or primary mortgage on Iowa real estate was as rare during this period as it had been in prior years. The basic value of Corn Belt land was still beyond question, and what few first-mortgage foreclosure actions were brought disturbed this confidence but little. During this same decade large drainage projects were inaugurated in the Corn Belt in order to bring large areas of "border" land under cultivation. Consolidated schools were erected to bring the highest type of educational facilities to the rural children. The proverbial little red schoolhouse became a modern brick building with enlarged faculties and increased facilities for education. Paved roads were built.

All these features had been demanded and are desirable; but the ability to pay for them has not continued. The general tax demands of school district, county, and State have equaled the interest on a thirty-dollar-per-acre mortgage over the entire State of Iowa; while special highway, drainage, and consolidated school assessments have increased the tax burden in areas affected by those improvements beyond bearing. For some years past, conservative mortgage lenders have hesitated to place loans on farms affected by these special levies, and in nearly every county the first of the flood of foreclosures was in such heavily taxed areas.

The drastic deflation of Iowa loans under orders from the Federal Reserve Board, upon which Smith Wildman Brookhart, depression Senator from Iowa, poured forth his venom, definitely marked the downward turn in the mythical prosperity of boom days. Despite our hopes for the better, conditions have grown steadily worse.

During the year after the great debacle of 1929 the flood of foreclosure actions did not reach any great peak, but in the years 1931 and 1932 the tidal wave was upon us. Insurance companies and large investors had not as yet realized (and in some instances do not yet realize) that, with the low price of farm commodities and the gradual exhaustion of savings and reserves, the formerly safe and sane investments in farm mortgages could not be worked out, taxes and interest could not be paid, and liquidation could not be made. With an utter disregard of the possibilities of payment or refinancing, the large loan companies plunged ahead to make the Iowa farmer pay his loans in full or turn over the real estate to the mortgage holder. Deficiency judgments and the resultant receiverships were the clubs they used to make the honest but indigent farm owners yield immediate possession of the farms.

Men who had sunk every dollar they possessed in the purchase, upkeep, and improvement of their home places were turned out with small amounts of personal property as their only assets. Landowners who had regarded farm land as the ultimate in safety, after using their outside resources in vain attempts to hold their lands, saw these assets go under the sheriff's hammer on the courthouse steps.

During the two-year period of 1931-32, in this formerly prosperous Iowa county, twelve and a half per cent of the farms went under the hammer, and almost twenty-five per cent of the mortgaged farm real estate was foreclosed. And the conditions in my home county have been substantially duplicated in every one of the ninety-nine counties of Iowa and in those of the surrounding States.

We lawyers of the Corn Belt have had to develop a new type of practice, for in pre-war days foreclosure litigation amounted to but a small part of the general practice. In these years of the depression almost one-third of the cases filed have to do with this situation. Our courts are clogged with such matters.

To one who for years has been a standpatter, both financially and politically, the gradual change to near-radicalism, both in himself and in those formerly conservative property owners for whom his firm has done business down the years, is almost incomprehensible, but none the less alarming. Friends and clients of years' standing have lost inherited competencies which had been increased by their own conservative management. Not only their profits, but their principal has been wiped out. The conservative investments in real estate which we Middle Westerners have for years considered the best possible have become not only not an asset, but a liability, with the possibility of deficiency judgments, that bane of mortgage debtors, staring us in the face. Not only have the luxuries and comforts of life been taken from us, but the necessaries are not secure.

Men and women who have lived industrious, comfortable, and contented lives have faced bravely the loss of luxuries and comforts, but there is a decided change in their attitude toward the financial and economic powers that be when conditions take away their homes and imperil the continued existence of their families.

The interests of insurance companies and outside corporations in Iowa real estate have resulted in a form of absentee ownership never before dreamed of. Large numbers of farms held by these outside interests are administered by men who do not have sympathetic appreciation of local conditions, and of the friendly relations which have been traditional between Corn Belt landlord and tenant.

The sympathetic, friendly inspection of the crops, the fences, and the livestock, which formed the Sunday afternoon diversion of the small landlord, has ceased. Now some young lad, clad like an English squire in riding boots and breeches, with a brief case and a Ford, drives up, hastily checks the acreage in corn and oats, inquires why the first payment of the cash rent has not been paid, tells the tenant that all checks for produce sold must be made out in the name of the company, and drives away. The personal element is gone.

Gone, too, is that pride of ownership which made possible the development of stock and dairy farms with their herds of fat cattle and hogs, their Jersey cows, their well-kept groves and buildings which beautified and developed the countryside. The former owners were willing to use a large part of receipts from a farm's income to increase its value and appearance, but the present absentee owner regards it only as a source of possible dividends.

It used to be that a quarter section of farm land and a few shares of stock in the community bank marked a successful man; now it is too apt to have placed him in the bankruptcy court, after an harassing experience of foreclosures and suits brought by the receiver of the little country bank to collect the double assessment on his stock.

It is thought by many people that these sweeping changes affect only the land speculator but have no bearing on the individual farm owner who lived on and operated his farm. When conditions were favorable, when taxes were not too high and when there was no mortgage to meet, those men in the main have been able to meet the crisis by applying on the taxes and assessments the bulk of the earnings of the farm above their meager living. But this has been accomplished only by a sacrifice of upkeep of farm buildings and by loss of fertility in the farm itself. What we out in the Middle West term "hay wire" repairs have taken the place of necessary renewals of farm machinery. Live stock has been sold at ruinous prices. The future has been sacrificed to the exigent moment.

From a lawyer's point of view, one of the most serious effects of the economic crisis lies in the rapid and permanent disintegration of established estates throughout the Corn Belt. Families of moderate means as well as those of considerable fortunes who have been clients of my particular office for three or four generations in many instances have lost their savings, their investments, and their homes; while their business, which for many years has been a continuous source of income, has become merely an additional responsibility as we strive to protect them from foreclosures, judicial receivership, deficiency judgments, and probably bankruptcy.

Thank heaven, most country lawyers feel this responsibility to their old clients, and strive just as diligently to protect their clients' rights under present conditions as they did in the golden days before the depression. Every time, however, when I am called to defend a foreclosure action filed against some client or friend, it is forced on my mind that an estate accumulated through years of effort has not merely changed hands but has vanished into thin air.

As I sit here my mind turns to one after another of the prominent land-owning families of this county who have lost their fortunes, not as a result of extravagance or carelessness, but because of conditions beyond their control, and which were not envisaged by the most farsighted.

Just after the Civil War one Johnson Burke came to our Iowa county from New York State, bringing with him what in those days was considered a comfortable fortune. His white hair, long beard, and patriarchal appearance resulted in his being termed Grandfather Burke; and as the years passed and Johnson the Second assumed that same patriarchal appearance, the founder of the family became Great Grandfather Johnson Burke to all of us. His York State shrewdness enabled him to buy tax titles and purchase farms at advantageous prices until he and his family were the leading land owners in the county. As the years passed he left his square-built frame house on the bank of the creek and spent his time in Long Beach, that second Capital of Iowa, in California.

The second generation did not get along so amicably, and extensive and expensive litigation was brought to determine the rights of the active head of the second generation and his brothers and sisters. As a young lawyer, I sat in the courtroom and listened intently to the long list of farms owned by Great Grandfather Burke and the estimates of their value which even in those pre-inflation days went into seven figures. Finally a settlement was made whereby Johnson the Second took over most of the Iowa real estate, paying off the other heirs in cash, mortgages being placed on the lands in order to make the settlements. In the long noonings we lawyers chatting in the courthouse commended the wisdom of young Johnson in the advantageous values at which he took in the farms.

Years passed and Johnson the Second grew feeble with oncoming age and the worries of rent collection and interest payments, and the third generation furnished the head of the family. Values of mortgaged land kept going down. Interest, general taxes, and special assessments for drainage projects whereby more land might be brought under cultivation to produce a greater surplus took a larger and larger share of the once ample income from this estate. Tax sales and foreclosures, judgments, and receiverships have followed in rapid succession until now most of the fertile acres which this family once owned are handled by a trustee who is waging a losing battle to save something from the wreckage. Mind you, the last generation did nothing which had not been considered good business by the preceding generations. Their management was sound, their loans were conservative. And yet their all is gone. This is but one of dozens of instances of more or less prominence in my home community.

The old maxim of three generations between shirt sleeves and shirt sleeves is finding a new meaning out here in the Corn Belt, when the return to very limited means in a formerly prosperous population is the result not of high living and spending, but of high taxes, high dollars, and radically reduced income from the sale of basic products.

Take, if you please, what seems to me to have been a typical case of the tenant farmer, one Johannes Schmidt, a client of mine. Johannes was descended from farming stock in Germany, came to this country as a boy, became a citizen, went over seas in the 88th Division, and on his return married the daughter of a retired farmer. He rented one hundred and twenty acres from his father-in-law and one hundred and sixty acres from the town banker. His live stock and equipment, purchased in the early twenties, were well bought, for his judgment was good, and the next eight years marked a gradual increase in his live stock and reductions in his bank indebtedness. During these years two youngsters came to the young couple and all seemed rosy.

In the year 1931 a drought in this part of the Corn Belt practically eliminated his crops, while what little he did raise was insufficient to pay his rent, and he went into 1932 with increased indebtedness for feed, back taxes, and back rent. While the crops in 1932 were wonderful and justified the statement that the Middle West is the market basket of the world, prices were so low as not to pay the cost of seed and labor in production without regard to taxes and rent.

Times were hard and the reverberations of October, 1929, had definitely reached the Corn Belt. The county-seat bank which held Johannes' paper was in hard shape. Much of its reserve had been invested in bonds recommended by Eastern bankers upon which default of interest and principal had occurred. When the bottom dropped out of the bond market the banking departments and examiners insisted upon immediate collection of slow farm loans, as liquidity was the watchword of bank examiners in the years 1929 to 1932. When Johannes sought to renew his bank loan, payment or else security on all his personal property was demanded without regard to the needs of wife and family. Prices of farm products had fallen to almost nothing, oats were ten cents a bushel, corn twelve cents per bushel, while hogs, the chief cash crop in the Corn Belt, were selling at less than two and one half cents a pound. In the fall of 1932 a wagon load of oats would not pay for a pair of shoes; a truck load of hogs, which in other days would have paid all a tenant's cash rent, did not then pay the interest on a thousand dollars.

This man Schmidt had struggled and contrived as long as possible under the prodding of landlord and banker, and as a last resort came to see me about bankruptcy. We talked it over and with regret reached the conclusion it was the only road for him to take. He did not have even enough cash on hand to pay the thirty-dollar filing fee which I had to send to the Federal Court but finally borrowed it from his brother-in-law. The time of hearing came, and he and his wife and children sat before the Referee in Bankruptcy, while the banker and the landlord struggled over priorities of liens and rights to crops and cattle. When the day was over this family went out from the office the owner of an old team of horses, a wagon, a couple of cows and five hogs, together with their few sticks of furniture and no place to go.

George Warner, aged seventy-four, who had for years operated one hundred and sixty acres in the northeast corner of the county and in the early boom days had purchased an additional quarter section, is typical of hundreds in the Corn Belt. He had retired and with his wife was living comfortably in his square white house in town a few blocks from my home. Sober, industrious, pillars of the church and active in good works, he and his wife may well be considered typical retired farmers. Their three boys wanted to get started in business after they were graduated from high school, and George, to finance their endeavors, put a mortgage, reasonable in amount, on his two places. Last fall a son out of a job brought his family and came home to live with the old people. The tenants on the farms could not pay their rent, and George could not pay his interest and taxes. George's land was sold at tax sale and a foreclosure action was brought against the farms by the insurance company which held the mortgage. I did the best I could for him in the settlement, but to escape a deficiency judgment he surrendered the places beginning on March 1st of this year, and a few days ago I saw a mortgage recorded on his home in town. As he told me of it, the next day, tears came to his eyes and his lips trembled, and he and I both thought of the years he had spent in building up that estate and making those acres bear fruit abundantly. Like another Job, he murmured "The Lord gave and the Lord hath taken away"; but I wondered if it was proper to place the responsibility for the breakdown of a faulty human economic system on the shoulders of the Lord.

When my friend George passes over Jordan and I have to turn over to his wife the little that is left in accordance with the terms of his will drawn in more prosperous days, I presume I shall send his widow a receipted bill for services rendered during many years, and gaze again on the wreckage of a ruined estate.

I have represented bankrupt farmers and holders of claims for rent, notes, and mortgages against such farmers in dozens of bankruptcy hearings and court actions, and the most discouraging, disheartening experiences of my legal life have occurred when men of middle age, with families, go out of the bankruptcy court with furniture, team of horses and a wagon, and a little stock as all that is left from twenty-five years of work, to try once more—not to build up an estate—for that is usually impossible —but to provide clothing and food and shelter for the wife and children. And the powers that be seem to demand that these not only accept this situation but shall like it.

13 • POVERTY AMID PLENTY

One of the most disheartening features of the Great Depression was that much of the product of field and orchard went to waste for want of a profitable market while millions were without enough food. Oscar Ameringer of Oklahoma City described some of this tragedy before a Congressional committee in February, 1932. Unemployment in the United States, Hearings *before a Subcommittee of the Committee on Labor, House of Representatives, 72nd Cong., 1 sess., on H.R. 206, H.R. 6011, H.R. 8088 (Washington: Government Printing Office, 1932), pp. 98-99.*

DURING THE LAST THREE MONTHS I have visited, as I have said, some 20 States of this wonderfully rich and beautiful country. Here are some of the things I heard and saw: In the State of Washington I was told that the forest fires raging in that region all summer and fall were caused by unemployed timber workers and bankrupt farmers in an endeavor to earn a few honest dollars as fire fighters. The last thing I saw on the night I left Seattle was numbers of women searching for scraps of food in the refuse piles of the principal market of that city. A number of Montana citizens told me of thousands of bushels of wheat left in the fields uncut on account of its low price that hardly paid for the harvesting. In Oregon I saw thousands of bushels of apples rotting in the orchards. Only absolute flawless apples were still salable, at from 40 to 50 cents a box containing 200 apples. At the same time, there are millions of children who, on account of the poverty of their parents, will not eat one apple this winter.

While I was in Oregon the Portland Oregonian bemoaned the fact that thousands of ewes were killed by the sheep raisers because they did not bring enough in the market to pay the freight on them. And while Oregon sheep raisers fed mutton to the buzzards, I saw men picking for meat scraps in the garbage cans in the cities of New York and Chicago. I talked to one man in a restaurant in Chicago. He told me of his experience in raising sheep. He said that he had killed 3,000 sheep this fall and thrown them down the canyon, because it cost $1.10 to ship a sheep, and then he would get less than a dollar for it. He said he could not afford to feed the sheep, and he would not let them starve, so he just cut their throats and threw them down the canyon.

The roads of the West and Southwest teem with hungry hitchhikers. The camp fires of the homeless are seen along every railroad track. I saw men, women, and children walking over the hard roads. Most of them were tenant farmers who had lost their all in the late slump in wheat and cotton. Between Clarksville and Russellville, Ark., I picked up a family. The woman was hugging a dead chicken under a ragged coat. When I asked her where she had procured the fowl, first she told me she had found it dead in the road, and then added in grim humor, "They promised me a chicken in the pot, and now I got mine."

In Oklahoma, Texas, Arkansas, and Louisiana I saw untold bales of cotton rotting in the fields because the cotton pickers could not keep body and soul together on 35 cents paid for picking 100 pounds. The farmers cooperatives who loaned the money to the planters to make the crops allowed the planters $5 a bale. That means 1,500 pounds of seed cotton for the picking of it, which was in the neighborhood of 35 cents a pound. A good picker can pick about 200 pounds of cotton a day, so that the 70 cents would not provide enough pork and beans to keep the picker in the field, so that there is fine staple cotton rotting down there by the hundreds and thousands of tons.

As a result of this appalling overproduction on the one side and the staggering underconsumption on the other side, 70 per cent of the farmers of Oklahoma were unable to pay the interests on their mortgages. Last week one of the largest and oldest mortgage companies in that State went into the hands of the receiver. In that and other States we have now the interesting spectacle of farmers losing their farms by foreclosure and mortgage companies losing their recouped holdings by tax sales.

The farmers are being pauperized by the poverty of industrial populations and the industrial populations are being pauperized by the poverty of the farmers. Neither has the money to buy the product of the other, hence we have overproduction and underconsumption at the same time and in the same country.

14 · SOUTHERN SHARECROPPERS:
THE AGRICULTURAL DEPTHS

Sharecroppers in the cotton belt, never a prosperous group, suffered from economic want during the 1930's as perhaps did no other group in America. On January 5, 1932, Congressman George Huddleston of Alabama told the so-called LaFollette-Costigan committee of the Senate of some of the conditions in his district. Federal Aid for Unemployment Relief, Hearings *before a Subcommittee of the Committee on Manufactures, United States Senate, 72nd Cong., 1 sess., on S. 174 and S. 262 (Washington: Government Printing Office, 1932), pp. 244-245.*

MR. HUDDLESTON. We have a great many tenant farmers there. We have a great many negro farmers, and practically all of them are tenants. Their ability to survive, to eat, to have a shelter, depends upon the ability of the landlord to supply them with the necessaries of life. They have a system under which they make a contract with the landlord to cultivate his land for the next year and in the meantime he feeds them through the winter, and at the end of the year they gather their crops and pay for their supplies and rent, if they are able to do so. Conditions in agriculture have been such for several years that the landlords have been gradually impoverished and their farms are mortgaged to the farm-loan system and to the mortgage companies in a multitude of instances.

In a very large percentage [of cases] the landlord is now unable to finance these tenants for another year. He is unable to get the supplies. He has no security and no money with which to feed and clothe his tenants until they can make another crop. They came to the end of the season—their chief crop is cotton which they sold at from 5 to 6 cents, and very few of them were able to pay for the supplies that it required for them to make the crop. They owe the landlord. Many landlords have said to them, generously, "Keep what you have made and go your way. I can not feed you another year. You will have to do the best you can, but keep whatever you have made." A great many of these landlords, no matter how well intentioned, are incapable of financing these tenants another year. The landlord is in almost as bad shape as the tenant. He owed for the supplies. He had to take what he received at the end of the season and turn it over to the merchant, or to the bank to pay them what he owed. He has been unable to pay in full, so that he can not advance them another year. Many of these people, especially the negro tenants, are now in the middle of a winter, practically without food and without clothes, and without anything else, and how are they going to live? Many of these local counties have no charitable organizations. They are poor people and impoverished. They have no county funds. There is no place to turn, nobody that has any money that they can turn to and ask for help.

Many white people are in the same kind of a situation. They beg around among their neighbors. The neighbors are poor and they have no means of helping them. They stray here and there.

Any thought that there has been no starvation, that no man has starved, and no man will starve, is the rankest nonsense. Men are actually starving by the thousands to-day, not merely in the general sections that I refer to, but throughout this country as a whole, and in my own district. I do not mean to say that they are sitting down and not getting a bite of food until they actually die, but they are living such a scrambling, precarious existence, with suffering from lack of clothing, fuel, and nourishment, until they are subject to be swept away at any time, and many are now being swept away.

The situation has possibilities of epidemics of various kinds. Its consequences will be felt many years. The children are being stunted by lack of food. Old people are having their lives cut short. The physical effects of the privations that they are forced to endure will not pass away within 50 years and when the social and civic effects will pass away, only God knows. That is something that no man can estimate.

15 • FARMERS ON RELIEF

This selection indicates the dimensions of the problem of rural poverty in 1935, even after two years of the New Deal's agricultural policies. Berta Asch and A. R. Magnus, Farmers on Relief and Rehabilitation *[WPA Research Monograph VIII] (Washington: Government Printing Office, 1937), pp. 6-12.*

THE 593,612 FARM OPERATORS receiving relief grants or rehabilitation advances in June 1935 constituted 9 percent of all farmers in the United States as reported by the 1935 Census of Agriculture. This proportion does not appear large when compared with the 18 percent of urban families on relief in June 1935. In 21 States, in fact, the combined number of farm operators receiving relief grants or rehabilitation advances was less than 6 percent of all farmers, and in 13 States the ratio was from 6 to 8 percent. In 14 States, however, farmers receiving relief grants or rehabilitation advances in June 1935 accounted for from 10 to 36 percent of the total farmers.

New Mexico had the highest proportion of its farm operators on relief or rehabilitation, 36 percent. South Dakota followed with 33 percent, and North Dakota and Oklahoma each with 27 percent. About one-fifth of all farmers in Colorado and Kentucky were receiving such aid. Florida, Idaho, Montana, Minnesota, Pennsylvania, Arkansas, South Carolina, and Wyoming reported 10 to 18 percent of their farmers on either relief or rehabilitation rolls. These 14 States, which contained approximately one-fourth of all farms in the United States, included over one-half of all farmers in rural areas receiving public aid in June 1935.

All but two of these States are in drought or poor land regions. Idaho, Montana, the Dakotas, and Minnesota form a belt across the northern part of the 1934 drought area. Wyoming forms a connecting link with Colorado, New Mexico, Oklahoma, and Arkansas, a chain of southwestern drought States cutting into the Dust Bowl and the cotton areas. Kentucky and Pennsylvania had large concentrations of farmers on relief in the Appalachian sections with their poor soil and abandoned mines. . . .

Rehabilitation clients in June were still concentrated to a large extent in the southern States, where the program was first developed. Of the 8 States with more than 10,000 clients receiving advances during the month, only 2 (South Dakota and Minnesota) were outside the South. The program had its smallest development on the west coast and in the northeastern States.

Part of the vast volume of rural need was due directly to depression factors. Farmers who had done fairly well in the past were victims of bank failures and vanishing markets. City workers and workers in rural industries lost their jobs and, without farm experience or capital, tried to make a living from the soil. Youth who would normally have gone to the cities and towns to work in industry stayed on the farm, crowding into an already overcrowded agriculture.

The depression was not directly responsible, however, for all the rural distress reflected in the heavy relief rolls. Federal relief brought to light a much more numerous group of farmers whose distress arose from long-run factors, who had led a precarious existence for some years prior to the depression because of these factors, or for whom the depression was the last straw in an accumulation of troubles outside their control.

Some of the accumulating hazards of American agrarian life have been enumerated here. They show the variety and complexity of the forces which underlie rural distress and indicate the regional differences involved.

In many parts of the country, farmers have been attempting for years to cultivate soil which was never suitable for farming or which has deteriorated beyond redemption. Such soil has given them only the barest living and has made it impossible for them to better their condition. Had Federal relief not been made available, they might have continued more or less inarticulately to endure their extreme poverty unaided. The relief program served to bring their condition to light and to focus attention on the need for removing the impoverished land from cultivation.

The National Resources Board has estimated that about 450,000 farms in the United States, including 75 million acres, are of this submarginal type. They are to be found for the most part in the hilly, dry, or forested parts of the country and in sections where the soil is light and sandy or seriously eroded. Over one-half of the total acreage proposed for retirement from arable farming is in the Western Great Plains and the southeastern hilly cotton and tobacco regions, although scattered concentrations are found throughout the United States.

Poor land in itself is a sufficient hazard to farming, but when, as in the Appalachian-Ozark highlands and parts of the cotton areas, it is coupled with an excessive birth rate, the problem is greatly aggravated, and individual and family suffering multiplied. In the past, the high farm birth rate served to populate new areas and the cities. But desirable free homestead land was exhausted years ago and the covered wagon is no longer a means of escape from an overcrowded shack in the hills. The depression shut off the opportunity to make a living by migrating to cities and towns. There was nothing for the surplus rural population to do but remain, causing serious unbalance between population and land in many sections.

Not only have some farmers been trying to grow crops on hopelessly poor soil, but others have been ruining good land by practices conducive to soil erosion or have failed to take necessary precautions to protect land subject to erosion. Warnings of soil erosion have been heard in many areas for years, but these have been ignored by farmers who were too eager for immediate results to care about the future. Other farmers could not afford the outlay necessary to prevent erosion or had such limited acreages that they had no choice but to use their land to the full, regardless of the danger of over cropping. In 1934, the National Resources Board reported that the usefulness for farming of 35 million acres had been completely destroyed, that the top soil was nearly or entirely removed from another 125 million acres, and that destruction had begun on another 100 million acres.

Excessive cropping has been especially destructive on the dry land of the Western Great Plains, where quarter sections allotted to the settlers under the homesteading laws were too small for economic use of the land. The farmers were further led astray during the World War when they were encouraged to break more and more sod in order to meet the world demand for wheat. No provision was made against the effects of the inevitable dry years, and vast acreages of dry soil were left unprotected by grass or trees against the ravages of wind and sun.

The southern and western corn belts also contain much easily eroded soil which is being destroyed because the many small farmers in the area have been concentrating on clean-cultivated row crops. In the hilly southeastern section, cotton and tobacco are being grown for the market on land from which the top soil has been completely worn away. Cultivating the subsoil requires extensive use of fertilizer, which makes farming on such land an expensive and precarious business. The cost of fertilizer consumes a large part of the farmer's income and credit, and when the crop fails he is ready for the relief rolls.

Small farms in areas which require large-scale methods often lead to practices conducive to soil erosion, as already pointed out. Even when soil erosion is not involved, the farms are often inadequate to make a stable income possible. Where productivity per acre is low, as in the western dry-farming regions and the hilly cotton areas, and where there is constant threat of drought, large acreages are required to compensate for low productivity and to build up reserves for years of crop loss. Famers whose acreages are too small to provide such surpluses in good years are brought to dependency at the first year of crop failure.

The recent trend in American agriculture has been toward absolute dependence on a single cash crop—cotton, tobacco, corn, or wheat—to the exclusion of production of food and feed crops for home use. The small farmer who follows this practice is rarely able to accumulate reserves in good years for the year when his one crop fails or the market falls. When that time comes, he is left not only with no alternative source of income but also with no products for home consumption.

During the World War and post-war years, farmers borrowed money and bought large acreages of land at inflated values in order to take advantage of high prices for foodstuffs. They also invested heavily in machinery to be paid for at some future date. But before they could realize on their investment, the depression sent prices and land values tobogganing. Many were unable to meet real estate and chattel mortgage payments and were left in the hands of their creditors.

Natural resources, such as timber, coal, and other minerals, have been progressively and often wastefully depleted in certain parts of the country. These formerly furnished small farmers with a means of earning the cash income necessary to supplement their limited agricultural production. When these industries declined, the farmers became completely dependent on farms too small or too unproductive to support them. This situation is found in the Lake States Cut-Over and Appalachian-Ozark Areas in particular, and accounts in part for the heavy relief loads in those regions.

An extremely low standard of living has been characteristic of tenant farmers in various parts of the country since long before the depression.

This has been particularly true of the South where the cotton tenant system, especially that phase of tenancy known as sharecropping, was developed to utilize the abundant supply of cheap and tractable labor.

Under the sharecropping system the tenant furnishes the labor of his entire family, as well as his own, for raising the cotton crop. The family receives in return the use of a piece of land, a house, work stock, equipment, subsistence goods, and the proceeds of half the crop, the other half being retained by the landlord. This system has become more and more widespread, until at the present time 50 percent of the tenants in some States are sharecroppers.

While cotton was booming, the extreme poverty of the southern cotton tenant attracted little attention, but the depression and pre-depression years brought a crisis in the cotton market. Cotton acreage was extended after the war. Increases in production, however, coincided with a relatively decreasing demand both at home and abroad. The competition of artificial silk, increased production in foreign countries since the World War, and increased tariffs were some of the factors responsible. The results were decreasing prices since 1925 and a large carry-over from one season to another.

When the depression brought these conditions to a climax, acreage was sharply reduced, and tenants, especially sharecroppers, were displaced from the land. With no resources of any kind, and accustomed to depend on the landlord for every want, large numbers of tenant farm families were left stranded, bewildered, and helpless.

The acreage reduction program of the Agricultural Adjustment Administration raised prices and helped the cotton growers by benefit payments. Most of the tenants' payments in the first years of the program, however, were applied by the landlords to old debts, and tenants continued to be displaced from the farms, although at a much slower rate than before.

Assuming a permanently decreased demand for cotton, the tenant system of the South has produced a "stranded" population, a group of landless people with undeveloped capacities, who, unless some scheme for rehabilitation is devised, will be permanently in need of public assistance.

Not so widely publicized, but more rapid of late, has been the increase in tenancy in the drought-stricken Great Plains Area, where discouraged owners are being replaced by tenants.

Insofar as farm laborers have formerly been employed by farmers now on relief, their need for relief is caused by the same factors that caused the need of their former employers. The depression also led to unemployment of farm laborers through restricting the demand for farm hands by farmers still able to carry on. It may be reasonably assumed, therefore, that the relief problem of farm laborers is to a greater extent a function of the depression than the result of long-run tendencies.

In addition, the problem of migratory labor has grown markedly with the increase of large-scale one crop commercial farming. Since under this system laborers are needed for only a brief period while the one crop is being harvested, they must move on to other areas after a few weeks, and so on throughout the season. At best they can find employment for only a few months a year and their wages are not enough to carry them through the months of idleness. Because of their wandering existence, they are without roots in any community and cannot turn to neighbors or neighborhood grocers for help in off-seasons.

III

America's Shame:
The Crisis of Relief

AMERICA'S SYSTEM OF RELIEF until long after the depression had settled over the land was one that had evolved in a preindustrial age. Fundamentally, the poor were dependent upon the charity of others more fortunate and upon their city or local government. The arrangement may have been satisfactory for more or less normal times, but after several months of depression neither private charity nor local government could begin to cope with the volume of poverty and tragedy created by the economic disaster. The result was that in well-endowed America people actually starved.

President Herbert Hoover believed firmly that relief was a matter for state and local government only. Not until the summer of 1932, after three winters of depression, did he consent to any federal relief action. The Emergency Relief Act of 1932 finally authorized the Reconstruction Finance Corporation to lend the states up to $300 million for relief purposes. By the end of 1932 the RFC had actually lent only $30 million for relief. When one remembers that in 1932 the RFC lent $90 million to the Central Republic Bank and Trust Company of Chicago, of which former RFC chairman and former vice-president Charles G. Dawes was an officer, one can appreciate the exasperation of the nation's hungry.

Even a partially satisfactory national relief policy had to await the arrival of a new Congress and a new administration.

16 • "NO ONE HAS STARVED."

This sentence was one not infrequently heard among people who were comfortable, despite such newspaper stories as the two reprinted here. Each of them is from The New York Times, *the first on Christmas Day, 1931, the second on September 7, 1932.*

MIDDLETOWN, N.Y., Dec. 24.—Attracted by smoke from the chimney of a supposedly empty summer cottage near Anwana Lake in Sullivan County, Constable Simon Glaser found a young couple starving. Three days without food, the wife, who is 23 years old, was hardly able to walk.

The couple, Mr. and Mrs. Wilfred Wild of New York, had been unemployed since their formerly wealthy employer lost his money, and several days ago they invested all they had, except 25 cents for food, in bus fare to this region in search of work. Finding none, they went into the cottage, preferring to starve rather than beg. They said they had resigned themselves to dying together.

An effort is being made to obtain employment for them, but if this fails they will be sent back to New York.

DANBURY, CONN., Sept. 6.—Found starving under a rude canvas shelter in a patch of woods on Flatboard Ridge, where they had lived for five days on wild berries and apples, a woman and her 16-year-old daughter were fed and clothed today by the police and placed in the city almshouse.

The woman is Mrs. John Moll, 33, and her daughter Helen, of White Plains, N.Y., who have been going from city to city looking for work since July, 1931, when Mrs. Moll's husband left her.

When the police found them they were huddled beneath a strip of canvas stretched from a boulder to the ground. Rain was dripping from the improvised shelter, which had no sides.

17 • INADEQUATE TAX BASE
FOR THE RELIEF LOAD

In the following selection one of the nation's most eminent economists analyzed the financial distress of American cities. Federal Aid for Unemployment Relief. Hearings *before a Subcommittee of the Committee on Manufactures, United States Senate, 72nd Cong., 2 sess., on S. 5125 (Washington: Government Printing Office, 1933), pp. 124-125.*

THE CHAIRMAN. Doctor Slichter, will you give your full name and address and your present occupation in the Harvard School to the reporter, for the record?

PROFESSOR SLICHTER. My name is Sumner H. Slichter, and I am professor of business economics, Harvard Business School.

THE CHAIRMAN. The committee would be grateful to you, Doctor Slichter, if you would, in your own way, comment upon the economic consequences and implications of the unemployment problem. We will then ask you any questions that occur to us.

PROFESSOR SLICHTER. Mr. Chairman, the need for national assistance, by this time, has become so self-evident that it would seem to me to be a waste of your time for me to offer anything along that line.

THE CHAIRMAN. Unfortunately, however, we do not find that to be the generally accepted opinion.

PROFESSOR SLICHTER. The tax base of the local communities is a somewhat narrow one. About nine-tenths of their income is derived from real estate taxation, and the difficulty, or one of the difficulties, with that base is that a man is liable for taxes simply because he owns the title to the real estate, quite regardless of whether or not he has any income from the real estate.

SENATOR COSTIGAN. Or able to pay it?

PROFESSOR SLICHTER. Yes, or from any other source.

The result one could predict without much difficulty is a steadily rising ratio of delinquent taxes throughout the country. In fact, delinquency ratios of from 20 to 30 per cent are not unusual.

The income from real estate, itself, of course, has gone down. It is one of the slower incomes to fall; but it is a fairly conservative generalization, I should say, to estimate that the rentals, in most places, are down about 20 per cent, in some cases more, and in some cases less.

Of course, the real estate owner bears a double burden in the case of unemployment, because it is almost the universal rule that relief agencies do not pay rent, except on eviction, and then they only pay for a month or two. In other words, there is a more or less national moratorium on rents, in so far as the unemployed are concerned.

The older the depression gets, the more unsatisfactory becomes this narrow base of public revenue. The private agencies have been compelled to conserve their resources, and to withdraw from the strictly unemployment field. They started out to help out the unemployed, more or less, but the burden became too great; and in order to conserve the permanent part of their work, they had to withdraw.

I made a compilation not long ago of some community chest drives for 1932 and 1933, and this covers 44 cities.

In 1932, the community chests in these cities raised about $24,900,000. This goal for 1933 is $23,100,000. That, of course, means that the burden on public relief funds is increasing.

18 • LOCAL RELIEF:
THE GENERAL SITUATION

The following selection, the testimony of a professional social worker to the LaFollette-Costigan committee in January 1933, describes the inadequacy of local relief in 44 American cities. Ibid., pp. 64-67.

THE CHAIRMAN. Mr. Lurie, please state your full name, address, and present position.

MR. LURIE. My name is H. L. Lurie, and I am director of the Bureau of Jewish Social Research in New York City.

I have been asked by a committee of the American Association of Social Workers to present a report which summarizes material recently obtained from social workers throughout the country describing present conditions of relief and perhaps something about the future uncertainties in the present relief situation. . . .

This report summarizes information which has been received in the last week from this group of consultants and applies to 44 cities and adjacent areas in 25 States and the District of Columbia. Since few professional social workers serve the smaller communities and the industrial and mining areas not incorporated in large cities, we were able to obtain this information, therefore, primarily from populous communities which possess relatively well organized programs of relief and social service. . . .

This report attempts to present a summary of present conditions with respect to unemployment relief in large industrial centers and the areas contiguous to large cities. The experience with unemployment relief has brought out strikingly the lack of organization for welfare in many parts of the country. There exists a great variation in organization, resources, policies, and standards of relief. Much of the recent organization is of an emergency and haphazard character and reflects the lack of a national program and the absence of minimum standards of administration.

Information which would bear upon conditions in entire States has not been available except in a few instances due to the fact that few States possess adequate organization for the gathering of information concerning general conditions of unemployment and relief within their boundaries.

It is safe to assume, perhaps, that in these areas which are not covered by the larger cities, conditions of need are at least equally serious. It is generally known that organized efforts for relief are less well established and effective in the smaller communities than in the area covered in this report. Even in the larger cities considered in this report there is a great diversity of standards, policies, and adequacy of resources.

It is believed that the depression has reversed the trend of several decades and has resulted in a shift of population from the larger urban centers to the areas of rural population. Prof. P. K. Whelpton, of the Scripps Foundation, Miami University, Ohio, has estimated that during 1932 urban centers have lost and rural areas have gained approximately 400,000 in population. He reports the use of farm houses formerly abandoned for human habitation, the erection of makeshift dwellings and doubling up of families in rural homes due to this return of an industrial population to the country. This additional population is creating a serious problem to the resources of relief and human welfare to the already overburdened rural sections. This drift to the more sparsely settled regions has to some extent been brought about by the inadequacy of relief available in the larger centers of population. Although the outlook for obtaining food and shelter may be thought to be somewhat better in the rural sections, this drift to the farms is intensifying the problem of maintaining essential standards of living for the rural population.

In the cities and counties specifically covered in this report, there has been a tremendous increase in the number of families and individuals receiving relief during the past year. This increase in number of families aided has been greater than the increase in the amount of relief expended, indicating a continuation of the conditions reported to this committee in May, 1932, when a tendency to stretch meager relief funds over an increasingly large number of applicants was already generally prevalent. With the beginning of this winter a number of cities report large increases in the number of applicants for relief and increasing relief loans. One city reports for the year an increase of 300 per cent in the number of families aided, with an increase of only 30 per cent in available funds.

There is a general expectancy that the number of families in need of relief will continue to increase during the winter months, although a few cities are anticipating a corresponding increase in relief funds to cover this expansion in relief responsibility. . . .

In general it may be said that the cities included in this report present a relief experience corresponding to the more comprehensive statistics which are regularly obtained by the agencies mentioned. The 43 cities and counties in this group are giving relief at this time to approximately 3,000,000 persons, consisting of 650,000 families and 100,000 unattached and homeless individuals and are expending approximately $17,500,000 a month on relief.

The committee attempted to obtain estimates of the proportion of those totally unemployed who were receiving relief from an organized source during December, 1932. Statistics on the number of families assisted are reasonably accurate, but information on the number of unemployed is frequently a crude estimate.

Discarding extreme cases at both ends of the table, the data submitted show a range from 18 to 58 per cent of the unemployed group receiving relief in December. The average city aided approximately 32 per cent of the totally jobless and in the 30 cities combined for which we have estimates of the number of unemployed, 25 per cent were receiving relief. Lower percentages in the large cities of Chicago and Philadelphia account for the difference.

Lawrence, Mass., Detroit, St. Louis, Philadelphia, Cleveland, Washington, and Chicago reported lower ratios of the unemployed on relief, while Seattle, Toledo, Akron, Syracuse, Hartford, and Milwaukee were among the highest percentages of relief cases to total estimated unemployed. Ratios for individual cities, however, must be considered as having less probability than the total which may to some extent balance errors due to under or over estimate of unemployed.

In these cities which have organized relief agencies an attempt is being made to supply at least food to all applicants who are found to be entirely destitute. In reply to the question as to the estimated number of families and individuals who were in need but not receiving relief, one informant replied that it was impossible to estimate the number since this would differ according to the standards of eligibility which might be applied. He indicated, however, that in his city, which is considered as having a more adequate organization than is usually to be found, families are forced into a position of extreme dependency before applications for relief are considered.

Homes are lost, insurance policies canceled, aid from relatives and friends has been terminated, families are forced to exhaust and destroy indefinitely their credit before relief is granted to them. This statement on the degree of destitution reached before relief is granted is applicable in practically all communities. A number of cities report that no work or home relief is being made available to adult families—that is, to childless couples or families without young children. No relief or very inadequate forms of relief are being given to the unattached men and women without family connections.

19 • LOCAL RELIEF:
YOUNGSTOWN, OHIO

The next five selections describe the relief situation and its consequences in five representative industrial cities. The first of these selections is excerpted from Joseph L. Heffernan, "The Hungry City: A Mayor's Experience with Unemployment," The Atlantic Monthly, *CXLIX (May, 1932), pp. 538-540, 546. Reprinted by permission of the publisher.*

IN DECEMBER 1929, when I was mayor of Youngstown, I attended a conference on unemployment at Cleveland, called at the request of President Hoover. It was held at the Chamber of Commerce, under the chairmanship of Mr. Elroy J. Kulas, president of the Otis Steel Company, and was attended by public officials of northern Ohio.

Speaker after speaker told what his community would do to end the depression, and how quickly it would be done. The unemployed were to be set marching gayly back to work without an instant's delay, and the two-car garage was to be made ready for further enlargement.

When it came my turn to speak, I said rather brutally: 'This is all plain bunk. We know that our cities and counties are in debt and have bond limitations imposed by the state. If all of us were to start this minute drawing up a programme of public improvements, it would require months to get the legislation through. Why not tell the people the truth?'

After the meeting many of the officials said to me: 'Mayor, you are right. There isn't much we can do. But we have to go along, don't we?'

Five months later I went to Germany and visited a number of cities. Everywhere I saw that the German people were in a bad way. On returning home, I made a public statement that Germany was on the verge of economic collapse, and predicted that the depression would take five years to run its course. Thereupon I asked for a bond issue of $1,000,000 for unemployment relief. Many leading business men went out of their way to show their disapproval. One of them voiced the opinion of the majority when he said to me: 'You make a bad mistake in talking about the unemployed. *Don't* emphasize hard times and everything will be all right.' An influential newspaper chastised me for 'borrowing trouble'; the depression would be over, the editor maintained, before relief would be needed.

Discussion dragged on for several months, and the gravity of the situation was so deliberately misrepresented by the entire business community that when the bond issue finally came to a ballot, in November 1930, it was voted down.

Thus we passed into the early days of 1931—fourteen months after the first collapse—with no relief in sight except that which was provided by the orthodox charities. Not a single move had been made looking toward action by a united community.

Strange as it may seem, there was no way in which the city government could embark upon a programme of its own. We had no funds available for emergency relief, and without specific authorization from the people we could not issue bonds. To get around that obstacle we urged the state legislature to amend the law so as to modify our bond limitation, but that body was reluctant to pass a relief bill. Finally, after a long delay, it agreed upon a halfway measure which permitted the cities to sell bonds for the limited purpose of providing for their indigents. It made no pretense of supplying new employment for the jobless, but it furthered this end to some degree by indirection. Up to this time all funds for poor relief had been appropriated from general receipts, such as taxes. The new bonds removed this strain upon taxes, so that the money which had formerly been set aside for this purpose was released for public works. A few of the unemployed were thus given part-time jobs improving the parks.

Inadequate as it was, this legislative relief was all that the great State of Ohio could bring itself to grant, and even this pittance was withheld until the crisis had already run through more than eighteen devastating months.

I have cited these instances from my experience as mayor of an industrial city because they illustrate perfectly the state of mind which has been America's greatest handicap in dealing with the depression. Everyone will remember the assurances that were freely given out in November and December, 1929, by the highest authorities in government and business. The country, we were told, was 'fundamentally sound.' Nevertheless, general unemployment continued to increase through the winter. Then in the spring of 1930 it was predicted that we might expect an upward turn any minute. Yet the summer slid past with hope unfulfilled. Winter came again, and conditions had grown steadily worse; still nothing was done, because we were reluctant to face the truth. Our leaders, having made a bad guess in the beginning, have been unwilling to admit their error. With the foolish consistency which is the hobgoblin of little minds, they have persistently rejected reality and allowed our people to suffer by pretending that all would be well on the morrow.

In spite of the insurmountable handicaps under which the cities have labored in trying to cope with the emergency, desperate men and women out of work have stormed city halls from coast to coast demanding jobs. It has been a waste of breath for mayors to explain that they have no authority to put men to work when municipal treasuries are empty. 'Don't hand us that,' is a response I have heard over and over again. 'Do you mean to tell us that the city couldn't raise the money if it wanted to?' This, of course, has been the real tragedy of the situation: the cities could *not* raise the money.

One man I had known for years stood at my desk and calmly said: 'My wife is frantic. After working at the steel mill for twenty-five years, I have lost my job, and I'm too old to get other work. If you can't do something for me, I'm going to kill myself.' I knew he was desperate. Through friends I managed to find him a little job where he could earn enough to keep body and soul together.

In another instance a newspaper man urged me to find work for one of his neighbors, a man who had a wife and four sons—all rugged citizens who preferred to starve rather than accept public charity. 'You could hardly believe what they live on,' the reporter told me. 'The mother mixes a little flour and water, and cooks it in a frying pan. That is their regular meal.' Eventually I found work for one of the sons, and he became the sole support of the others.

To my home came a sad-eyed woman, the mother of nine children. No one in the family had had work in more than a year. 'How do you manage to live?' I asked her. 'I can't tell you,' she replied simply; 'I really don't know.' Christmas 1930 was marked by the usual campaign for the most needy cases, and this family was included in the list. They got their Christmas basket all right, but when the holidays were over they were no better off than they had been before.

As time went on, business conditions showed no improvement. Every night hundreds of homeless men crowded into the municipal incinerator, where they found warmth even though they had to sleep on heaps of garbage. In January 1931, I obtained the cooperation of the City Council to convert an abandoned police station into a 'flop-house.' The first night it was filled, and it has remained filled ever since. I made a point of paying frequent visits to this establishment so that I could see for myself what kind of men these down-and-outers were, and I heartily wish that those folk who have made themselves comfortable by ignoring and denying the suffering of their less fortunate neighbors could see some of the sights I saw. There were old men gnarled by heavy labor, young mechanics tasting the first bitterness of defeat, clerks and white-collar workers learning the equality of misery, derelicts who fared no worse in bad times than in good, Negroes who only a short time before had come from Southern cotton fields, now glad to find any shelter from the cold, immigrants who had been lured to Van Dyke's 'land of youth and freedom'—each one a personal tragedy, and all together an overwhelming catastrophe for the nation. . . .

This descent from respectability, frequent enough in the best of times, has been hastened immeasurably by two years of business paralysis, and the people who have been affected in this manner must be numbered in millions. This is what we have accomplished with our bread lines and soup kitchens. I know, because I have seen thousands of these defeated, discouraged, hopeless men and women, cringing and fawning as they come to ask for public aid. It is a spectacle of national degeneration. That is the fundamental tragedy for America. If every mill and factory in the land should begin to hum with prosperity to-morrow morning, the destructive effect of our haphazard relief measures would not work itself out of the nation's blood until the sons of our sons had expiated the sins of our neglect.

Even now there are signs of rebellion against a system so out of joint that it can only offer charity to honest men who want to work. Sometimes it takes the form of social agitation, but again it may show itself in a revolt that is absolute and final. Such an instance was reported in a Youngstown newspaper on the day I wrote these lines:—

FATHER OF TEN DROWNS SELF

JUMPS FROM BRIDGE, STARTS TO SWIM
GIVES UP, OUT OF WORK TWO YEARS

Out of work two years, Charles Wayne, aged 57, father of ten children, stood on the Spring Common bridge this morning, watching hundreds of other persons moving by on their way to work. Then he took off his coat, folded it carefully, and jumped into the swirling Mahoning River. Wayne was born in Youngstown and was employed by the Republic Iron and Steel Company for twenty-seven years as a hot mill worker.

'We were about to lose our home,' sobbed Mrs. Wayne. 'And the gas and electric companies had threatened to shut off the service.'

20 • LOCAL RELIEF:
DETROIT, MICHIGAN

Detroit, like many other cities dependent upon a single industry, was a poor place to be broke and jobless. This newspaper story by Gladys H. Kelsey, "Problem of Relief Acute in Detroit," The New York Times, June 26, 1932, indicates some of the auto city's financial difficulties. Reprinted by permission of the publisher.

DETROIT, June 23.—The Department of Public Welfare, after an uneven career of attempting to give the city's unemployed men care which would maintain their morale until such time as conditions became normal, is at length faced with the situation of being unable to provide even groceries for a bare sustenance diet to the families under its care without the most complex planning.

Affairs became acute May 24, when the Emergency Relief Fund ceased to function. The Welfare Department, under the balanced budget demanded by New York bankers who loaned money to Detroit, received a $7,000,000 allowance. In November the Emergency Relief Committee, a volunteer organization functioning at the request of the Mayor, reported that $2,250,000 additional would be needed to run the department.

In January the Emergency Relief Committee announced that the Welfare Department would have to get along with an additional $1,125,000. Ultimately they turned over a total of $645,000 to the Welfare Department, which had in the meantime been carrying 6,000 cases that it would not have carried without hope of financing from that committee.

So on May 24 the Welfare Department owed $800,000 and had on hand $8,000. . . .

21 • LOCAL RELIEF:
PHILADELPHIA, PENNSYLVANIA

On May 9, 1932, Karl de Schweinitz, executive secretary of the Community Council of Philadelphia, described for the La-Follette-Costigan committee what happened in the spring of 1932 when relief funds in the City of Brotherly Love were entirely exhausted. Federal Cooperation in Unemployment Relief, Hearings *before a Subcommittee of the Committee on Manufactures, United States Senate, 72nd Cong., 1 sess., on S. 4592 (Washington: Government Printing Office, 1932), pp. 20-26.*

MR. DE SCHWEINITZ. When I appeared before the Subcommittee of the Committee on Manufacturers [*sic*] last December, I stated that there were 238,000 persons out of work in Philadelphia and that we estimated unemployment in the city in ordinary times to be between 40,000 and 50,000. There are now 298,000 persons out of work. In other words, whereas in December our unemployment was a little less than five times what one might call normal unemployment, to-day it is six times normal unemployment.

In December I told you that 43,000 families were receiving relief. To-day 55,000 families are receiving relief.

In December our per family grant was $4.39 per week per family. It ₃s now $4.23 per family. Of this $4.23 per family, about $3.93 is an allowance for food. This is about two-thirds of the amount needed to provide a health-maintaining diet. . . . I want to tell you about an experience we had in Philadelphia when our private funds were exhausted and before public funds became available.

On April 11 [1932] we mailed to families the last food orders which they received from private funds. It was not until April 22 that the giving of aid to families from public funds began, so that there was a period of about 11 days when many families received nothing. We have received reports from workers as to how these families managed. The material I am about to give you is typical, although it is based on a small sample. We made an intensive study of 91 families to find out what happened when the food orders stopped.

In a little less than 9 per cent of these families there were pregnant mothers and in a little more than one-third of the families children of nursing age.

This is how some of these families managed.

One woman said she borrowed 50 cents from a friend and bought stale bread for 3½ cents per loaf, and that is all they had for eleven days except for one or two meals.

With the last food order another woman received she bought dried vegetables and canned goods. With this she made a soup and whenever the members of the family felt hungry they just ate some of the soup.

Here is a family of a pregnant mother and three children. They had only two meals a day and managed by having breakfast about 11 o'clock in the norming [sic] and then advancing the time of their evening meal. Breakfast consisted of cocoa, and bread and butter; the evening meal of canned soup.

One woman went along the docks and picked up vegetables that fell from the wagons. Sometimes the fish vendors gave her fish at the end of the day. On two different occasions this family was without food for a day and a half.

One family had nothing the day the food order stopped until 9 o'clock at night. Then the mother went to a friend's house and begged for a loaf of bread. This woman finally got two days' work at 75 cents a day. She bought a little meat and made a stew from vegetables picked up which they cooked over again every day to prevent its spoiling.

Another family's food consisted of potatoes, rice, bread, and coffee, and for a period of a day and a half they had no food at all.

SENATOR COSTIGAN. Are the cases you are citing typical or extreme?

MR. DE SCHWEINITZ. They are typical. I could tell you about many others, but while tragic it would become monotonous, and a few will illustrate the situation as well as many.

Here is another family which for two days had nothing to eat but bread, and during most of the rest of the time they had only two meals a day. Their meals consisted of bread and coffee for breakfast, and bread and raw or cooked carrots for dinner.

The gas company was careful not to turn off gas in a great many of these families, so in some instances food could be cooked.

Another family did not have food for two days. Then the husband went out and gathered dandelions and the family lived on them.

Here is another family which for two and a half days went without food.

Still another family thinking to get as much as possible with their last food order bought potatoes and for 11 days lived only on them. . . .

I should also like to say that when we talk to people who ask about unemployment they say, "Well, people manage to get along somehow or other don't they? You do not have very many people who really drop dead of starvation." That is perfectly true. Actually, death from starvation is not a frequent occurrence. You do not often hear about casualties of that sort. This is because people live in just the way that I have described. They live on inadequacies, and because they live on inadequacies the thing does not become dramatic and we do not hear about it. Yet the cost in human suffering is just as great as if they starved to death overnight.

SENATOR COSTIGAN. What you say is not only shockingly true but Senator Copeland, of New York, has recently reported cases of known starvation this past winter.

MR. DE SCHWEINITZ. The hospitals have had definite cases of starvation. . . .

A great many people raise the question as to whether the unemployed are a good-for-nothing lot and are out of work because of their own fault. They are not. We have definite studies to show that they had had long and good work records and that they are active, earnest human beings. All they want is a job.

SENATOR WAGNER. No really intelligent person asserts that to-day.

MR. DE SCHWEINITZ. No intelligent person, no; but lots of persons raise that question.

SENATOR WAGNER. I said intelligent persons.

MR. DE SCHWEINITZ. Yes; we are agreed on that.

I want to repeat that to-day the unemployed are upstanding, intelligent, earnest, capable people, but if we put the children in these families under a period of malnutrition such as they are going through to-day, what sort of people are we going to have 20 years from now, and what will we say at that time about them? What kind of working people will they be if we continue treating them as we are treating them now? . . .

SENATOR COSTIGAN. . . . One other question, Mr. de Schweinitz. Are World War veterans among the recipients of your relief?

MR. DE SCHWEINITZ. Oh, yes; a great many.

SENATOR COSTIGAN. They are suffering with the rest?

MR. DE SCHWEINITZ. There is no distinction. We have all creeds, all groups, all races; everybody is suffering together.

In Philadelphia, in large areas, no rent is being paid at all, and the landlords, the small landlords, are suffering terribly in a great many instances and sometimes by reason of their own losses they have been obliged to come to us for help.

22 • LOCAL RELIEF: BIRMINGHAM, ALABAMA

Congressman George Huddleston, whose testimony on share-croppers was reprinted in document 14, here describes the relief problem in his home city. Federal Aid for Unemployment Relief, Hearings *before a Subcommittee of the Committee on Manufactures, United States Senate, 72nd Cong., 1 sess., on S. 174 and S. 262 (Washington: Government Printing Office, 1932), pp. 239-240.*

MR. HUDDLESTON. The best I can get at it, we have about 108,000 wage and salary earners in my district. Of that number, it is my belief that not exceeding 8,000 have their normal incomes. At least 25,000 men are altogether without work. Some of them have not had a stroke of work for more than 12 months . . . practically all have had serious cuts in their wages and many of them do not average over $1.50 a day.

A few weeks ago, my city decided as a measure of relief to dig a little canal from some funds that they had left from another improvement. They advertised that they wanted 750 laborers . . . to do the hard, dirty work of digging and other laborious and unpleasant work. The men were to work 10 hours and to get $2 a day. They had over 12,000 registrations for those jobs and they were supposed to be only men who live in my city.

Since that happened, the Woodward Iron Co., which is a large producer of pig iron, has shut down and 3,000 men were thrown out of work. Previously, they had been operating two and three days a week. . . .

We are hard put to it for money. We have a very efficient worker in charge of the family relief that we are distributing, and to get it the applicant must have to have it. Nobody gets it who does not make an ironclad showing. Many are deterred, of course, by the rigid investigating and the various humiliating circumstances attending the situation and do not ask for it. They ask their neighbors. Some are too proud. They go into remote quarters of the community and beg from door to door where they think they are not known, trying to get a little something to eat.

The scale of relief ranges for an average family of four and three-tenths persons from $2.50 to $4 per week. Possibly, in some cases, there is something additional given for house rent, but I think that I may say that such cases are rare.

Ordinarily, many landlords do not expect to get any rent. Men have houses and the choice is between leaving them vacant or allowing somebody to live in them free of charge. When they are vacant long they are subjected to vandalism and frequently the landlord prefers to have somebody living there free of charge rather than to have the house torn down or burned up for fuel. That is a very general condition.

23 · LOCAL RELIEF: NEW YORK CITY

The nation's largest city had one of the best relief systems in the nation. But as the following story, from The New York Times, *July 9, 1932, indicates, to be down-and-out in New York was as tragic as elsewhere.*

SOMEWHERE IN TIN MOUNTAIN, the four-acre jungle on the Red Hook waterfront in Brooklyn, Louis Bringmann put down his old sea chest last night and looked about him for a place to sleep. He was 60 years old, penniless, friendless and jobless.

Up to 9 A.M. yesterday Louis Bringmann had had a home on the top landing of the Atlantic Theatre, at Flatbush Avenue and Dean Street, but the Fire Department inspector on his monthly round discovered it.

Patrolman Richard Palmay of the Bergen Street police station climbed the fire-escape stairs at 8 A.M. with orders to "remove the fire hazard." At the top landing he peered over the walls of corrugated cardboard which Bringmann had built around the grille work. The tenant was fast asleep.

On the cardboard wall was a neat sign, done in old-school flourishes and shading:

NOTICE

Please be kind enough not to destroy or take anything from this resting place. I am out of work and this is all I have. I have no money and I can't find a job, so please leave me alone. I'll appreciate your kind consideration and

THANK YOU.

Patrolman Palmay looked down on the tired old face, the slight figure outlined beneath the worn but clean-looking blankets, at the socks and spotless shirt fluttering in the breeze on the short clothes-line overhead. He had his orders, but—

An hour later, doubling back on his post, Palmay saw Louis Bringmann leaving his cardboard shelter. He watched him as he dipped into the rain barrel he had fixed under the copper leader, to make his morning ablutions. Then he walked over.

"You'll have to move, old man." He hated the job.

"I can't stay? I'm not bothering any one. And they don't use the theatre in the Summer time. I keep everything clean. I—"

"They gave me orders," replied Palmay. "It's against the fire laws."

The snow-white head nodded. Louis Bringmann was too patient a man to vent his bitterness in vain argument.

He rolled his blankets carefully and dressed. He took his little sea chest under one thin arm. The other meager chattels dangled from his white fingers. He started to move.

Palmay thrust a half dollar into the free hand and walked away. . . .

The white-haired Bringmann plodded up the avenue, immaculate in his worn brown trousers and blue jacket, heading toward the river.

He had known of Tin Mountain before, but he was proud. In Tin Mountain, a sprawling village of tin huts and makeshift dugouts at the foot of Henry Street, are all types of men—brawny Scandinavian seamen, husky Irish longshoremen—good men, but a bit rough. One of its streets has the bitter legend on a placard, "Prosperity Boulevard."

Late in the afternoon he was still sitting on the little chest that contains the meager souvenirs of better days—a few faded menus he had made up when he was head chef of one of the big Manhattan hotels. He wouldn't tell which one.

"The past," said Louis Bringmann, "is a turned-over page. When I read it I read alone. They tell me now that I'm even too old for dish-washing—that's the whole story. I have no friends and my money is gone."

24 • HUNGRY CHILDREN

Growing children, who certainly had no responsibility for the dismal world their elders created for them, were the most tragic figures of the Great Depression. In this account, Grace Abbott, Chief of the Children's Bureau, Department of Labor, describes in general terms malnutrition among the nation's children. "Children and the Depression: A National Study and a Warning," The New York Times, December 18, 1932. Reprinted by permission of the publisher.

. . . EVEN THOSE WITH LITTLE IMAGINATION know how no employment or underemployment, the failure of banks and building and loan associations have affected many children whose parents faced the future self-reliant and unafraid a few years ago. In the millions of homes which have escaped the abyss of destitution fear of what may still happen is destroying the sense of security which is considered necessary for the happiness and well-being of children.

Great effort has been made to prevent suffering. Last year probably more than a billion dollars was expended by public and private agencies for the relief of the unemployed. Although this is probably some eight times as much as was spent for relief in normal times, no one who has been going in and out of the homes of the unemployed in large urban centres or in the single-industry towns and mining communities has reported that it has been adequate to insure shelter, clothes and reasonably adequate diet for all needy children. . . .

Although the death rate [of infants and children] is low, there is much evidence that the health of many children is being adversely affected by the prolonged depression. For example, hospitals and clinics report an increase in rickets among children; in New York City, where relief for the unemployed has probably been more nearly adequate than in any other of the largest cities, the city Health Department reports that 20.5 per cent of the school children examined were suffering from malnutrition in 1932. . . .

Undernourishment is even more widespread in areas of extreme depression, where the available relief has been quite inadequate, such as the coal-mining communities and "one-industry towns," where there has been little or no work for several years, or in districts where the depression has been added to the economic losses brought by flood and drought.

In a recent report of the Surgeon General of the Public Health Service on the rural health work in the drought-stricken areas in 1931, the reports of the health officers as to health conditions in the counties are summarized. Here one finds the health officers of Alabama and Arkansas, for example, reporting for county after county an increase in pellagra due to inability to purchase the necessary food; and "dietary diseases" and widespread undernourishment were frequently referred to in the reports for these and other States. The bulletin, "Health Briefs," of the Tennessee Health Department for August of this year says that "the increase in deaths from pellagra that has been forecast since the beginning of the reduced economic conditions is now beginning to show on the tally sheets of vital statistics." . . .

Recently the director of the Child Hygiene Division of the Children's Bureau was called into a conference to discuss how the reduced relief budgets should be expended so as to insure the health of the children. Protective foods for children include milk, fruits, some fresh vegetables, and eggs, and the problem was how to purchase these as well as the foods that supply energy for a family of five when the total income is $11 a month. Some families are managing to exist on a smaller per capita than $2 a month, but at the cost of greatly lowered vital capacity and resistance to disease.

It is the future effects of undernourishment among children that are to be feared. As Dr. William H. Welch has put it, "The ground lost by undernourishment in childhood may never be regained." That many children have suffered such losses during the past three years is certain. . . .

25 • CHICAGO'S UNDERNOURISHED
SCHOOL CHILDREN

Of the nation's major cities, Chicago was one of the hardest hit by the depression and had one of the worst records for relief. The city of the World's Fair of 1933, the Century of Progress Exposition, allowed its unpaid teachers to supplement the inadequate diets of its children from their own pocket. These two accounts are from The New York Times, *April 12 and June 19, 1931.*

CHICAGO, April 8.—A group of University of Chicago faculty members warns against the ravages of undernourishment among children in the public schools. It appears that principals and teachers in many schools have for several months been contributing from their salaries in order to provide free lunches for hungry children. Allowances have been made to the schools from the fund raised by the Governor's Commission on Unemployment, but the money has been insufficient to meet the need.

Meantime, the Board of Education announces that it has exhausted its fund for the payment of teachers and other educational purposes. This fact, however, has not prevented it issuing an elaborate report on the schools at a cost of $13,000, which is generally regarded as a campaign document contributed to the cause of Mayor [William H.] Thompson.

CHICAGO, June 18.—Shortly after a check-up of the city schools revealed today that 11,000 hungry children were being fed by teachers, Superintendent William J. Bogan dispatched a plea to Frank Loomis, secretary of Governor Emmerson's Relief Committee, pleading "for God's sake, help us feed these children during the Summer."

Mr. Bogan originally appealed to the Governor's committee for $100,-000 to feed hungry school children. Today his letter asked for "at least

$10,000." The Governor's committee sent a group of social investigators to study the situation.

In the meantime teachers are seriously handicapped by the failure of the Board of Education to pay them. Collections taken up among the more fortunate children have also aided in feeding those not so fortunate.

26 • CHILDREN
IN THE COAL MINING TOWNS

The bituminous coal industry was sick even in the 1920's. The Great Depression brought appalling conditions among the soft coal miners. In this selection Clarence E. Pickett, secretary of the American Friends Service Committee, describes the work of the Quakers in relieving the hardship of miners' children. Federal Aid for Unemployment Relief, Hearings before a Subcommittee of the Committee on Manufactures, United States Senate, 72nd Cong., 1 sess., on S. 174 and S. 262 (Washington: Government Printing Office, 1932), pp. 58-60.

MR. PICKETT. We are now doing relief work in the bituminous coal fields.

THE CHAIRMAN [Sen. LaFollette]. What areas are being covered?

MR. PICKETT. We are actually feeding in West Virginia and Kentucky, two counties in Illinois, with prospects of expanding into western Pennsylvania and eastern Ohio within the next couple of weeks. . . .

You might be interested to know something of the form of organization that we have followed. We feed through the public schools. We go only to schools where the mine is operating two days a week or less, feeling that the worst cases of need are not likely to appear in large number where the mines are operating three days or more.

THE CHAIRMAN. How much would a miner make in this bituminous field if he got three days' work a week? Do you know?

MR. PICKETT. He gets on an average about 30 cents a ton, and a good day's work will be 10 tons in these mines where we are operating. That is about $3 a day, with perhaps $2.50 or $2.40 left after his equipment is paid for. That means, say, $7.50 or $8 a week. That is very low.

THE CHAIRMAN. Do you think a man can support a family on $8 a week in that area?

MR. PICKETT. No; he can not do it. We are not holding a brief for this situation.

THE CHAIRMAN. I am not implying any criticism, but I gathered from the unqualified statement you made that you had come to the conclusion that where a man was getting three days a week work the distress would not be great.

MR. PICKETT. Well, let me put it in this way: That the area of need is so great that we are facing, that we drew an arbitrary line to hit the worst spots first. Now we are making a second study in each of these areas and that is spreading out into some of these slightly more favored communities. Of course, within a given school district you may have a mine that is operating one day a week and another that is operating three days. Now, we are studying each community, so that we probably will have to include a good many more, because we are putting our feeding on the basis of the weight of the child, and also certain other factors which we discover by a case study of families. The first thing we do is to weigh all the children in the school, and automatically put on the list to be fed all who are 10 per cent underweight.

THE CHAIRMAN. In these surveys of the schools, what percentage of the school children did you find underweight?

MR. PICKETT: It ranges from 20 to 90 per cent. We found in one school of 100 children that 99 were underweight. That is the worst we have found. We have found a good many that were 85 and 90 per cent, and then ranging down to as low as 20.

THE CHAIRMAN. Did you make any other tests of health aside from weight?

MR. PICKETT. We have not yet been able to make anything like an adequate study of health statistics. There isn't any doubt, from what we have found out, that over the past three years there has been a steady decline in the health conditions in these areas. We know that to be true, although we are not satisfied yet to quote data, because we have not finished our studies.

SENATOR COSTIGAN. Are the children retarded in their physical development?

MR. PICKETT. I do not think you would find many cases of seriously retarded physical development. We find drowsiness, lethargy, and sleepiness.

SENATOR COSTIGAN. A mental retardation?

MR. PICKETT. A mental retardation, but not often physical retardation.

IV

Nomads
of the Depression

AMERICANS HAVE ALWAYS BEEN a footloose people, but the Great Depression created a new kind of wanderer, the poverty-stricken nomad seeking escape from an intolerable life at home. Optimism had been a characteristic of earlier wanderers, the colonist, the immigrant, the westward-trekking farmer, the gold seeker; there was little optimism among the boy and girl tramps or the "Okies," uprooted from the land by drought, dust storms, and tractors that landlords had purchased with their Agricultural Adjustment Administration checks. Desperation, rather than optimism, was the main characteristic of the nomads of the 1930's.

Many of the wanderers were homeless youngsters, only recently out of school, who in normal times would have been beginning workers, living with their parents. Many were families forced off the land. Many were men without families, living out a futile life by going from one poor and temporary job to another. None of them lived what most Americans consider a normal life, within a family, with an established community and a regular routine to give stability to their lives.

27 • ANXIETY
ABOUT THE VAGRANTS

In this article Newton D. Baker, former mayor of Cleveland, Secretary of War during World War I, and a contender for the Democratic presidential nomination, reveals concern for what the nomads may mean for America. "Homeless Wanderers Create a New Problem for America," The New York Times, *December 11, 1932. Reprinted by permission of the publisher.*

A CURIOUS SOCIAL PHENOMENON has developed out of the present depression. All over the country hordes of young people and entire families are found wending their way along the highways and byways. They are the people whom our postoffices label "address unknown," and whom we call transients, lacking a more adequate term by which to describe them. Every group in society is represented in their ranks, from the college graduate to the child who has never seen the inside of a schoolhouse. Expectant mothers, sick babies, young childless couples, grim-faced middle-aged dislodged from lifetime jobs—on they go, an index of insecurity, in a country used to the unexpected. We think of the nomads of the desert— now we have the nomads of the depression.

At least 25,000 families in our country and more than 200,000 boys and young men are reported by the United States Children's Bureau and the National Association of Travelers' Aid Societies as recruits in the present transient army. Because of the difficulties which lie in the way of a "head-to-head" census, these figures are generally conceded as telling only a part of the story. The actual count, beyond doubt, is several times the reported figures. One thing we know positively: that is, this army is gaining rapidly in numerical strength.

One-quarter of the present transient army, we are told, is made up of boys ranging between 16 and 21 years of age. Girls flock to the city in numbers, but the desire to travel long miles across country has not as yet proved as contagious to them as it has to their brothers.

Russia's experience with her vagabond youth should prove a warning to us. The shelterless, or bezprizorni, as they were called, came into being after the overthrow of the Russian monarchy in 1917 and increased so rapidly that they were estimated in a few years' time to number from 2,000,000 to 3,000,000 boys and girls. This army of children, many of them as young as 10 years, terrorized whole villages and cities and became known for their murders, robberies and other acts of violence. The "wild children of Russia" the press termed them. . . .

The reasons which have made our transient youth take to the road seem mild in comparison with those which caused the Russian children's exodus. The quest for jobs, the lure of adventure, escape from broken, unhappy or poverty-stricken homes or personality difficulties are the causes behind most youthful flights in America. The average young American transient of today, we are told by social workers and others who come into daily contact with him, is a normal boy from a substantial family. He differs from the hobo of yesterday in that his goal is apt to be a "chance to work" not an escape from it. In contrast to the bezprizorni, a considerable proportion of our boys have had high school educations, while most of the wild children of Russia, we are told, were unable to read or write.

Of the 7,512 transients served by the Salvation Army in Washington, D.C., during the first quarter of 1932, it was found that 1,866 had had an eighth-grade education, 260 had been in high school and 258 were college trained.

Reports submitted on the transient seem to agree that he is on the whole an honest, self-respecting person. Railroads record few thefts as a result of recent transient migrations. Communities through which they pass connect them with only occasional misdemeanors or crimes.

America's vagabonds, however, share this quality in common with Russia's wild children: having tasted the poison of a wandering life they find it difficult to give it up. In all probability the bezprizorni, when they first started out, were a harmless group of young people also, but finding it impossible to secure food and shelter by honest means, they resorted to other methods. No doubt they were helped in their activities by criminals and degenerates of their country just as the social workers report our transients are being contaminated today.

It is impossible to travel across any country, to live in box cars or "jungles," as the camp sites near the railroad yards are called, or even in municipal shelters, without meeting men whose influence is destructive. All too easily impressionable young people thrown into these environments without home guidance or direction pick up the vices and crimes of the underworld—gambling, stealing, drug addiction, prostitution and sexual perversion. . . .

The health hazards of the road are also many for the transient. Often he arrives in town sick from exposure or lack of food. Last winter in one Western city thirty-five men and boys were removed from box cars seriously ill, some in advanced stages of pneumonia. One railroad alone reported fifty men and boys killed and more than 100 crippled along its route. Hospitals treat the transient only if he is seriously ill. The demands for free care on these institutions are so great and their resources so limited that, unless it is a case of absolute necessity, they feel that their first obligation lies to the needy sick of their own community.

The drifting family in our country about whom we hear so much less than the transient youth has but one reason generally for its vagabondage, and that is the loss of a job by its breadwinner. Unable to find work or to continue the rent or payments on the home, the family piles itself into the old car and takes to the highway. Its philosophy, if any exists, probably runs like this: "We know what to expect if we stay at home, but who knows what our luck may be further on?"

Human nature is such that almost anyone will give a handout once with some little grace, but continuous handouts day after day are often not so generously bestowed. So we have the family making its way as best it can, looking for the elusive job, the unexpected stroke of luck or the pot of gold at the end of the rainbow, and as a rule ending its pilgrimage in some remote spot miles away from the starting place, miserable and destitute.

The children of these families perhaps suffer most of all. They are dazed, bewildered bits of humanity driven from town to town by a strange force called a "depression," which has upset the stability of their past and is dangerously threatening the safety of their future.

So suddenly has the seriousness of the transient problem thrust itself upon us and so rapidly has it increased in size that it may be said to have taken the average American community completely by storm. Busily coping with welfare and relief problems of their own and pondering how the multitude can be fed on the loaves purchasable with their limited resources, communities have been inclined to consider the transient as some other city's problem. And so, what is one city's problem today, by a system of "passing on," becomes another city's difficulty tomorrow. . . .

We are all interested in reducing budgets—personal, municipal, State and national—but it is well to remember that ruthlessly slashing essential services is both a costly and hazardous undertaking. If there is any doubt in our mind of the seriousness the present transient problem brings with it, we have only to turn to Russia for a somewhat similar tragedy for which that government paid dearly.

The question which every American community faces today and which demands an immediate answer is, can we afford to permit permanent injury to the character of this generation of youth? . . .

28 • THE DANGERS OF THE ROAD

Freight cars were not designed for passenger travel, and the dangers such travel presented young depression nomads concerned the railroad detective whose testimony is reprinted here. Relief for Unemployed Transients, Hearings *before a Subcommittee of the Committee on Manufactures, United States Senate, 72nd Cong., 2 sess., on S. 5121 (Washington: Government Printing Office, 1933), pp. 35-38.*

SENATOR COSTIGAN. Please give your name and address.

MR. MITCHELL. R. S. Mitchell, chief special agent, Missouri Pacific Railroad; resident, St. Louis.

SENATOR COSTIGAN. Mr. Mitchell, you are particularly familiar with certain phases of the transient problem?

MR. MITCHELL. Yes, sir.

SENATOR COSTIGAN. Will you tell the committee what you have observed and give us the benefit of any conclusions to which you have been led?

MR. MITCHELL. On the Missouri Pacific Railroad we have been trying to pay some attention to what we at one time called migratory labor; that is, the transient movement, and I have some figures here that my department has gathered from 1928 through 1932.

We took official notice, in 1928, of 13,745 transients, trespassers that we found on our trains and property.

In 1929 that figure was 13,875.

In 1930 we took a record of 23,892.

In 1931 that volume jumped to 186,028.

In 1932 it receded a little bit to 149,773, or a total, for the five years, of 387,313 persons that we found trespassing upon our trains and property.

I would like to call your attention to one serious result of this trespass.

In 1928 we unfortunately killed 102 trespassers and injured 172.

SENATOR COSTIGAN. Are you referring now to railroad accidents?

MR. MITCHELL. Railroad accidents to trespassers. . . . In 1929 there were 103 killed and 156 injured, or a total of 259.

In 1930 there were 114 killed and 221 injured, making a total of 335 killed and injured.

SENATOR COSTIGAN. Is there a typical accident among transients?

MR. MITCHELL. Too often it is an attempt to catch a train—get on a moving train—and the person not being an expert at that sort of thing, will miss his step and lose his leg. . . .

SENATOR COSTIGAN. There is not so much riding of rods, as formerly?

MR. MITCHELL. No, sir; the steel underframe car has decreased the rod riding possibility, probably 50 per cent.

In 1930 we killed 114 and injured 221, a total of 335.

The largest year was 1931. There were 125 killed and 247 injured, or a total of 372.

In 1932 there were 91 killed and 214 injured, or a total of 305.

SENATOR COSTIGAN. What has been the attitude of your company toward transients and has that attitude changed from time to time? I have in mind, more particularly, trespassers on railroad property.

MR. MITCHELL. A few years ago—to be exact, prior to the depression or prior to 1929—it was the policy of our railroad, and it was the policy of most railroads in the West, to rid certain classes of trains of trespassers and in some instances to arrest them for trespass. The volume became so large in 1929 and since then, that the railroads did not feel that these men should be arrested, and they were not arrested in the sense that they were turned over to officers and fined. They were arrested in the sense, Senator, that they were asked to get off our trains and were conducted from the property, but never was there any curtailment of liberty. . . . That continues to the present time.

SENATOR COSTIGAN. In many parts of the country men do not seem to be ordered from trains. Is that practice general?

MR. MITCHELL. Some railroads absolutely look the other way and do not order them from the trains. We feel we should say to those people when we find them on trains that they are not welcome visitors. . . . That is because, should they be injured, there is more of a responsibility when we invite them—tacitly invite them by not saying anything to them. . . . We have had one instance in five years of these men throwing a brakeman from the train. We found the men that did this and they were criminals. They are not of this younger class of transients that has been referred to here.

SENATOR COSTIGAN. In other words, men ordinarily told to leave have been responsive to the suggestion and have not resisted?

MR. MITCHELL. In very few instances have we had forcible resistance.

SENATOR COSTIGAN. What have they done? Have they immediately left and later attempted to board the trains?

MR. MITCHELL. That was usually the case when they were ordered off by train crews and other people. They would walk around the train and try to get on at another place, and they usually did so.

SENATOR COSTIGAN. It is apparent that merely ordering men from trains does not rid the community or nation of transients. What else have the railroads done with respect to this problem?

MR. MITCHELL. Illustrating the truth of your statement, Senator, at the beginning of this large increase in travel by trespassers, the railroad officers would threaten these men with arrest and in most instances, they would laugh at the officers and say, "That is what we want. That will give us a place to sleep and eat."

That is one of the reasons why the arrests were not carried out.

We have found in my territory, sir, that not only individuals but whole families are traveling in empty cars. One of the ways we have tried to curtail this is by insisting that our employees keep empty cars closed and securely fastened by wire. That has cut down our travel of this character to some extent. . . .

SENATOR COSTIGAN. It is fair to conclude from your testimony that you consider it a national problem?

MR. MITCHELL. Yes, sir; and a very serious problem.

There is this that I did not touch on: I feel there is an altogether different character of persons traveling in the warm weather than we find in the cold weather. In the summer time we find younger people and, as has been said here, the majority of these people so traveling can not be called "bums." They are not that sort of people. They are people who would actually work if they could find work.

SENATOR COSTIGAN. You are satisfied that they prefer work to charity?

MR. MITCHELL. Yes, sir. There is one big feature that has not been touched on. These tender persons who get into the jungles with the old "bums" and, too often, hardened criminals, get a bad influence in that way that eventually will be serious to this country. It is going to cause criminals and that element—

SENATOR COSTIGAN. In other words, you do not restrict your testimony to accidents and deaths; you feel that serious effects on character are involved?

MR. MITCHELL. Absolutely, sir.

SENATOR COSTIGAN. Have you observed any ill effects on the health of people traveling under these conditions?

MR. MITCHELL. The health conditions in the winter, I imagine, is a very serious thing. It is a very serious thing for a tender individual not properly clothed, to ride outside in winter weather. I do not see how they can escape pneumonia.

SENATOR COSTIGAN. There is considerable exposure?

MR. MITCHELL. Yes, sir.

29 · BOY AND GIRL TRAMPS

In the early 1930's a graduate student at the University of Minnesota dressed in old clothes and traveled with youthful tramps to gather material for his thesis. This selection describes how they got food and clothes on the road. Thomas Minehan, Boy and Girl Tramps of America *(New York: Farrar and Rinehart, 1934), pp. 67-71, 78-83. Reprinted by permission of Rinehart and Company.*

THE AMERICAN YOUNG TRAMPS, if one may judge by appearances, are not hungry. To a casual observer, they seem in good health and not bad spirits. When you talk to them, however, or listen to their talk, you realize the important part food plays in their lives. Almost one-fourth of all their conversation concerns food. When you live with them, eating at the missions or in the jungles, you understand almost too well why they are so concerned with food.

The young tramps, I repeat, are not starving. But for growing, healthy boys engaged in strenuous outdoor life, the food they eat is shamefully inadequate. Many relief stations serve but two meals a day, others three, and some only one. No station ever serves second helpings and the Oliver who asks for more is expelled before breakfast. Jungle food is better in quality and, if the pickings are good, more generous in quantity, but meals are uncertain. One day the boys may gorge themselves. The next there may not be a slice of bread or a cup of coffee.

Travel interferes with meals. A youth shivers all night in a gondola. Next day he falls asleep on a hillside and sleeps the sleep of exhaustion until dusk. On awakening he is hungry, but where can he get food? The bread lines are closed. The police have, in one of their weekly raids, cleaned out the jungles. At none of the customary places are there friends or food. The youth can beg on the streets, walking miles perhaps before he gets a nickel. A boy can steal, but the chances are that he will be caught. A girl can offer her body, but as likely as not she will find nobody in the market with desire and a dime. The usual course is to remain hungry until breakfast at a mission for a boy, or until breakfast can be begged by a girl. If the boy is very hungry, he may glom a grub from garbage cans.

The breakfast at the mission, if he remains there, is a thin bowl of gruel containing too few vitamins and calories to replace the energy lost on a twenty-four-hour fast. In one day's fast the boy's body has been definitely robbed of much strength. With work and walking, sleeping out of doors, and riding in box cars, it may be a long time before that lost energy can be replaced. Yet, unlike the adult tramp, all the time the boy is growing. He needs enough food not only for the repair and replacement of tissue oxidized in daily activity, but for growth, development, and future use. He does not get it.

Not only does he fail to receive food enough for a growing, healthy boy, but because he is constantly calling upon reserves he is definitely undernourished. The signs of malnutrition may not be so evident to the casual observer. A dozen child tramps in a shower room or swimming hole appear merely a group of lean and lanky boys. But if the observer is critical, he will note the too-prominent ribs, an abdomen too concave, and legs and arms on which the skin, strange phenomenon in the young, is loose and baggy as if there were not enough muscle and flesh underneath. He will notice, too, the tired, hungry eyes, the nervous mannerisms, and the habitual posture of weariness and want.

Communities differ in their systems of caring for all transients. Almost all, however, give one free meal, work for the second meal, a bed on the floor, and eviction before a second or third day.

A boy tramp arriving in any large city walks from the railroad yards to the bread line. The bread line may be a mission, a Salvation Army flop house, or a municipal welfare station, or, literally, a bread line. Some cities have two bread lines; others, only one. The more bread lines, the better for the boy tramp. Rivalry between them forces each to give better service. Meals are varied, privileges and accommodations greater, and sometimes on lucky days it is possible to get food in both. All agencies follow more or less the same procedure. Generally there is some form of confidential exchange, so that the agencies can compare records and information, keep from being imposed upon, and force the young tramps out of the city in two or three days.

As soon as he arrives at the station the boy registers, receiving a slip of identification. Generally the registration is a mere formality to keep a record of the number of transients accommodated. After the registration, the youth is usually entitled to something. Some agencies give him a card for the next meal; others, a bowl of soup immediately; still others, merely an opportunity to work for a meal. Before a second meal is served, however, the young tramp must work two to four hours. The work is not onerous, but for a tired boy laboring on a bowl of beans or soup it is difficult enough. The soup is invariable—I write from experience—thin, watery, lukewarm, tasteless, and served without even stale bread, and never with soda crackers. A portion equals about a small cupful. No second bowl is ever given, no matter how tired and hungry the boy.

Meals vary from city to city, but the two old reliables are stew and beans. Stew and beans, beans and stew. Sandwiches are sometimes given instead—usually cheese or peanut butter. Once a week, perhaps, a boiled vegetable dinner or hash is on the bill. Bread accompanies the meal. The bread is almost always bakery returns, stale and unpalatable, or Red Cross flour bread baked by the missions in their own ovens. Fresh, wholesome, and appetizing, the latter bread is good—but there isn't enough of it. . . .

And while some missions in their publicity claim to serve pie, it is sky pie. I have never had any, have never seen any served to other transients, nor have any of the men and boys to whom I have talked ever encountered a mission meal with pie—save one old hobo. He asserts that on Christmas in Chicago in 1911 he received a small piece of mince pie in a mission, but his memory—rapidly failing—cannot recall the place, he is not sure of the time, and it may not have been mince pie after all.

While pie is entirely mythical in a mission meal—so mythical indeed that songs have been written about it, meat seems to have a more tangible although evanescent quality. Meat is something that was served yesterday, or last week, or is to be served next Sunday. For myself, after scores of mission and relief station meals, I must say, so far as the young tramp's meals are concerned, I have tasted it but once—meat loaf in a sandwich. It is true, I have seen meat cooked almost every day at missions and served regularly at meals. The meals, however, were for local homeless men and not for transients. Mission stew served to boy tramps always has in it a hint of meat. There is an inevitable sliver of bone that sticks between your teeth and small diced squares of tripe, but of flesh-and-blood meat, of muscle and sinew, I have tasted none. . . .

But when a boy is hungry and unable to obtain food by begging or working he must steal or starve.

To date, stealing has not developed many complicated techniques among the young tramps. In summer, the farmer's gardens and orchards are raided regularly. Chickens, turkeys, ducks, and even small pigs are picked up when they stray from the farmyard into a grove. They are run down, snared, or caught in any convenient fashion with as little noise and fuss as possible. Seldom, I suspect, do farmers miss the fowl. If they are missed, the farmer most likely blames a skunk or a fox.

Farmer John, it is true, is the most frequent and common victim of the young tramp's thievery, but there are others. Bakery trucks parked early in the morning before stores, vegetable trucks on the way to market before dawn, all furnish the youthful vagrant with some of his needed food. Sidewalk counters and tables inside stores are raided but not often. Produce trucks going to market early in the morning are the boy's best regular supply. Boys hiding in the culverts at grade crossings rush out, board the truck and are gone with an armful of supplies before the driver realizes he is being raided.

With what they receive at missions, beg at back doors, and steal from farmers and others, the young tramps manage to keep alive. Some meals the youths cook in jungles are very good meals indeed. . . . At other jungle meals I have eaten potatoes burnt to a cinder, coffee full of sand, ants, and flies, chicken poorly dressed and sourly cooked, and boiled salt fish that tasted like something inexpressibly evil and diseased.

The relief stations for transients in the large cities feed but do not clothe the young tramps. Clothing is for the local homeless, not for the travelers. A boy or girl tramp must be not only in rags but half-naked to obtain a patched and dirty shirt or a worn cap. How difficult it is to obtain clothing nobody who has never tried can know. I have tried. For almost a week in two important cities of this country noted for their large transient populations and their advanced and humane policy of handling transients, I tried to get clothing in return for honest labor and in response to obvious need.

It was in December and very cold. Snow covered the ground. The thermometer had touched zero more than once the preceding night and morning saw its continued descent.

Dressed as a transient, registered and living at the missions, eating and sleeping with the men and boys, working for my soup and bed, taking the compulsory shower and fumigation, I attempted to obtain needed clothing. Without an overcoat beyond a well-worn blazer, buttonless and out at one elbow, with a pair of trousers out at the knee and in the seat, with an old summer cap that had hung for years in a furnace room, with worn tennis shoes covered by patched rubbers, with a pair of unmatched canvas gloves, I attempted to get some clothes through the regular relief agencies and to no avail.

My journey started in a reefer where Boris and I huddled together with three older men transients in the front of the car, the animal heat of our bodies making an ineffectual effort to keep us warm. We have been riding only two hours, but it has been a long cold two hours, and no swaddling of newspapers can keep us warm. Boris wears a sawed-off sheepskin over two old coats, three shirts and two pairs of patched trousers. I wear a long old sheepskin over a collection of rags.

"Today might be a good day to hit the stem for some clothing," he suggests as we leave the yards and make for a mission. "It's cold and people sometimes give you clothes when it's cold. I need shoes."

And he does. But so do I. My feet are covered with four pairs of heavy socks under tennis shoes and old rubbers patched with adhesive tape. A layer of oiled Manila paper between the top two pairs of socks, keeps my feet warm enough, but the tennis shoes and rubbers look cold as an Arctic night.

We leave our sheepskins at the mission and in ten below weather solicit every agency in the city. The missions, the Clothing Center, the Travelers' Aid, the Salvation Army, the Y.M.C.A., and a dozen other smaller agencies are visited with no success. It seems to make little difference what story Boris and I tell them. The answer is invariably No. No clothes for bums. No clothes for boy tramps.

"But we gotta leave in the morning," objects Boris to the thin young college graduate behind the desk in the Clothing Center. "Lots of folks can't stand the cold in a box car and especially me. I'll freeze tonight without a coat. Don't you think so?"

No, the young man does not think so. If it remains below zero we can most likely stay another day or two at the mission. No, we cannot work for clothing. There are more calls from local cases than can be filled. We are bums and we must be on our way.

Nor was our experience unusual. In all my association with adult transients and child tramps I have never known one who received any apparel from any agency—except a girl who appealed to a Travelers' Aid Society for transportation home and whose case was publicized in a drive for clothing. . . .

It is well perhaps to keep my experience in mind. Unless you have something concrete to judge by it is difficult to realize that the child tramps must get their clothing mainly by begging and stealing. The road is hard on clothes. A few days on the cinders or cement and a pair of shoes are well worn. Clothes slept in, in jungles or box cars, boiled and fumigated at missions, soaked in the rain, soon disintegrate. Rents and tears appear. Patches will not hold. Replacements are needed.

But if the child tramp cannot get clothing by working at agencies, how can he get it? He can beg or steal. He must beg or steal. Begging is the method used most often. The child tramps beg clothing at back doors, on the streets and at second-hand stores.

30 • THE WANDERING WAGE EARNER

This selection provides information on the wages and jobs of migratory workers. John N. Webb, The Migratory-Casual Worker *[WPA Research Monograph VII] (Washington: Government Printing Office, 1937), pp. xvii, 3-4.*

IT IS A COMMON PRACTICE among migratory-casual workers to spend part of each year on the road, working or seeking work, and then to withdraw from the labor market during the period, usually in the winter months, when the chances of finding work are small. This practice was followed by a majority of the 500 workers in the study. The median length of the migratory period was 41 weeks. Workers in agriculture had the longest off-season period—averaging 13 weeks; and the combination workers, the shortest—averaging 7 weeks in 1933, and only 4 weeks in 1934.

Necessarily, the migratory-casual worker wastes much time and motion during his migratory period both because of a scarcity of jobs and also because of the lack of proper direction to such jobs as are available. Among the 500 workers, the portion of the migratory period spent in employment averaged 24 weeks in 1933 and 21 weeks in 1934.

In exchange for his labor the migratory-casual worker obtains a meager income at best. When the earnings of the 500 workers were reduced to net yearly income to exclude the uncertain value of perquisites, it was found that although the range was from maintenance to $1,350 a year the most frequent earning was between maintenance and $250 yearly. The agricultural worker had the lowest yearly net earning, averaging $110 in 1933 and $124 in 1934. Industrial workers averaged $257 in 1933 and $272 in 1934. Workers combining agricultural and industrial employment earned on the average $223 net in 1933 and $203 in 1934. . . .

The migratory-casual worker in agriculture, the largest employer of mobile labor, is clearly defined in the following work history:

July-October 1932. Picked figs at Fresno, Calif., and vicinity. Wages, 10 cents a box, average 50-pound box. Picked about 15 boxes a day to earn $1.50; about $40 a month.

October-December 1932. Cut Malaga and muscat (table and wine) grapes near Fresno. Wages, 25 cents an hour. Average 6-hour day, earning $1.50; about $40 a month.

December 1932. Left for Imperial Valley, Calif.

February 1933. Picked peas, Imperial Valley. Wages, 1 cent a pound. Average 125 pounds a day. Earned $30 for season. Also worked as wagon-man in lettuce field on contract. Contract price, 5 cents a crate repack out of packing house; not field pack. This work paid 60 cents to $1 a day. On account of weather, was fortunate to break even at finish of season. Was paying 50 cents a day room and board.

March-April 1933. Left for Chicago. Stayed a couple of weeks. Returned to California 2 months later.

May 1933. Odd-jobs on lawns, radios, and victrolas at Fresno. Also worked as porter and handy man.

June 1933. Returned to picking figs near Fresno. Wages, 10 cents a box. Averaged $1.50 a day, and earned $50 in 2 months.

August 1933. Cut Thompson's seedless grapes near Fresno for 7 days at 1¼ cents a tray. Earned $11. Picked cotton 1 day, 115 pounds; earned $1.

September-November 1933. Cut Malaga and muscat grapes near Fresno. Wages, 25 cents an hour. Made $30 for season.

December 1933. Picked oranges and lemons in Tulare County, Calif. (Earnings not reported.)

January 1934. Picked oranges at 5 cents per box for small jobs and 25 cents per box for large jobs, Redlands, Calif. Earned $30. Picked lemons at 25 cents an hour.

January 1934. Went to Brawley, Calif. Picked peas at 1 cent a pound. Picked 125-150 pounds a day for 15-day season.

February 1934. Picked grapefruit at 25 cents an hour, Koehler, Calif. Worked 8 hours a day on three jobs for a total of 22 days. Also hauled fertilizer at 25 cents an hour.

March 1934. Worked as helper on fertilizer truck at $2 a day for 20 days, Brawley, Calif.

June 1934. Worked as circus hand with Al G. Barnes Circus for 4 weeks at $4.60 a week and board, Seattle to Wallace, Idaho.

July 1934. Tree shaker at 25 cents an hour, averaged $2 a day for 25 days, near Fresno.

August-October 1934. Picked oranges and lemons at 25 cents an hour, working an average of 6 hours a day, for 60 days, near Fresno.

December 1934. Houseman in hotel, Fresno. Received 50 cents a day and board for 1 month, and 25 cents a day and board for 2 months.

The migratory-casual worker following industrial, as distinct from agricultural, employment is equally well defined by the work history presented below:

June-August 1932. Jackhammer operator, railroad construction, Liberty, Mo. Wages $4.80 a day.

September 1932. Extra gang laborer, railroad, Hays, Kans. Wages $3.20 a day.

October 1932. Extra gang laborer, railroad, Cheyenne, Wyo. Wages $4.50 a day.

February-March 1933. Laborer, pipe-line construction, Topeka, Kans. Wages $3 a day.

April-October 1933. Watchman, building construction, Kansas City, Mo. Wages $1.25 a day.

February-May 1934. Extra gang laborer, railroad, Wamsutter, Wyo. Wages $2 a day.

June-September 1934. Extra gang laborer, railroad, Topeka, Kans. Wages $2.80 a day.

31 • THE "OKIES"

The best known nomads of the Great Depression were the "Okies," made famous by the novelist John Steinbeck. Reprinted here is Chapter 12 of The Grapes of Wrath (*The Viking Press, 1939*). *Reprinted by permission of the publisher.*

HIGHWAY 66 is the main migrant road. 66—the long concrete path across the country, waving gently up and down on the map, from the Mississippi to Bakersfield—over the red lands and the gray lands, twisting up into the mountains, crossing the Divide and down into the bright and terrible desert, and across the desert to the mountains again, and into the rich California valleys.

66 is the path of a people in flight, refugees from dust and shrinking land, from the thunder of tractors and shrinking ownership, from the desert's slow northward invasion from the twisting winds that howl up out of Texas, from the floods that bring no richness to the land and steal what little richness is there. From all of these the people are in flight, and they come into 66 from the tributary side roads, from the wagon tracks and the rutted country roads. 66 is the mother road, the road of flight.

Clarksville and Ozark and Van Buren and Fort Smith on 64, and there's an end of Arkansas. And all the roads into Oklahoma City, 66 down from Tulsa, 270 up from McAlester. 81 from Wichita Falls south, from Enid north. Edmond, McLoud, Purcell. 66 out of Oklahoma City; El Reno and Clinton, going west on 66. Hydro, Elk City, and Texola; and there's an end to Oklahoma. 66 across the Panhandle of Texas. Shamrock and McLean, Conway and Amarillo, the yellow. Wildorado and Vega and Boise, and there's an end of Texas. Tucumcari and Santa Rosa and into the New Mexican mountains to Albuquerque, where the road comes down from Santa Fe. Then down the gorged Rio Grande to Los Lunas and west again on 66 to Gallup, and there's the border of New Mexico.

And now the high mountains. Holbrook and Winslow and Flagstaff in the high mountains of Arizona. Then the great plateau rolling like a ground swell. Ashfork and Kingman and stone mountains again, where water must be hauled and sold. Then out of the broken sun-rotted mountains of Arizona to the Colorado, with green reeds on its banks, and that's the end of Arizona. There's California just over the river, and a pretty town to start it. Needles, on the river. But the river is a stranger in this place. Up from Needles and over a burned range, and there's the desert. And 66 goes on over the terrible desert, where the distance shimmers and the black center mountains hang unbearably in the distance. At last there's

Barstow, and more desert until at last the mountains rise up again, the good mountains, and 66 winds through them. Then suddenly a pass, and below the beautiful valley, below orchards and vineyards and little houses, and in the distance a city. And, oh, my God, it's over.

The people in flight stream out on 66, sometimes a single car, sometimes a little caravan. All day they rolled slowly along the road, and at night they stopped near water. In the day ancient leaky radiators sent up columns of steam, loose connecting rods hammered and pounded. And the men driving the trucks and the overloaded cars listened apprehensively. How far between towns? It is a terror between towns. If something breaks—well, if something breaks we camp right here while Jim walks to town and gets a part and walks back and—how much food we got?

Listen to the motor. Listen to the wheels. Listen with your ears and with your hands on the steering wheel; listen with the palm of your hand on the gear-shift lever; listen with your feet on the floor boards. Listen to the pounding old jalopy with all your senses: for a change of tone, a variation of rhythm may mean—a week here? That rattle—that's tappets. Don't hurt a bit. Tappets can rattle till Jesus comes again without no harm. But that thudding as the car moves along—can't hear that—just kind of feel it. Maybe oil isn't gettin' someplace. Maybe a bearing's startin' to go. Jesus, if it's a bearing, what'll we do? Money's goin' fast.

And why's the son-of-a-bitch heat up so hot today? This ain't no climb. Le's look. God Almighty, the fan belt's gone! Here, make a belt outa this little piece a rope. Let's see how long—there. I'll splice the ends. Now take her slow—slow, till we can get to a town. That rope belt won't last long.

'F we can on'y get to California where the oranges grow before this here ol' jug blows up. 'F we on'y can.

And the tires—two layers of fabric worn through. On'y a four-ply tire. Might get a hundred miles more outa her if we don't hit a rock an' blow her. Which'll we take—a hunderd, maybe, miles, or maybe spoil the tubes? Which? A hunderd miles. Well, that's somepin you got to think about. We got tube patches. Maybe when she goes she'll only spring a leak. How about makin' a boot? Might get five hundred more miles. Le's go on till she blows.

We got to get a tire, but Jesus, they want a lot for a ol' tire. They look a fella over. They know he got to go on. They know he can't wait. And the price goes up.

Take it or leave it. I ain't in business for my health. I'm here a-sellin' tires. I ain't givin' 'em away. I can't help what happens to you. I got to think what happens to me.

How far's the nex' town?

I seen forty-two cars a you fellas go by yesterday. Where you all come from? Where all of you goin'?

Well, California's a big State.

It ain't that big. The whole United States ain't that big. It ain't that big. It ain't big enough. There ain't room enough for you an' me, for your kind an' my kind, for rich and poor together all in one country, for thieves and honest men. For hunger and fat. Whyn't you go back where you come from?

This is a free country. Fella can go where he wants.

That's what *you* think! Ever hear of the border patrol on the California line? Police from Los Angeles—stopped you bastards, turned you back. Says, if you can't buy no real estate we don't want you. Says, got a driver's license? Le's see it. Tore it up. Says you can't come in without no driver's license.

It's a free country.

Well, try to get some freedom to do. Fella says you're jus' as free as you got jack to pay for it.

In California they got high wages. I got a han'bill here tells about it.

Baloney! I seen folks comin' back. Somebody's kiddin' you. You want that tire or don't ya?

Got to take it, but Jesus, mister, it cuts into our money! We ain't got much left.

Well, I ain't no charity. Take her along.

Got to, I guess. Let's look her over. Open her up, look a' the casing—you son-of-a-bitch, you said the casing was good. She's broke damn near through.

The hell she is. Well—by George! How come I didn't see that?

You did see it, you son-of-a-bitch. You wanta charge us four bucks for a busted casing. I'd like to take a sock at you.

Now keep your shirt on. I didn' see it, I tell you. Here—tell ya what I'll do. I'll give ya this one for three-fifty.

You'll take a flying jump at the moon! We'll try to make the nex' town.

Think we can make it on that tire?

Got to. I'll go on the rim before I'd give that son-of-a-bitch a dime.

What do ya think a guy in business is? Like he says, he ain't in it for his health. That's what business is. What'd you think it was? Fella's got—See that sign 'longside the road there? Service Club. Luncheon Tuesday, Colmado Hotel? Welcome, brother. That's a Service Club. Fella had a story. Went to one of them meetings an' told the story to all them business men. Says, when I was a kid my ol' man give me a haltered heifer an' says take her down an' git her serviced. An' the fella says, I done it, an' ever' time since then when I hear a business man talkin' about service, I wonder who's gettin' screwed. Fella in business got to lie an' cheat, but he calls it somepin else. That's what's important. You go steal that tire an' you're a thief, but he tried to steal your four dollars for a busted tire. They call that sound business.

Danny in the back seat wants a cup of water.

Have to wait. Got no water here.

Listen—that the rear end?

Can't tell.

Sound telegraphs through the frame.

There goes a gasket. Got to go on. Listen to her whistle. Find a nice place to camp an' I'll jerk the head off. But, God Almighty, the food's gettin' low, the money's gettin' low. When we can't buy no more gas— what then?

Danny in the back seat wants a cup a water. Little fella's thirsty.

Listen to that gasket whistle.

Chee-rist! There she went. Blowed tube an' casing all to hell. Have to fix her. Save that casing to make boots; cut 'em out an' stick 'em inside a weak place.

Cars pulled up beside the road, engine heads off, tires mended.

Cars limping along 66 like wounded things, panting and struggling. Too hot, loose connections, loose bearings, rattling bodies.

Danny wants a cup a water.

People in flight along 66. And the concrete road shone like a mirror under the sun, and in the distance the heat made it seem that there were pools of water in the road.

Danny wants a cup a water.

He'll have to wait, poor little fella. He's hot. Nex' service station. *Service* station, like the fella says.

Two hundred and fifty thousand people over the road. Fifty thousand old cars—wounded, steaming. Wrecks along the road, abandoned. Well, what happened to them? What happened to the folks in that car? Did they walk? Where are they? Where does the courage come from? Where does the terrible faith come from?

And here's a story you can hardly believe, but it's true, and it's funny and it's beautiful. There was a family of twelve and they were forced off the land. They had no car. They built a trailer out of junk and loaded it with their possessions. They pulled it to the side of 66 and waited. And pretty soon a sedan picked them up. Five of them rode in the sedan and seven on the trailer, and a dog on the trailer. They got to California in two jumps. The man who pulled them fed them. And that's true. But how can such courage be, and such faith in their own species? Very few things would teach such faith.

The people in flight from the terror behind—strange things happen to them, some bitterly cruel and some so beautiful that the faith is refired forever.

V

The Middle Classes:
Bank Failures and Unemployment

INDUSTRIAL WORKERS AND FARMERS clearly suffered more from want during the depression than other economic groups. Nevertheless, the deprivations of middle-class families were serious. Most people who made their living from their invested capital, from their business, or from their professional work did not go hungry—although some did—but many lost a considerable part of their fortune and took a major loss of income.

Few working men and dirt farmers lost substantial amounts of money in the decline of stock prices or in bank failures, because few such people had ever had substantial amounts of money. The collapse of the market and of many banks—more than 5,000 banks closed their doors in the three years, 1930-1932—fell hardest upon that rather ill-defined group we call the middle classes. Professional men on salary frequently suffered a drastic loss of earning power, and unemployment among college trained people was not uncommon. So numerous were cases of hardship among formerly comfortably well to do families, so frequent were cases of descent from the middle classes, that there was widespread concern that the middle classes might shrink to political and social insignificance.

32 • DISENCHANTMENT
IN HIGH PLACES

The tone of this article by Frank A. Vanderlip, former president of the National City Bank of New York, indicates a disillusion with American financial institutions that would have been unthinkable by a business leader only a few years earlier. Frank A. Vanderlip, "What About the Banks?" The Saturday Evening Post, CCV (November 5, 1932), pp. 3-4. Reprinted by permission.

THE PRESENT ECONOMIC DISTURBANCE has been so severe that it has made even some changes in our language. No longer is it an apt metaphor to say that anything is "as safe as a bank." The word "securities" has almost become obsolete. An investment that drops in price to a tenth or, perhaps, even to a twentieth of its former range is not a security; it is a jeopardy. The page of stock-and-bond quotations might well be headed Quotations of Risks and Hazards. To call them securities in the light of their fluctuations is ironical.

In 1720, a financial debacle added to the English language a phrase which has persisted in common world-wide use for two centuries. A hopelessly exploded financial venture is to this day called a South Sea Bubble.

The South Sea Company in its time was the rival of the Bank of England. It was the ambition of the Tories that it should supplant the Bank of England. When the bubble burst, the extreme decline in the price of the stock was from 1000 to 135. The company withstood the shock, however, and continued in business for eighty years.

Here is an example from our own times: United States Steel and General Motors stocks, the two leading industrials of the country, declined from the high quotations of 1929 to 8 per cent of that price. The decline in the stock of the South Sea Company was only to 13½ per cent of its highest quotation. Take another example: The stock of what has long been one of the premier banks of the country declined from 585 to 23½. That is to say, it fell to 4 per cent of its highest quotation. The decline in the market price of this great American banking institution was therefore more than three times as severe as was the fall in the stock of the South Sea Company.

That illustration is by no means a unique one. There were innumerable American bank stocks which made a more distressing record. Between October 1, 1929, and August 31, 1932, 4835 American banks failed. They had deposits aggregating $3,263,049,000. The stocks of many of those banks not only fell to zero; some did worse than that, for they carried on to the shoulders of the stockholders further liability, which had to be met, in addition to the complete loss of the money which had been invested when the stocks were bought.

If I draw illustrations from the banking field to indicate the limits to which the depression reached, it is only because I am writing about banks and not because the banks are the one glaring example marking the extent of the financial cataclysm. The railroads, the insurance companies, the building-and-loan societies and mortgage companies would quite as well depict the situation.

The decline in the price of bank stocks was only a minor phase of our debacle. The quoted value of all stocks listed on the New York Stock Exchange was, on September 1, 1929, $89,668,276,854. By July 1, 1932, the quoted value of all stocks had fallen to $15,633,479,577.

Stockholders had lost $74,000,000,000. This figure is so large that not many minds can grasp it. It is $616 for every one of us in America. It is, roughly, three times what we spent in fighting the World War. The bursting of the South Sea Bubble concerned a single company. In the bursting of the New York Stock Exchange bubble, the value of all stocks fell to 17 per cent of their September 1, 1929, price—almost as great a drop as the South Sea Company stock, with its fall to 13 per cent of its top price. Remember that this calculation is not a selected example. It is made from the average of all stocks listed on the Exchange.

The South Sea Bubble wasn't so much! We have done pretty well in the way of bubbles in our own time. All financial history shows no parallel to what we have been going through. Never before, in this country or anywhere else, has there been such a general loss in "security" values.

The decline in the quoted value of New York listed stocks is only part of the story. The total of real-estate mortgages in default, particularly mortgages on city property, is unexampled. The value of real estate can no longer be accurately appraised, because the market for real estate has been practically paralyzed.

The loss of $74,000,000,000 in the value of New York listed stocks is something more than a mere item of financial data. Implicated in it are ten million cruel heartaches. I am using "million" as an adjective, and making an understatement. The laborious savings of an uncounted number of lifetimes have been swept away. Prudent provision for the future has been made to contrast unfavorably with the pleasures of spendthrift waste. . . .

Not only did our investments shrivel in the last three years but we even frequently lost our pocketbooks. Cash in hand, left for safekeeping in a bank, often went the way of our investments, and worse. Almost $3,000,-000,000 of our daily-used cash funds were sequestered in the doubtful assets of the 4835 insolvent banks. Widespread communities were left with only the mattress as a safe depository, and with little to put into it. People became so frightened in regard to the safety of the banks that they locked up in safe-deposit vaults, or secreted elsewhere, more than $1,500,000,000.

This is a shameful and humiliating exhibition. It is uniquely bad. Across the border in Canada, there was not a single bank failure during our period of depression, and one must go back to 1923 to find even a small one. Nowhere else in the world at any time, were it a time of war, or of famine, or of disaster, has any other people recorded so many bank failures in a similar period as did we. We were not experiencing a war, a famine or any other natural disaster. All the economic tribulations we have undergone in the past three years have been man-made troubles, and Nature has continued to shower us with an easy abundance—more, indeed, than we have known how to distribute with economic wisdom.

Human stupidity and cupidity were the taproots of this great financial disaster. Those are evils which will always beset us. There have, however, been revealed faults and weaknesses in our banking and investment practices that account in part for the extreme nature of this experience. Isn't it about time that we began thoughtfully to examine some of the fundamentals of our banking and investment theories and methods?

33 • THE MIDDLE CLASS OF A SMALL CITY

The business men of the community described in this selection managed to save themselves and their town from ruin, but their attitude toward America's business civilization changed nevertheless. George R. Clark, "Beckerstown: 1932. An American Town Faces the Depression," Harper's, CLXV (October, 1932), pp. 580, 583-589, 591. Reprinted by permission.

ASK ANYONE IN BECKERSTOWN how the town has been hit by the depression and the answer invariably is, "We'd be pretty well off if the banks hadn't failed."

There is more than a little truth in this statement. For until the autumn of 1931, when two of the local banks of Beckerstown succumbed to the national epidemic of bank failures and closed their doors, tying up four million dollars of the townspeople's money, Beckerstown had not suffered greatly. During the first two winters of our discontent, when coal towns and steel towns and textile towns were in cruel straits, its balanced economic life had been in its favor. For Beckerstown, a town of some thirty-five thousand inhabitants, is not dependent upon any one industry, or any one farming crop, or on deposits of coal or oil or metals: it is a town of small and highly diversified industries set in the middle of a rich farming district. Its numerous factories, almost all of them independent of outside control, make a wide variety of products; and while a few of them employ in prosperous times as many as five hundred men, most of them have less than a hundred. Since Beckerstown is also the county seat of a fertile county and the most important town in a radius of thirty miles, it serves as the trading center for the farms and villages of the whole smiling valley in which it lies. As a community it is thus unusually compact, self-supporting, and self-contained.

Yet the very balance of Beckerstown's life makes it a peculiarly interesting place in which to study the effects of the depression. Partaking somewhat of the character of our industrial towns and somewhat of that of our farming areas, and representing a complex of business interests, it offers perhaps as fair a sample of American economic life as one could find in a small compass. It has, of course, a marked individuality of its own; nevertheless, the story of what has happened to Beckerstown during the past few years may suggest what has happened to innumerable other American towns, and its present condition may give a clue to the condition of the country at large. . . .

Speculating among all classes and kinds of people in Beckerstown had by this time [1929] become very nearly universal. The inbred conservatism of the town prevented its business men from over-expansion in their businesses, but they felt perfectly free to employ their private funds as they pleased. Mr. Hubert continued to run his drug store according to the principles laid down by his grandfather, but of his personal capital he was prodigal indeed. Cheerfully he removed the savings of his lifetime from their modest quarters in the People's Loan and Savings Institute in response to a compelling circular, and invested them in Cities Service and Montgomery Ward (bought on margin). Nor were the ladies of the town less eager to participate in the delightful new game. Mrs. Meredith in her box-hedged garden listened with wellbred attention and the pretty credulity of the gently nurtured to the suave arguments of the polite young city salesman, and the next day transferred the comfortable sum left her by her devoted husband from the Government and municipal bonds of his selection to the more stimulating media of fancy foreign bonds and still fancier investment trusts.

The city salesmen reaped a rich harvest in Beckerstown and in the county surrounding. With flattering regularity they visited the banks and individual investors and hypnotized them into buying anything that promised large and quick returns. And what investments did not? Beckerstown people who were known to have money received long-distance telephone calls daily from brokerage houses in New York and other large cities. The firm of Harris Forbes alone is said to have extracted a million dollars from Beckerstown. Even those who were entrusted with the handling of funds of public institutions were urged by New York brokers to invest them in highly speculative ventures.

It is difficult for one who has never lived in a small town to realize to what extent personalities direct the general habits of thought there. Judge Cantrell, a wealthy and highly respected man, believed in American Founders. Everybody who learned of this promptly bought American Founders. It was rumored that old Mr. Sennenbaugh had bought Goldman Sachs. There was immediately a tiny bull market in Goldman Sachs. And so it went. People who had been brought up to believe that a mortgage on the house was a serious misfortune if not, indeed, a disgrace, enthusiastically staked all that they had on the slenderest possible margins. . . .

Then came the autumn of 1929, and the stock-market crash; and down came American Founders, Goldman-Sachs Trading, and the rest of them.

During the two succeeding years, when the rest of the country was floundering deeper and deeper into the slough of economic despond, business in Beckerstown was a little pinched—but only a little. Until late in 1931 it was chiefly the well-to-do, the victims of the Wall Street mania and of the young security salesmen from the city, who suffered. As for the town as a whole, its self-sufficiency stood it in good stead. Webster, forty miles away, was far worse hit than Beckerstown: Webster, which is supported by huge automobile works and an artificial-silk factory, and which depends upon national rather than local markets. The factory-owners of Beckerstown—who, after all, had known most of their employees since they were boys together—were reluctant to turn men off when sales languished, and were staggering them or providing them with at least part-time work. There was a little wage-cutting, but not much. In spite of gloomy predictions, business in Beckerstown was holding up better than might have been expected.

In March, 1930, the Beckerstown Chamber of Commerce, under energetic and intelligent leadership, formed a committee to bring new industries to the town. Until June of that year, the committee was very busy; some twenty-six new industries were likely prospects; and though the campaign which was to expand the town's business died a sudden death in the fresh slump of June, 1930, a general feeling of optimism remained in the air. Things would pick up before long.

The drought of 1930 was followed in 1931 by a season of bumper crops, and once more Beckerstown profited from its location in a fertile valley. Arlington County had never known such a year. The farmers advertised in the town papers, offering to give away food to all who would come and gather it. Consequently, although unemployment was at last beginning to appear, nobody was hungry. The charitable organizations of the town combined their forces in a joint campaign for funds for relief, and this campaign took on the tone of a religious revival and exceeded its quota by forty per cent. Despite the dismal state of the investment markets and the lagging pace of the town's industries, people could still say with a measure of truth, "Beckerstown does not know that there is a depression."

Then suddenly the blow fell. In the autumn of 1931, hard upon the heels of the successful Welfare drive, almost without warning two of the Beckerstown banks closed their doors, and the people of the town suddenly realized for the first time what the depression could do.

These two bank failures resulted from a peculiar chain of circumstances. Early in September, 1931, a bank in Williamsburg, twenty miles away, failed, carrying down with it seventeen small country banks which it had absorbed in the golden era of bank mergers. Eighteen million dollars went to glory and every third family in the county was ruined—a not unimpressive performance for an institution in a town considerably smaller than Beckerstown. Mr. Saunders, the president of this Williamsburg bank, was a man of unquestioned ability and vaulting ambition. Some believe that he was inspired with a genuine desire to add lustre to his native town by making it the capital of a small financial empire, and that his difficulties arose when he tried to take too many short cuts to financial power. Others hold to a harsher estimate, claiming that he was a miniature Kreuger whose personal financial operations encroached upon his bank operations until the two became hopelessly entangled. The truth of his complicated affairs may come to light when his case—he is charged with no less than forty-nine indictments—is tried. Be that as it may, his bank over-expanded and undertook too many glamorous investments, and the bear market demolished it.

The collapse of the Saunders bank was a stunning blow to the people of Beckerstown. They began to wonder where the lightning would strike next. A feeling of uneasiness spread through the town. Mr. Saunders was known to have been on friendly terms with certain directors of two of the Beckerstown banks. It was whispered that they were on his note. Cautious citizens began quietly to withdraw their money from these banks. On September 12 the Beckerstown Clearing House Association issued a reassuring statement expressing "unbounded confidence" in the local banks; but the tide of rumor continued to seep through the town.

Steadily it began to undermine the People's Loan and the Merchants National. These two banks were of different types. The People's Loan and Savings Institute, founded in 1860, was the place where the smaller merchants and the working people of the town kept their savings. Its directors were men of unquestioned integrity; and although events proved that they had been over-optimistic in taking the second mortgage bond on the Jefferson Hotel, they were generally considered men of sound and prudent judgment. ("As conservative as Lee Higginson," one might have said in those days.) Aside from this ill-advised investment, the bank had a list of good mortgages; but with the real estate market as quiet as the grave, the mortgages were mostly frozen.

The other bank about which rumor was gathering so persistently was more representative of the new era spirit of finance. For some time such Beckerstown people as still held to old-fashioned ideas about banking had regarded the Merchants National with some apprehension. The story went about that some of the directors had been lent large sums of the bank's money without security of any sort and had invested it in enterprises in which they were personally interested. Doubtless there was precedent for this sort of thing in the operations of some of the large city banks, but Beckerstown was disturbed.

The ten thousand deposits in these two banks represented four million dollars, and if they closed their doors a sum of about $3,700,000 in loans would have to be called in—to say nothing of the potential loss to their 750 stockholders. People talked and shook their heads, and quietly drew out more and more money.

The times were hardly auspicious for liquidation. On September 21 England left the gold standard. During the following week other European countries followed it, several European exchanges closed, and the international credit panic raged in full force. But though this panic made things no easier for the bankers who were trying to set their houses in order, the people of Beckerstown were hardly aware of it. The banner headlines of their local papers were announcing from day to day the new developments not in international finance, but in the mystery of the disappearance of one Benjamin P. Collings from a yacht in Long Island Sound. The fears of the men and women of Beckerstown were purely local. Were the Beckerstown banks going to last? As talk went about, many depositors learned for the first time, with a gasp of fright, that "the bank's investments" were made not with funds of its own, as they had vaguely supposed, but with the depositors' money—*their* own.

On Monday morning, September 28—three weeks after the closing of the Saunders bank and a week after England's departure from the gold standard—all who came to the People's Loan found the door closed, and upon it a notice which said that the bank had been placed in the hands of the Bank Commissioners. Later in the morning, while crowds of hatless and bewildered men were milling in the street outside, the directors of the People's Loan announced that they had closed the bank for the protection of the depositors and stockholders. "It was impossible," said they, "to liquidate our mortgages and other investments rapidly enough to meet the unusual demands made upon us, resulting from false and unfounded rumors recently circulated by irresponsible persons."

On the following day, the daily paper (still devoting its biggest headlines to the Collings case) editorially urged the citizens of Beckerstown to stop drawing money out of the banks. "Take your money back to your bank, where it has been kept with safety for over a century," said the editorial, "and you won't have any regrets." The whole last page of the same paper was given to an advertisement of the largest and most important bank in town, the Beckerstown Bank. The advertisement began with a letter from a certified public accountant, well known in town, who said that from his knowledge of the affairs of the bank there was "no question in my mind that the resources are sufficient to amply secure all of its depositors." This was followed by a paragraph in 24-point boldface type which read, "We have been depositors for years in the Beckerstown Bank and Trust Company and now are. We will not withdraw our money because we have confidence in the bank." This statement was signed by twelve of the wealthiest and most influential people in town.

Neither chastening editorial nor encouraging advertisement, however, could stem the rising tide of hysteria, and two days later—on Thursday, October first—the Merchants National Bank was closed. The statement of the directors echoed the words of the directors of the People's Loan, ascribing the troubles of the bank to "unprecedented withdrawals as a result of untrue and absolutely false rumors."

This fresh catastrophe threw the people of the town into a state very near panic. There had never been such a thing as a bank failure in the whole history of Beckerstown. To have "money in the bank" had always meant to them complete security. The collapse of two banks within four days brought a shock more profound than the loss of the money, which was in itself considerable: it unsettled all their fundamental beliefs.

Meanwhile, with the mass of the townspeople caught in a blind, uncomprehending terror, the leaders of Beckerstown faced the deepening crisis. They were neither blind nor uncomprehending. Terrified, they may well have been, for they knew very well that the fortunes of the town now hung upon the fate of the Beckerstown Bank.

Founded in 1810 and housed in one of the few really beautiful Colonial buildings still standing in the town, the Beckerstown Bank not only listed among its stockholders and depositors a large proportion of the influential citizens, but was far and away the most important industrial bank of the town. As a natural result, much of its money was in industrial loans—perfectly sound, but not readily callable without grave trouble for its clients. It was safe to assume that if the Beckerstown Bank were to fail, the remaining banks of the town would inevitably go, and the town itself would be ruined.

And ruin was anything but improbable. The restless crowds still filled the streets; men and women kept moving in a small, quiet, stubborn stream to take their money out of the institutions in which they no longer believed.

On Friday afternoon—the day after the second bank failure—the directors of the Beckerstown Bank held an emergency meeting. At such a time, in a town like Beckerstown, it is natural for hard-pressed men to turn for counsel to some elder statesman of the community, to someone whose life runs a little apart, perhaps, from that of the majority of the townspeople engaged in active business, but whose character, experience, and judgment command universal respect. The directors of the Beckerstown Bank did this. That it was a woman to whom they turned might seem strange to one who knew how little interest Beckerstown has in feminist doctrines; but it would not seem strange to one who knew Mrs. Jane Kennedy Whitcomb. Mrs. Whitcomb lived in the largest and finest house in town. A descendant of an old aristocratic family, she was a person of social consequence. But she was much more than this. It was she whom her father had chosen, of all his gifted and intelligent children, to care for the family estate, and under her wise and vigorous management its value had quadrupled. The business men of Beckerstown knew that her grasp of finance was equal to that of the best of them, and that when she spoke it was with authority. They invited Mrs. Whitcomb to meet with them; and when she suggested that they adjourn to her house, they duly trooped up the hill and filed into her big back parlor with its Aubusson carpet and gilded cornices.

Mrs. Whitcomb dominated the meeting. The situation was acute: unless the directors could lay hands on a million dollars before the next morning, the bank would probably fail. A long-distance telephone call to the nearest large city, some seventy miles away, had brought the city bankers' terms—they would provide the million if the people of Beckerstown would *in the meantime* underwrite half the amount. Sixteen hours to raise half a million dollars in a town of 35,000 people already in the throes of panic.

Mrs. Whitcomb, her small compact figure very straight in a brocaded chair, laid down the law. "You must go at once to all the stockholders. Tell them that this is not a matter simply of saving the bank, but of saving the town. They must put up cash, securities, jewelry, whatever they have. Telephone all night if you have to. The bank cannot be allowed to fail."

It was decided that each stockholder should be asked to contribute a sum equal to ten per cent of the value of his stock. One of the directors, a local manufacturer, immediately put up $110,000 of his own funds. Another director, Mr. Shriver, volunteered to drive to the city to bring back fifty thousand dollars in cash to be ready when the bank opened the next morning. Mr. Shriver threw an empty suitcase into his car and set out on his one-hundred-and-fifty-mile errand. The rest of the directors left for their round of visits and their vigil of telephone calls.

It was an anxious and a thrilling night. All night long the weary men telephoned, explained, argued. The people of the town responded heroically. For it *was* heroic for men and women who had already lost thousands of dollars in the stock market crash, and whose incomes were dwindling, to stake what remained of their capital on what must have seemed to many of them a hundred to one chance.

In the course of that night's work, many curious things came to light. It was then that many of the most severe losses of individuals of the town were first discovered—losses which in some cases dated back to the ill-fated projects engineered by Mr. Newman's associates in the nineteen twenties. A man who had been supposed to be extremely wealthy confessed that he did not have five thousand dollars to put up. A woman who had always lived more than comfortably was found to have no securities of any value whatever.

But by four o'clock the next morning, Saturday, October 3rd, the seemingly impossible task had been accomplished. Half a million dollars had been put up by the people in the town; Mr. Shriver had driven back over the mountains with fifty thousand dollars in bank notes in the suitcase beside him; and the morning paper was printing the announcement that a million dollars had been added to the resources of the Beckerstown Bank, adding a stinging invitation to all uneasy depositors to withdraw their money if they still wished to. The following week all the banks of Beckerstown were almost as busy taking in money as they had been paying it out.

And so the crisis passed, and people began to breathe more easily. The town was not ruined—not yet. Like a horse that has had a bad fall, Beckerstown pulled itself together, found that no bones were broken, and once more set about its daily living. But the shock and fright of the bank failures and the monetary loss have left their mark. Beckerstown now knows there is a depression.

Eight months after the collapse of the two banks, a visitor who had known the town well would be struck by the absence of obvious outward manifestations of the depression and by the marked psychological change in the people. . . .

Let the former leaders of finance make speeches about recovery in terms of getting back to pre-depression days. The Beckerstown man listens quietly and without conviction. He is determined to turn his back on big business, promotion, and nation-wide banking. He feels that he must begin again, and this time he is going to deal with those whom he knows and trusts, and put his money where he can keep his eye on it.

34 • MAIN STREET REVISITED

The Melrose of this selection was a Middlewestern Beckerstown. The author, the newspaper columnist Marquis Childs, emphasizes the changing social attitudes of the community. "Main Street Ten Years After," The New Republic, LXXIII (January 18, 1933), pp. 263-265. Reprinted by permission of the publisher.

THE CASUAL VISITOR viewing Melrose for the first time in four years would observe few changes. There are the current phenomena of the depression, empty stores, For Rent signs, smokeless factories, closing-out sales. But on a fine summer evening, an endless procession of cars, and many of them are new, passes out along Washington Boulevard to the Spring Valley Highway. And on any Saturday afternoon, the group waiting to drive off from the first tee at the country club is apparently as large as ever, as jovial, as well fed, as carefree. There is, however, a startling disparity between this familiar surface and what is really happening as a result of the depression.

This town of nineteen thousand, located in a rich farming community, might be anywhere in the Middle West, Minnesota, Ohio, Iowa, Illinois. Along with the other Main Streets, it had its boom, a whole series of booms. There was the War, with fat contracts for the steel-castings company and the wire-cloth factory. It was in 1924 that Main Street was made Main Avenue, paved drives were put through Sunset Park, the new half-million-dollar high school was finished and the Kiwanis public golf links and swimming pool were opened. Then came the stock-market boom.

The majority in Melrose were not lured away from rock-ribbed safety— savings banks and real-estate bonds. The collapse of the banks and the bonds the bankers sold was the immediate cause of the deflation in Melrose. School teachers, insurance salesmen, small wage earners, dentists, retired farmers, saw life savings disappear, security vanish. An entire generation, with striking exceptions, has been stripped; and not by some remote force a thousand miles away but, so the reasoning is, by the man who used to live in the big house on the corner of South Main Avenue and Washington Boulevard.

What is surprising is the passive resignation with which the blow has been accepted; this awful pretense that seeks to conceal the mortal wound, to carry on as though it were still the best possible of all worlds. Before the depression, one of the principal pleasures was to discover how much one's neighbor was spending; now the game is to find out how much he has lost and how he is standing his losses. This curiosity is almost a form of psychopathology; sympathy is all too often an ill concealed form of triumph, a kind of "Thank God, someone is worse off than we are."

The First National Bank of Melrose was the first to go. There was no warning; in the middle of the banking day the doors were closed by the examiners. It was one of the oldest banks in the state, regarded as a branch of the United States Treasury. Within two or three hours everyone knew of the disaster. Depositors, stunned and disbelieving, gathered in small groups to read the notice on the door. There were wild rumors. It was said that Mr. Johnson, the new president, had fled to Canada with his blonde secretary. Someone brought a report that the closing was only temporary, someone else spread word that there would be nothing left for the depositors. The other three banks, forewarned, withstood heavy runs.

There was little public lamentation. The most shocking example was old Mrs. Gearman. She beat with her fists upon the closed plate-glass doors and screamed and sobbed without restraint. She had in a savings account the $2,000 from her husband's insurance and $963 she had saved over a period of twenty-five years from making rag rugs. Nothing was left but charity. For a week neighbors did not see her. A policeman found her sitting in the middle of the kitchen of her small, scrubbed house. They took her to the insane asylum a few days afterward.

Others were more successful in concealing the tragic extent of their losses. For fifty-two years Amy Blanshard taught the fourth grade. Her sister kept house for her. They lived in the upper half of the old Blanshard home, renting the lower half. Amy had more than $11,000 in a savings account in the First National Bank. On a salary which was never more than a thousand dollars a year, it is plain what heroic economies this must have required. As a direct result of the closing, twelve families, most of them elderly couples, were forced onto the county. School children had on deposit about $25,000 in small accounts; these were repaid in full before any other claims "to retain the faith of the youngest generation in our banks."

There were charges and counter-charges. It was said that all the directors withdrew their deposits before the bank failed and that more important business men were warned, too. In the first bitter reaction there was talk of criminal prosecution against one director, Davis, who, according to rumor, succeeded in tapping the bank before it collapsed, for a sum greater than the amount of his stock. There was a public meeting in the armory which ended on a note of reassurance from President Johnson. There would be sufficient assets to cover virtually the entire amount on deposit at the time of the bank's closing. Gradually the whispered rumors were forgotten.

"Do you see any of the bankers themselves ruined?" Jeffery Fagan demands, with fire in his eye. (He dropped $17,000.) "They're still riding around in their big cars. I can remember the day when it was the banker that went to the poorhouse and the depositors got their money. It takes about as much brains and honesty to run a bank now as it used to take to run a peanut stand." This last is a concise expression of opinion in Melrose. The spectacle of the Davises whizzing about in their expensive car is not one to cheer the losers. Reason has no part in this reaction; the fact that the capitalization of the bank was absurdly low and Davis' share of the stock only a small percentage of the total of deposits is not considered. What no one can forget is that only 31 per cent of the deposits were paid after a delay of eight months. The prospect for a further dividend is slight.

The collapse of the Merchants' Bank and Trust Company was less spectacular. It had long been weak, and when a plan to merge it with the Melrose National Bank failed, it wilted away. There were other calamities to take public attention. One was the failure of the Ryder Furniture and Carpet Company. Like the First National Bank, it had been regarded as a Gibraltar of stability. Edward Ryder represented the third generation in the business; the Ryder store occupied one of the four principal corners at Main and Washington. After the grand closing-out sale, people were not slow to discover that the Ryders had nothing left. The bank got the property, tore down the old building and put up a new one that is occupied by a chain clothing store.

The Ryders themselves offered a more complex problem which no one undertook to solve. The envious said they had long lived beyond their means and it served them right. Mrs. Ryder sold Chevrolets until she exhausted the roster of her friends. The town watched them slip from one subterfuge to another, recalling with little charity the days when the Ryders went on Mediterranean cruises and Bermudan holidays. They lost their home on South Main Avenue. For a time, an aged aunt sent money for apartment rent. When this failed, the Ryders took refuge in a friend's third floor. There were stories. People said that while she ate at the Busy Bee Cafe, he waited outside in the car and she brought out what she could in a paper napkin; that for three days he lived on peanuts from a penny slot machine. He grows thinner and grayer; she tries to maintain the surface pretense.

Perhaps the most appalling blow of all was reserved for early in 1932. R. William McSwirtle was in more ways than one the town's leading citizen. The Melrose National Bank was long known as McSwirtle's bank. He was the personification of the small-town Middle Western banker, gray, respectable, shiny, with cold, fish-colored eyes concealed behind pince-nez, and a pompous smile. The very sight of this pious man was for a long time enough to reassure depositors. He was the chief angel of the Episcopal Church. Not a young boy in the past thirty years has escaped hearing R. William's famous lecture, "Banks and the Churches."

But there were rumors about his bank all through the fall and winter of 1931. The women of the town drew most assurance from the fact that the McSwirtle household was maintained on the same scale as before. R. William certainly tried. He even fought off another threatening run. But the end was close at hand. Early in March of this year The Melrose Advocate announced he had resigned as president of the bank, because of ill health, but would continue in an advisory capacity. Two days later the bank failed and R. William left for parts unknown.

It developed that he had looted the bank of some $300,000. In addition he had extracted about $100,000 from various personal accounts. He had managed the finances of a number of persons of comparatively large income: Dr. Maxwell, the leading surgeon; a half-dozen of the more prosperous professors at Cremona College; old Mrs. Tompkins. Shock followed upon shock until it seemed that God himself had fallen from his throne. Mrs. McSwirtle, Dorothy and young Ted had signed for R. William a number of mysterious papers which proved to be promissory notes. The late neo-Georgian home on South Main Avenue, Dorothy's undyed sealskin coat, the new Packard convertible coupe, everything melted away and the McSwirtles sought shelter with relatives in Decatur.

It is impossible to convey the blasting effect this had upon Melrose. The City National, the only remaining bank, promptly called a thirty-day moratorium on deposits above $100 and convinced the town that, as is true today, it would be possible to pay off every depositor in full in cash. "But," the president added grimly, "we wouldn't have any bank left." Two of the directors of this bank died of nervous strain. . . .

Even to maintain a pretense of the old standard has become a desperate kind of endurance contest for many. A number have succumbed; they have given up, withdrawing from the social and economic life of the town in a kind of living death, pariahs, outcasts, disregarded in even the humblest councils. Their condition is more fortunate than that of those who still struggle. It is, in a sense, as though the whole town were entrenched behind a false front. How much longer they will be able to hold out is a question that no one dares to ask—openly. There is now little consolation in knowing that Chestnut Springs, with all its banks and all its furniture factories closed, is in a worse condition. With the majority, the battle is too grim for such easy consolations. There is small solace in the plight of the Fergusons next door; their condition is prophetic. What will happen next spring Melrose does not venture to guess; next month is too close at hand.

35 · THE DESCENT FROM THE MIDDLE CLASS

To many observant people of all shades of political opinion, it appeared in the early 1930's that the American middle class was doomed to extinction. Actually, within a generation the middle class was as strong as ever, but the future was no clearer to people then than it is now. Arthur Pound, "Bankruptcy Mill," The Atlantic Monthly, CXLIX (February, 1932), pp. 173-175. Reprinted by permission of the publisher.

WHEN MILLTOWN WAS GROWING rapidly, a few years ago, the citizens felt a little aggrieved at having to go elsewhere to obtain the benefits of Federal justice. The situation has recently been relieved, though hardly in the way to rouse local pride, by regular visits from the Referee in Bankruptcy and his assistants. Quite suddenly Milltown, which had been booming broadly and handsomely, began to spawn so many bankrupts that the United States found it advisable to install local service, with regular sittings.

The Referee sat in one of the courtrooms of the new county building, his mercy seat being directly under a rather astonishing mural painting of agricultural blessedness. In this scene of beaming plenty, stalwart humans of the hardy stock which settled this county are revealed at their pioneering tasks—chopping trees and bringing in the harvest sheaves. Court attendants, who perforce study this painting closely while the lawyers are talking, point out all manner of minor anachronisms in it, both of anatomy and of costume, but there is no mistaking the atmosphere of placid plenty which it exudes, and its hale glorifying of the good old ways of Man to Earth.

Beneath this massive painting living men seemed dwarfed as they came and went, telling their brief, sad stories on the stand. Even the lawyers, though speaking with authority, seemed scarcely of the same race as the Anaks and Goliaths in the picture. The Court himself, possessed of a countenance and bearing elsewhere commanding, appeared little more than a pygmy here, in spite of his elevation on the bench. His comments were brief and hurried, and while he neved failed to show either kindliness or shrewdness, one could see that he would relish the end of this sorry business.

A young man, almost a boy, took the stand. Married, out of work for months, owed money he couldn't pay, family sickness the cause of debt, no assets, no automobile. If garnisheed, he would lose his present job. Excused. A discharge will be issued.

A somewhat older man, grocer, small store somewhere in a Polish quarter, had bought at top price a decrepit building, quarter down and pay as you earn. When he tried to repair it, the building sagged from age and swallowed his reserve. What's it worth now? Not half he paid for it. Question arises: his equity is in his wife's name now; when did he put it there, and was it to defraud creditors? Case put over, but the Judge seemed not very hearty about delay. Wife or no wife, come what may, the man's ruined. All that remains is to paw over his small assets, and divide mites.

Came a man named Lincoln, gaunt as Abraham; anyone could see he would stand by his debts as long as he could. Had been a farmer, and ruddier then, no doubt, but now carrying the dirty pallor which comes from indoor work around oil. Not much work, too many to feed, no automobile, not much of anything but debts and children. He wouldn't mind the debts except that his creditors were bothering him with garnishees on his pay at the factory. So he had to get clear or starve his children. The Law waved him promptly off the stand; in due course Mr. Lincoln will get his discharge.

A wrangle develops over the failure of a Hungarian merchant to list a debt he owes a neighboring baker. Both men are almost scared out of their voices. The Referee tries to make them talk up, cups his ear, calls for silence, cannot get at the root of it, small matter anyway, but he must postpone the case. Chides the lawyers for wasting his time, but is gentle and kind even with them.

Only once does he lose his judicial serenity. This is when one who seems willing to fish in these troubled waters offers one-third face value for a long list of accounts due a debtor. The Court barked him down, but in general the personification of the Law appeared to be every inch a gentleman performing with swift precision the most merciful of all legal activities.

When the last case was called, I left hurriedly, to avoid embarrassing a friend, a gentlewoman of the old school, who was about to appear for her final hearing. No doubt the Court placed her case last on the docket so that there would be few observers of the last act in her financial tragedy. She sat, a forlorn, huddled figure, by the only exit, as I hurried past, our eyes not meeting.

Mrs. Clare, after her husband's death, took to speculating. An extremely thrifty person in all respects, her initial successes convinced this delicate, quiet woman that she was a second Hetty Green. She pyramided her winnings with what might be considered the coolness of a professional gambler, except that events showed it to be merely the courage of ignorance. At the peak of stock prices she might have sold out for close to a million, but she could not let go. She never spent any profits, never grew extravagant, never had any fun out of her money. Her bank wisely sandbagged her out of the market at a point where she still had a choice home and enough income left to finance a standard of living well above her desires or needs. But she would not stay out. Presently she was back in the market on broker's margins, and in the end lost everything, even her home. With her fortune wiped out, she still owed money; and there, under the pioneer scene her forefathers knew so well, she waited for the final hearing that would establish her as a bankrupt.

Nothing new, I grant you, in her case; merely the old story of the widow grown mighty in her new freedom. She was in the grasp of the spirit of a mad time, when even men deemed wise talked of a New Era, when foolish youngsters actually believed in the stocks they were selling, when everyone with an axe to grind tried to make us believe that his cutlery was responsible for Prosperity. But, having known more than one generation of Clares, I see in the rise and fall of Mrs. Clare something more than merely the downfall of an individual.

Mrs. Clare's grandparents entered this state while it was still a territory. They took up land from the government in goodly quantities, tilled the best acres, sold the rest, acquired the position of good farmers in a day when a good farmer stood as high as a village merchant. They sent their sons to college, where they became doctors, lawyers, teachers, engineers. Mrs. Clare's father was a doctor and she married a doctor's son. Both her father and her father-in-law were substantial men, looked up to as learned in the county seat where they settled. Though neither pursued the main chance too hotly, being healers first and business men second, some excellent real estate came their way and settled in their laps. One of the two died well off, and stores now grace the corner where he lived; but they are not, at this writing, Mrs. Clare's stores. In other words, a vast amount of risk, labor, and thrift, persevered in by their ancestors to improve the lot of present and coming Clares, has gone for naught, and the Clares of 1932 will be poorer, both actually and by contrast with their neighbors, than were the Clares of 1832.

In her dizzy climb with the boom, Mrs. Clare passed from the middle to the upper economic class, and then dropped clear through the middle bracket into the proletariat, from which it is unlikely that either she or her descendants will emerge for some time, if ever. Of the other cases under review that day, three were those of merchants gone bankrupt, sliding from the middle class into the lower level. Two represented the defeat of efforts to climb from the cellar to the ground floor, while three revealed merely the misfortunes of toilers caught in the wash when the cellar flooded.

36 • VAGRANT CIVIL ENGINEER

The next four selections have to do with unemployment among people trained for professional careers. The first one appeared in The New York Times, *May 4, 1932.*

A HEAVILY BEARDED MAN in a faded brown suit, who said he was a graduate of the University of Colorado and had held responsible positions as a civil engineer in this country, China, Panama and the jungles of Venezuela, was arraigned yesterday on a charge of vagrancy in Flatbush Court, where he told such a dramatic and straightforward story of his experiences that he held the attention of the crowded courtroom for nearly an hour. Magistrate Eilperin adjourned the case until Friday so that a thorough investigation could be made.

The defendant said he was Langlan Heinz, 44 years old. He was arrested at 4 A.M. by a policeman who found him sleeping on an improvised cot in a vacant lot near Flatbush Avenue, between Fillmore Avenue and Avenue R, Brooklyn. Heinz said he had made this lot his home for forty-six days.

In a well-modulated voice, Heinz began the recital of his experiences by saying that he was born in Dodge City, Kan., had received his early schooling there and then had entered the University of Colorado from which he was graduated with a Bachelor of Science degree in 1911. He worked in various parts of the country as a civil engineer until 1921, when he came to New York City and worked for the city for seven years as a structural draftsman.

In 1929, Heinz said, he went to Shanghai where he worked as a draftsman for ten months at $450 a month. Most of his earnings he sent to his mother, who is living . . . [in] Los Angeles, Cal. When the Shanghai job was finished, Heinz continued, he went to Panama, where he got occasional employment, and then worked for an oil company in Maturin, Venezuela.

While at Maturin Heinz was sent into the jungle territory but contracted fever after a few months and was idle for a long period. When he recovered he went back to Trinidad and then, his money almost depleted, worked his way by ship back to Los Angeles and to his mother's home. After several months in California he sailed for Cairo, Egypt, in December, 1930, but lost his passport en route and was not allowed to land.

He next went to Naples where he worked for ten months in a wine factory and learned the Italian language. On New Year's Day, 1932, he landed in this country at Jersey City. He said he remembered that he had left about $1,000 worth of tools in the office in which he had worked for the city and stayed at a hotel in Manhattan during his attempts to find them. He was unsuccessful, however, and when his savings were used up he left the hotel and started walking the streets.

A month and a half ago he made the Brooklyn lot his home. Firemen at a firehouse near by gave him occasional shower baths, he said, and housewives and school children in the neighborhood gave him food. Each day he went to the Brooklyn waterfront in an effort to obtain employment on some outgoing ship.

Heinz, who substantiated his story from time to time with names and dates, said he had two brothers and two sisters living in different parts of the country. One brother, he said, was a member of the Board of Education in Los Angeles.

37 • COMMITTEE ON UNEMPLOYMENT
AND RELIEF
FOR CHEMISTS AND CHEMICAL ENGINEERS

Since World War II America has been troubled by the problem of how to educate a larger number of qualified scientists. America's concern for scientists in the early 1930's was somewhat different. The New York Times, *May 22, 1932.*

MORE THAN ONE-FOURTH of the 455 qualified chemists who have applied for jobs to the Committee on Unemployment and Relief for Chemists and Chemical Engineers, 300 Madison Avenue, have been placed, it was announced yesterday. The committee said that it has funds for only five more weeks and estimates that $20,000 is needed to carry the work through the Summer.

An appeal for $5 contributions from members of the profession has brought $3,000 so far.

Approximately 109 of those registered with the committee are said to be destitute, about 130 others are in need and 158 have funds for a short time. Jobs obtained for applicants average in salary from $35 to $50 a week. Four have been obtained at $100 or more a week and one at $60. Forty-seven of the positions are permanent and 74 temporary.

Among the applicants, it was said, are men who have never before had to look for positions. Yet some have been sleeping in the subway for nights. One of these was a chemist who had worked for nine or ten years with the biggest companies in the country. . . .

38 · UNEMPLOYED COLLEGE GRADUATES

These two selections give some idea of the extent of unem-
ployment among college alumni and the kinds of colleges from
which the unemployed came. The first item is from The New
York Times, *July 27, 1932. The second, "A Survey of Unem-*
ployed Alumni," is from School *and* Society, *a professional*
educational journal, XXXIX (March 10, 1934), p. 307. Re-
printed by permission.

ORGANIZATION OF THE ASSOCIATION of Unemployed College Alumni was announced yesterday after a meeting of graduates of nine Eastern colleges at the offices of the League for Industrial Democracy. Estimating the number of unemployed alumni in this city alone at more than 10,000, the association made public a plan of action designed to enlist members throughout the country.

In a statement prepared at the meeting the group pointed out that since June, 1929, it had become increasingly difficult for university graduates to obtain positions. Distress consequent upon unemployment was more acute among college-trained men and women, according to the announcement, because of their relatively high standards of living and education. . . .

Colleges represented at the meeting included Columbia, Harvard, New York University, Vassar, Hunter, City College, Swarthmore, Columbia Law School and New York Dental School.

THOUSANDS OF COLLEGE GRADUATES, many with high-grade professional training, are among the ranks of the unemployed, as disclosed in a recent survey conducted by the American College Personnel Association. Under the direction of Dr. Esther Lloyd-Jones, assistant professor of education at Teachers College, Columbia University, and Clyde R. Miller, director of the Bureau of Educational Service, the study embraced fifty-four colleges and universities located in every section of the United States. The confidential records of these fifty-four institutions revealed that at the present time 21,974 men and women holding degrees from these colleges are without positions.

"The figures revealed by this survey do not pretend to completeness," Mr. Miller reports. "They include only those individuals who have notified the appointment bureaus of their colleges that they are without work. Scores of colleges are not included in the association, and the appointment bureaus of the member colleges have no information concerning the status of large numbers of their alumni who have not communicated with them. It is safe to say that at the present time hundreds of thousands of college graduates are unemployed. Many of them are technically trained men and women of proven ability and splendid achievement."

Many professions are represented, the teaching profession leading with 12,420 unemployed. Engineers are next in rank, listing 2,845 unemployed graduates, the larger number being electrical, mechanical and civil engineers. Business graduates also suffer greatly, the survey showed, as 2,436 business executives are unemployed.

Over 100 different occupations are listed, together with the number of unemployed graduates in each field. Some of the most frequent groups include architects, agriculturalists, bankers, chemists, educational administrators, dietitians, journalists, librarians, social workers, salesmen, laboratory technicians, religious educators, advertising men, draftsmen, artists and biologists.

Of the colleges and universities which listed unemployed alumni, the Ohio State University has the greatest number, with 2,097. The University of Chicago has 1,798; the University of Illinois, 1,445; Teachers College, Columbia University, 1,255; Princeton University, 450; the Carnegie Institute of Technology, 844; New York University, 575; the University of Minnesota, 528; Temple University, 687; the College of the City of New York, 550.

VI

The Depression
and Education

PEOPLE NEVER ENJOY paying taxes. With the lower incomes of the depression came widespread demand for retrenchment and lower local taxes. Indeed, many citizens and property owners were quite unable to pay their taxes at all.

Since a large part of the revenues of local government is spent for public education, it was perhaps inevitable that the tax crisis should produce cutbacks in the schools. Many communities decreased their school spending severely. In effect, they passed the burden on to the teachers, the students, or both. No one will ever be able to calculate the cost to American civilization that resulted from inadequate education of the nation's children during the Great Depression.

The colleges' problems were somewhat different. Although the budgets of almost all colleges, public and private, were not what they should have been, a greater problem was that of students who were destitute. Rare was the college that did not have several cases of severe student poverty. Thousands of students in the 1930's made important sacrifices to stay in college. Because the students of the depression constituted, on the whole, a hungry campus generation they gave college life a new and earnest tone. The goldfish gulpers may have got the big headlines in the late 1930's, but they were not typical depression undergraduates.

39 · CHEAPER AND CHEAPENED
PUBLIC SCHOOLS

*This article by a Kansas woman describes the national pub-
lic school crisis. Avis D. Carlson, "Deflating the Schools,"
Harper's, CLXVII (November, 1933), pp. 705-713. Reprinted
by permission.*

DURING THE FIRST TWO YEARS of the depression the schools did business
about as usual. By September, 1931, the strain was beginning to tell.
Salary cuts were appearing even in large towns, and the number of pupils
per teacher had definitely increased. Building programs had been postponed. In a few communities school terms had been considerably shortened, and in others some of the departments and services were being
lopped off. But, on the whole, the school world wagged on pretty much
as usual.

During the 1932-33 term the deflation gathered momentum so rapidly
that many communities had to close their schools. By the end of last March
nearly a third of a million children were out of school for that reason. But
the number of children affected, shocking as it is, does not tell the story
so vividly as does the distribution of the schools. Georgia had 1,318 closed
schools with an enrollment of 170,790, and in Alabama 81 per cent of all
the children enrolled in white rural schools were on an enforced vacation.
In Arkansas, to cite the case of another sorely pressed State, over 300
schools were open for *sixty days or less during the entire year.* By the last
of February more than 8,000 school children were running loose in sparsely
settled New Mexico. And over a thousand West Virginia schools had
quietly given up the struggle.

These are, of course, States which for one reason or another have always
lagged educationally. But consider the case of Ohio, which formerly was
near the other end of the procession. According to authentic information,
some of it compiled by the Cleveland *Plain Dealer* and some by the State
Director of Education, practically every school in the State had to shorten
its term. Numbers of county schools shut down at the end of seven months.
Findlay and Cuyahoga Falls, towns of 20,000 population, closed after
seven months. Akron worried on a little longer, to the first week in May,
owing its teachers $330,000. During the first part of the year the Dayton
schools were open only three days a week. Youngstown closed three weeks
earlier than usual, with a half million dollars in overdue salaries on its
books. Every school in Carroll County clipped a month from its term.

In various other American communities where the schools continued open to the end of their 1932-33 term, it was only because teachers went stoutly on with their work even when they knew their salaries would not be forthcoming at the end of the month. The Chicago situation is so well known that there is no need to discuss it. But the average citizen who read of it somehow got the notion that it was unique. It was unique only in the size of the town and the length of time the drama had dragged on. Scattered throughout the nation last year were hundreds of school districts in which the Chicago plan of issuing tax-anticipation warrants which finally became uncashable worked out to its bitter end. In Oklahoma scores of teachers cashed only one or two warrants all year. In the whole of Apache County, Arizona, not a single warrant was cashed. In Mississippi, Northern Minnesota, Idaho, South Dakota, Alabama, Ohio, and probably other States that I do not know about, some of the rural teachers managed to exist by "boarding around" at the homes of their patrons, much as in the days of *The Hoosier Schoolmaster*. If the schools had been on a pay-as-you-go basis there is no estimating how many of them would have been closed during a greater part of the year. . . .

Some governmental expenditures are more essential than others, of course, and some are less wastefully made than others. But the average taxpayer is never disposed to investigate and make discriminations. Recently he has been in such straits that he is less than ever inclined to pause for discrimination. He may suspect or know that certain branches of his local government are shot with waste and graft of the most flagrant sort and that others are outworn and useless; but in that field he is either indifferent or convinced of his helplessness. He surely knows that an enormous bonded indebtedness is involving a staggering annual bill for "fixed charges"—but the capitalistic system being what it is, he supposes that fixed charges must remain fixed and sacrosanct. So far as he can see, there is only one thing he can do. He can kick and kick hard about all these governmental trimmings like county nurses and school gymnasiums which have been growing up under his eyes in the last twenty years. Use the knife, legislator, send it deep!

Thus adjured, the legislator has responded nobly.

Take the case of Iowa. In that home of fat cornfields and distraught corn growers, 95 per cent of the cost of the public schools came from the property tax. As farm prices have dropped, banks closed, and delinquent taxes mounted, the strain has become unbearable. If any State in the Union should have been interested in modernizing its tax system, that State was Iowa. The 1933 legislature brought forth much legislation. But an analysis of the 32 new laws that affect the schools shows that all but one were concerned solely with economy. The millage levies were limited to 80 per cent of the 1930 level. Agriculture, home economics, and manual training were taken from the list of required subjects, and kindergartens were made optional instead of mandatory. The appropriations for the

State department of public instruction were reduced by 30 per cent. Permission was given for the discontinuance of junior colleges, and regulations were laid down for the disestablishment of county high schools. A flat minimum salary of $40 a month was fixed for teachers, regardless of their training or experience—which, interestingly enough, is just about half the annual minimum income the government has assigned to industrial workers. Every conceivable kind of budget whittling was done, but nothing whatever was accomplished in the way of correcting the basic tax trouble.

Kansas, true to her genius for engaging in reforms on a heroic scale, had an economy legislature that really did things. None of the Iowan attention to small details in economy sullied their record. In spite of words of caution from the governor, they kept their eyes on the main job. They made a four-million-dollar cut in State appropriations, a large share of which must be borne by the State schools. They ordered the tax commission to reduce real property values 20 per cent, and they sternly limited school levies. And, to make all things doubly sure, they required every governmental agency to tot up its indebtedness, issue bonds to cover it, and forthwith go on a strict "cash basis." Having started from scratch, it must stay absolutely within its income. No more tax-anticipation warrants for Kansas.

Naturally such a legislative job is received in various ways. The taxpayers' associations that forced it are jubilant. School boards are bewildered. No one knows what to count upon, because the amount of delinquent taxes is nowadays unpredictable.

In smaller communities over the State the situation is still [August] uncertain. The "cash basis" system comes particularly hard just at this moment, for Kansas is going through one of the worst drouths in her drouth-ridden history. Two years of twenty-five cent wheat followed by a year of drouth make a sad combination for Kansas. Out through the wheat country great level fields are being foreclosed by the thousands. In the eastern part of the State, where diversified farming is practiced, the condition is no better. Naturally, then, taxes dribble into the courthouses in slow, thin streams. In the face of all this some rural school boards have decided that it is not worth while trying to open their schools. More than one rural teacher has contracted to teach for $35 a month, which in an eight months' school year means an annual income of $280. How many books and magazines these teachers, who are supposed to form the cultural leadership of rural Kansas, can afford to buy during the next year is open to any one's estimate. Their teaching will consist of a plodding sort of routine drill—when they are not worrying about the problem of how to replace the shoes which have just sprung leaks.

In general, the urban districts have the choice between cutting down to the Three R's, putting the teachers on a subsistence level, or shortening the term. At Horton, a town of about 4,000, the superintendent and teachers were hired at the rate of $50 a month. In a typical countyseat town of

3,500 the plan is to eliminate the kindergarten, school nurse, and one grade school, cut salaries sharply again, then run along until near the holidays, when the officials will say to the teachers, "We have only so much money on hand. If you want to prorate it among yourselves, well and good. If not, you'll have to go." The assumption back of this plan is that on the present crowded teacher market it will always be possible to get teachers no matter what salary is offered.

In other States the school legislation may not have been so extreme, but much of it was to the same point. In Idaho the appropriations for all educational institutions were reduced from 20 to 39 per cent of the 1931 level. In Oregon the teachers' minimum salary law was invalidated for two years. In Wyoming the legislature provided for the distribution of the government royalty fund (derived from mineral leases on federal lands) for a six months' term instead of eight months. In Michigan a severe tax-limitation law was passed. In Delaware there was proposed a measure which would make it unlawful to employ any person to teach art, music, or athletics.

In Arkansas, where the school situation was last year so bad that in late November a tourist driving across the State saw few rural schools open, the legislature set itself to the task of relieving the schools. The line of reasoning was apparently thus: "In the good old days when the schools were in politics we did not have such messes as this. Therefore, we will return them to the politicians, and incidentally save some money on them." Accordingly, the offices of County Board of Education and County Superintendent were abolished. The powers and duties of the former were vested in that picturesque institution, the County Court, and the powers and duties of the latter in a county examiner appointed by the county judge. This county examiner is required to remain in active teaching service, and for his extra-professional chore is to be paid a fee of $650 a year! Another backward step of the same sort was taken in the abolition of the State Board of Education and throwing of the office of State Superintendent back into State politics.

In Oklahoma an economy measure requires the adoption of text books for a period of ten years. On a mad-hatter arrangement like that a whole generation of children would have grown up without knowing that the state of Poland exists or that the form of government in Russia has changed! Another interesting new law establishes a schedule of *maximum* salaries for schools which are to have State aid. According to this schedule the teachers with the lowest permissible training and experience are to be limited to $40 a month, while the upper limit for an experienced, college graduate, elementary teacher is $85, or an annual income of $680, if State funds can hold out for eight months. An inexperienced high school teacher with an A.M. is entitled to $90. The most any such teacher can ever get with no matter how many years of experience is exactly $100. . . .

In general, there are four points at which a Board of Education sitting down to work out its annual budget may apply the knife: in building and repairs, in text books and classroom equipment, in salaries, and in services and curricula.

The first need not detain us long. It is no longer available at all as a method of economy. At the onset of the depression building programs were abandoned and repairs reduced to a minimum that in many a town will prove a costly economy in the long run, if not an actual danger to life and limb. The results of this three-year stretch of thrift are beginning to be apparent. Since the average school district had spent heavily for building during the decade before 1930 (to compensate for the war years when no construction went on and to accord with the general spirit of "bigger and better") probably no great harm has yet been done by this halt in building. But depression or no depression, the school population continues to increase by more than 200,000 a year. Present building equipment will not long continue to house a family that grows so rapidly. In many city systems room-shortage is already an acute problem. In fact the 1932-33 term saw about 250,000 children attending school on a part-time basis for lack of school rooms and approximately 150,000 others housed in temporary or portable shacks. To enjoy the Century of Progress one must forget that the eccentric metropolis which stages the show used seven hundred tin shacks in housing its school-children last year and has just junked its entire junior high school system in order to gain classroom space for the senior high schools.

The next items to be considered by our hypothetical Board in desperate search for something to reduce are text books and classroom equipment. Here, too, economy was early in the game carried as far as it could be without serious injury to the quality of instruction offered. It is safe to say that whatever further reduction is being made for the 1933-34 term does offer that injury. With a million more pupils than in 1930, the sale of textbooks had dropped off 30 per cent by the beginning of 1933. Such a contrast in figures can only mean that youngsters are using dog-eared, dirty books, crudely defaced and probably with missing pages. A fine chance they have to learn to respect books! It can also only mean that many schools are already seriously crippled by the lack of books. Supplementary readers and reference books fall to pieces after a while, and if they are not replaced, instruction in the courses which depend upon them must cease.

And now the Board comes to salaries. Three courses are open. Salaries may be cut all round, teachers may be released, or at the worst both devices may be resorted to. The first method was the one most often chosen in 1932-33. According to a study made last spring by the United States Office of Education, teachers' salaries had already dropped from 12 to 43 per cent—besides, of course, the discount levied by bankers who cashed the warrants. This fall salaries fell sharply again. In many regions the teachers are now literally on a subsistence level. Throughout the country as a whole the classroom teachers who still have jobs, who are paid in cash and with some degree of regularity, and who have an annual income of as much as $1200 may count themselves among the plutocrats of the profession. The rise of commodity prices, which the administration is so assiduously fostering, will materially add to the troubles of the pedagogues. . . .

In preceding depression years new teachers were not hired, but this year has seen a wave of actual releases. Chicago has trimmed her teaching force by more than a thousand. With the $2,200,000 cut Boston is making from last year's budget many teachers will surely have to be eliminated. So small a city as Tulsa has had to let 60 go. In villages and cities everywhere the teaching force is smaller this year than in 1930, when the school population was about a million less than this year. To the cynic who asks, "What of it?" one has to reply that Mark Hopkins on the end of a log may be only a romantic ideal, but Susan Smith facing 50 or 60 pupils in a room designed to seat 35 or 40 comfortably is so far at the other extreme that it is nonsense to think she can do much teaching.

And finally, the Board approaches the items most loaded with emotional dynamite: services and curricula. Here enter for attention the celebrated "fads and frills" about which every critic of the public schools is so deeply exercised. Now a fad or a frill seems to be anything in the school system which was not there thirty years ago. Last year the schools began reluctantly to relinquish them, in other words, to retreat to the educational customs of 1900. This year a veritable axe has descended upon them. Night schools and special schools for physically and mentally handicapped children have been eliminated or drastically curtailed. At the present rate of mortality, kindergartens will soon be a thing of the past. Supervisors are being blown out like chaff in the wind. Health services are being abandoned and visiting teachers becoming a luxury few cities can afford. Many towns have eliminated music entirely and others have greatly reduced their offerings. Art, home economics, manual training, physical education, trade and vocational classes, and even foreign languages are all being eliminated or curtailed.

40 · TEACHERS
FOOT THE EDUCATIONAL BILL

The following testimony summarizes the financial plight of the teachers of Chicago, who had several "payless paydays" in the early 1930's. It was nearly a decade before the Chicago teachers received all their back pay. Federal Cooperation in Unemployment Relief, Hearing *before a Subcommittee of the Committee on Manufactures, United States Senate, 72nd Cong., 1 sess., on S. 4592, May 9, 1932 (Washington: Government Printing Office, 1932), pp. 48-51.*

SENATOR COSTIGAN. What is your name?

MR. WILSON. Irvin A. Wilson.

SENATOR COSTIGAN. Are you president of the Chicago Principals Club?

MR. WILSON. I am president of the Chicago Principals Club, and am here officially representing that organization.

SENATOR COSTIGAN. Have you a statement for the committee?

MR. WILSON. I have no statement. I will speak from notes, Mr. Chairman.

SENATOR COSTIGAN. Please proceed.

MR. WILSON. In the first place, gentlemen of the committee, the credit of the Chicago board of education has completely collapsed. The taxes which are now in process of collection on the penalty date, which was the 1st of June, were collected only to the extent of less than 50 per cent.

SENATOR WHEELER. You say the financial structure has completely collapsed. How much of that has been due to the misapplication of funds by those in charge of the school board, if any?

MR. WILSON. I should say a very small part of it from that standpoint alone. It is pretty largely from the fact which Mr. Stillman brought out. In a period of two years no taxes whatever have been collected, and we have been borrowing money for the last several years at least a year ahead, and for the last three or four years two years ahead in order to meet expenses.

SENATOR WHEELER. One hears so much these days about the corruption and crookedness of city officials and school boards, that I was wondering as to the making of money of those interested in school boards on private contracts—I was wondering how much, if any, you had knowledge of in Chicago; just in a general way, without specific instances, has there been much of that?

MR. WILSON. The schools have recently been surveyed by Dr. George D. Strayer, of Columbia University, and in his survey report just submitted to the board of education this week, he makes several recommendations for economy in the board of education, and the board of education already ahead of that survey put into operation a great many economies under the present stress period of financial depression.

SENATOR WHEELER. I hope an aroused public opinion will come about in Chicago and other large cities that are suffering from lack of funds, against these thieving public officials who have been responsible to some extent, at least, in breaking down the finances of the cities, counties, and States of our country.

MR. WILSON. I want to address myself, gentlemen, to two or three things. In the middle of February the Chicago Principals Club, in order to acquaint the people of Chicago with the critical financial situation facing the school people, sent a questionnaire to each of the 14,000 teachers in the city. We had replies from 263 of the city's schools, and from 6,315 teachers, covering their own financial situation, beginning with the first of last May, when salaries ceased to come through on time.

Over the period of the last 13 months the Chicago school system has paid in cash to school employees only 5 months out of 13.

SENATOR COSTIGAN. When you refer to the 1st of last May, what year have you in mind? Is that of this year?

MR. WILSON. The 1st of May, 1931. These are some of the results we have on the questionnaire.

The teachers of Chicago, 3,177 of those teachers, out of 6,315, reported a total loss of $2,367,000 in bank failures. Two thousand eight hundred and sixty-nine of those teachers reported a loss of time of $621,293, because of personal illness, this at a time when salaries were not forthcoming.

SENATOR WHEELER. How many lost money by investing in the Insull Securities Cos. in Chicago?

MR. WILSON. I imagine a large number of them did that. Two thousand two hundred and seventy-eight reported losses to the extent of $7,800,-000, by lapsed life insurance policies, as the result of this critical financial situation. Seven hundred and fifty-nine lost their homes, lost an equity in the homes which they were buying. There were large amounts due on rent and food, doctors' and dentists' bills, and all those things.

Insurance companies have loaned teachers at Chicago on their policies, $1,128,000. Many of the teachers had been forced to allow their life insurance policies to lapse. Eight hundred and five teachers reported having gone to what we call the loan sharks and procured money to the extent of $232,000, and were therefore paying an interest rate equal to a maximum of 42 per cent a year on that.

I want to say to you that the situation of the Chicago school teachers has been critical for the past year. A year ago we went into the summer vacation period with two months' back salary unpaid. This year, unless something unexpected happens in the next few days, we will go into the summer vacation with six months' unpaid salaries.

Twenty million dollars to-day is owing the teachers, 14,000 teachers, of Chicago. That is an average of $1,400 for each teacher in the Chicago school system that that community owes to the teachers. If every citizen in the United States were assessed an equal tax, that would bring in the stupendous total of $150,000,000,000, enough to operate the entire public-school system of the United States of America for three-quarters of a century.

SENATOR WHEELER. I did not get that statement.

MR. WILSON. Each teacher in Chicago is owed by that community $1,400;

each of the 14,000 teachers. If every citizen in the United States were assessed an equal tax, that would bring in the stupendous total of $150,-000,000,000, which would be enough to operate the entire public-school system of the United States for three-quarters of a century. That is the load, gentlemen, the Chicago public-school teachers are carrying to-day. That is the load the Chicago public-school teachers have carried almost continuously for the past 12 months.

I say to you that we have reached the breaking point. I believe that it is impossible for the Chicago school situation to go on as it is without some form of relief. We can not see any relief immediately ahead in the city. We are appealing to you as representatives of the United States Government, because we believe that education is fundamental to the preservation of the ideals of this Nation.

We are certain that anything that wrecks, cripples the school system of this Nation can not but have an effect upon the citizenship in all times. We believe the second largest city in the country, with such a school situation that we are certain is absolutely unique and tremendously dangerous, tremendously serious; we believe that that situation if permitted to continue will finally result in but one thing, the complete collapse of the Chicago public-school system, which would be a blot upon the good name, not only of that city, but upon the records of this Nation.

We believe that education and citizenship must go hand in hand. We believe that anything that interferes with the proper carrying out of the educational system of this Nation will finally have its effect upon the citizenship and upon the State as a whole.

This we believe to be a real crisis, a crisis that demands the most expert thinking, the most expert acting, and the most expert remedy. We are, therefore, appealing to you wholly on the ground that the United States of America can not afford to permit 500,000 boys and girls to remain out upon the streets of the second largest city in this Nation. We are certain that is imminent unless some relief comes, and comes immediately.

Certainly the ideals of America support public education. We believe that that city of ours is supporting public education. We are willing to make any sacrifice, and we have made all sacrifices in order that the schools of that city be kept open during the past year.

SENATOR COSTIGAN. Mr. Wilson, the problem of the boys on the street is further complicated, is it not, because many of them belong to families the members of which have long been and still are unemployed?

MR. WILSON. Absolutely. That is a very, very important point in connection with that.

SENATOR WHEELER. What has the appeal been to the bankers out there to take up these warrants?

MR. WILSON. The warrants which are now given to teachers—I have a half of one month's salary in my pocket at the present time that I have not been able to dispose of, that I would have to dispose of, if I were putting it on the market to-day, at 12 to 20 per cent discount. That is the answer of the bankers.

SENATOR WHEELER. Will the bankers take these warrants?

MR. WILSON. The bankers will not take the warrants at all. You have to sell them through private investment companies.

SENATOR WHEELER. They will not take them at all?

MR. WILSON. Not at the present time.

SENATOR WHEELER. Why will they not take them? What is the excuse they will not take them, the reason for it?

MR. WILSON. Very largely because of the muddle the tax situation is in, out of which we have not emerged in Chicago.

SENATOR WHEELER. But eventually it seems to me the city of Chicago, certainly the people of the city of Chicago, are not going to let the complete city government collapse there.

I want to remind you that the Congress of the United States has passed a reconstruction bill for the purpose of helping the bankers of the country. We have passed the Glass-Steagall bill for the purpose of helping the bankers of the country, and to keep the banks open, and we have passed other legislation, all of it with the idea of helping the big banks of the country, and it seems to me that when a community is in the situation that you have described, that at least there ought to be patriotism enough among your bankers in Chicago to take up these warrants and keep it going until such time as your tax muddle is straightened out.

MR. WILSON. Of course, as a matter of fact, over the last several years the bankers have carried the situation completely, but when this so-called tax strike came on, and with less than 50 per cent of the taxes due, and on which the penalty date began June 1, with less than 50 per cent of those taxes paid, the bankers find it impossible to carry the situation longer.

41 • COLLEGE STUDENTS
OF THE DEPRESSION

Many students during the 1930's devised ingenious ways to make or save a dollar. This article describes some of the students' practices during the school year 1932-1933. Gilbert Love, "College Students Are Beating the Depression," School and Society, XXXVII (June 10, 1933), pp. 749-751. Reprinted by permission of the editor.

ACROSS THE CAMPUS of Oklahoma A. and M. College moved a weird procession. At the front was an ancient open flivver, sufficiently battered to be termed "collegiate." In its front seat were two boys; in its back seat a bale of hay. There followed another car, differing from the first only in the number and kind of dents in its fenders and body. It was also manned by two boys. Its back seat was occupied by a large crate of protesting poultry. Then came a fifth boy leading a Jersey cow. The cow refused to be influenced by the obvious impatience of the motorized portion of the procession, so it was hours later when the strange group finally arrived in front of a house on the outskirts of the college town. The poultry was given a back yard coop in which to live and, presumably, to lay eggs. The cow was tethered in an adjoining field. Then from some recesses in the battered hulls of the flivvers the boys pulled out some 200 quarts of canned fruits and vegetables and a dozen cured hams. With meat and vegetables in the cellar and prospective eggs and milk in the back yard, the five were ready for higher education.

College students have probably developed more ingenious ways of beating the depression than any other group in America. Using their wits to earn money or cooking their own meals and living in shacks to save it, Joe College and Betty Co-ed are getting educated in spite of technological unemployment, bank moratoria, impoverishment of agriculture and a general scarcity of cash. For instance:

Two male students at Ohio State University have started a "dog laundry." They call for Fido, Bruno or Towser, take him to their "plant" and return him all nicely bathed, combed and manicured. . . .

A Notre Dame student who found that all the regular "hashing," janitorial and secretarial jobs were taken when he arrived in South Bend, created a business for himself by becoming a campus guide. He spends his Sundays at the entrance to the university, picking up groups of visitors and taking them to points of interest around the famous school.

A student at Western Reserve University, Cleveland, has been able to hold a comparatively lucrative position right through the depression because he is becoming accustomed to hold-ups. The large gasoline station at which he is night attendant has been robbed three times by gunmen.

A couple of husky freshmen at West Virginia University who probably didn't know the difference between a casserole and a wash tub when they left home, have been going to school on less than $1.60 a week apiece by renting a back bedroom with a small stove in it and cooking cheap but nourishing foods.

Eight boys at the University of Washington are getting their meals at very small cost by cooking them in a basement and "taking in" several other students as boarders.

An examination of a single small school reveals the wide variety of occupations that students have taken up to support themselves. In Duquesne University, Pittsburgh, one student is an undertaker's helper, one a railroad fireman, one a laborer in a steel mill, one cuts granite tombstones and another sells newspapers. A student who has become an expert on glass works a regular eight-hour shift in a glass factory 40 miles from Pittsburgh and "commutes" to take a full-time course at Duquesne. A pharmacist who has changed his mind about professions is keeping his corner drug store to pay his way through a law course. An enterprising student buys old text-books from sophomores and sells them to freshmen. An athletic young man is serving as first aid instructor for a coal company. One Duquesne student is reputed to hold 27 odd jobs on the campus and in the city. Among other things he is editor-in-chief of the school newspaper and official announcer at the major league baseball games at Forbes Field.

The student wage-earners at Duquesne are mostly male. But, throughout the country, girls are showing as much initiative and courage as their masculine fellow-students in making their own way. Take Northwestern co-eds, for example. One girl living in a Northwestern cooperative dormitory earns her expense money by remodeling hats and dresses, washing and waving hair and doing any odd mending wanted. Two girls have become so well known for their adeptness at catering that they can not take care of all the calls they receive from hostesses in Evanston and near-by sections of Chicago. Another girl is housekeeper—"home manager" would be more accurate—in a household in which there is a grandmother who is so seriously ill that she must have two nurses, a father and mother who must be away on business most of the time, and three small children who are left in Evanston to attend school. An exclusive apartment hotel employs a co-ed as hostess in its tea room. For working about four hours a day the girl is given a luxurious apartment, maid service and meals. Another girl makes several hundred dollars a year by tinting photographs for an out-of-town company.

Student occupations at the University of Pennsylvania, Philadelphia, range all the way from historical research to handling boats. A recent survey disclosed the fact that students were engaged in 84 kinds of gainful activity. Dish washing, furniture moving, painting, tutoring, pantry work, scraping floors and soda dispensing seem to be favorites, if numbers are any indication. To take care of some of the students who could not find work in Philadelphia, the student placement service started an automobile washing and polishing establishment on the campus.

The University of Pennsylvania took action at the start of the present school year to turn over as many campus jobs as possible to students. As a result, collegians are now acting as night watchmen, janitors, secretaries, mail carriers, switchboard operators, locker room attendants, technicians and clerks. Students have also been appointed to act as gate men and ushers at athletic contests and to handle all parking on university grounds. They handle trunks in the dormitories at the beginning and end of each academic year and have been authorized to sell certain articles at service stands placed in university buildings.

As a matter of fact, schools everywhere are taking heroic measures to help their students through the period of economic difficulty.

Costs at the University Commons, University of Kentucky, have been reduced to such an extent that students can now live there for $3.50 a week. Through the intervention of the dean of men at West Virginia University, the standard rate of board charged in private homes near the university has been reduced from $7 to $4 a week.

At the University of Pittsburgh a number of boys are being allowed to live rent-free in unused garages and other buildings near the campus. And, although it was not officially sanctioned by the university, a group of athletes lived for several months last winter in a drafty campus building used for dressing room purposes.

Officials of Carthage College, in Illinois, let a miner pay his daughter's tuition in coal this past winter. At Notre Dame 300 students are earning their board by waiting on tables in the dormitory dining halls. They are so numerous that they serve a meal to their 2,000 fellow students in 20 minutes.

Statistics compiled last fall indicate that fully half the men and one fourth of the women attending the nation's 48 land-grant colleges are working for at least part of their funds. More than 13,000 men and 3,000 girls in these colleges are earning all their expenses. Their total earnings are $7,000,000 a year.

At the University of Wisconsin, three fifths of the students earned part of their expenses during the last school year, and 23 per cent were wholly self-supporting. At Yale, during the last school year, students earned $553,701. The institution contributed another $683,378 in scholarships and loans.

When the economic depression is finally over and commendations for valor are being passed around, some sort of special recognition should be given the student who, with only enough money to last until June if he spent but 35 cents a day for food, quit a $100 a month job because it was keeping him from his studies.

42 • A NEW DEMOCRACY
IN COLLEGE EDUCATION

The New Deal's aid to poverty-stricken college students helped enable college enrollments to climb back to normal and then surpass the numbers of the 1920's. The Roosevelt administration's FERA and NYA did more than any national measure undertaken before to make a college education possible for young people from poor families. Excerpted from Betty and Ernest K. Lindley, A New Deal for Youth: The Story of the National Youth Administration *(New York: The Viking Press, 1938), pp. 156-163. Reprinted by permission of the publisher.*

THE AMERICAN DREAM of equal educational opportunity has never fully materialized—not even in the elementary schools. The gap between aspiration and fact has been the widest at the college level. Even at the state institutions, laboratory fees, books, and incidentals are more costly than in the high schools, and most students must meet the additional expense of board and lodging away from home. A bridge of scholarships and loan funds has carried a few promising but poor young people across the gap. A wider bridge has been built by the energetic and ambitious youths who have worked their way through college. Entirely or partly self-supporting students have been respected members of undergraduate communities. They have not been unknown even at the high-tuition private colleges catering chiefly to the children of families in the upper-income brackets.

For a decade before the great depression the difficulty of working one's way through college had been increasing somewhat. Between 1920 and 1930 college attendance more than doubled. Many colleges are situated in small communities where the number of part-time jobs did not increase in proportion to the number of students seeking them. Nor, on the average, was there a decrease in the cost of a college education to the individual student.

With the advent of the depression, the number of students partly or entirely dependent on their own earning capacities sharply increased, and the number of jobs open to them sharply decreased. Most institutions made all the concessions that their own often dwindling resources permitted to promising students with little or no money. Some of the State universities were able to provide living quarters in limited quantity at extremely low cost. Some university cafeterias sold balanced dinners to needy students at ten or twelve cents. Yet this scale of living was beyond the means of many youth. At one State university, the authorities found that one young man had been trying to feed himself on fifty cents a week and that another was sleeping during a cold winter in an old automobile parked on the edge of the town. Yet these ambitious young people hung on grimly. Many of them would have been no better off anywhere else. At the colleges they could suffer undernourishment in attractive surroundings; and in the classrooms and college libraries they could at least find warmth. Thousands of other capable young people remained in idleness at home because they could not scrape together even enough money for incidental fees at the least expensive colleges.

In spite of all that was done, the enrollment in colleges and universities dropped about 10 per cent between 1932 and 1934, and would have dropped further if the Federal Government had not begun to supply aid to needy students in February 1934. If this drop had meant a weeding out of the least fit, perhaps it could have been considered as not undesirable. But it was not. It meant only the loss of some of those who lacked financial means and could not find the jobs with which to pay for their own education.

With the creation of the Civilian Conservation Corps various educators began to suggest that a small amount of money be made available to help young people to go to college. Until the unused capacity of the colleges was filled, it obviously was less expensive to keep youths in college than to put them in CCC camps. Indeed, there was no cheaper way to keep a large number of people of college age off the labor market and usefully occupied. And for those capable of benefiting from a higher education, this way probably held the greatest promise of gain for society as a whole.

These considerations led President Roosevelt to approve the use of enough Federal relief money to help approximately 75,000 young people to attend college during the second half of the college year 1933-34. With a slight expansion this aid was continued by FERA during the next college year and since then has been provided through NYA.

The principal terms of the college aid program have remained unchanged since the program was instituted in February 1934. In return for work, the Federal Government pays to a needy student a maximum of $20 a month during the college year. The average of payments within any institution may not exceed $15 a month. Every bona fide non-profit-making and tax-exempt institution which requires a high school diploma or the equivalent as the minimum for entrance is eligible to participate. Each is given as a quota a percentage of its enrollment of regular students.

Unlike the work program for out-of-school youth, NYA college student aid has never been restricted to youth from relief families. The colleges and universities themselves select the students to be aided. The Federal Government requires that these students possess the ability to do good scholastic work, that they be regular students carrying at least three-fourths of the normal academic schedule, and that they be unable to enter or remain in college without Federal assistance. The institutions themselves also arrange and supervise the work which these youths do to earn their Federal wage checks. The pay is at the hourly rates for comparable work in the college or community. The chief Federal requirements are that this work be useful and that it be work not formerly done by regular employees or which could be done out of regular budgets.

Under NYA the college aid program has been expanded to include graduate students under the age of 25. The graduate students are permitted to earn a maximum of $40 a month each. For two years, graduate aid was segregated, and the graduate students assisted in any one institution were allowed to earn up to an average of $30 a month. During 1937-38, graduate aid was lumped with college aid. While an individual graduate student may still earn up to $40 a month, the funds allotted to any institution are sufficient to permit average earnings for college and graduate students combined of only $15 a month. A small special fund has been created for Negro graduate students.

Approximately 98 per cent of the eligible institutions, including junior colleges and normal schools, have participated in the student aid program. Most of the handful of exceptions are privately controlled colleges with limited enrollments and high tuition. A few institutions in this class accepted Federal aid for a year or two but have now dropped it. Others continue to take advantage of it, but in many cases not to the full extent of their quotas. . . .

For a limited number of students, NYA aid pays all, or substantially all, expenses during the college year. Before Federal aid was established, the University of Iowa had provided dormitory space in a field house, where 100 students were sheltered for $1.00 a week each. Subsequently this university assisted in the organization of 10 co-operative houses for a total of 300 young men and women. During 1935-36, these co-operative houses charged $15 a month for board and room, and at the end of the year were able to refund approximately one month's board to each participating student. Several State institutions have assisted in making similar provision for a few students with little money. At the University of Idaho two years ago, more than 200 students paid for all their living expenses, fees, and necessary incidentals with $18 a month each.

NYA students who live at home while going to college, as many do in the cities, often are able to pay most or all of their fees and incidental expenses from NYA earnings. For the great majority, however, NYA earnings will pay only from 50 per cent to as little as 10 per cent of their expenses. At the tax-supported institutions the NYA assistance usually meets from 25 to 60 per cent of the total expenses of students who do not live at home. At the privately controlled colleges the percentage is lower.

In some cases, NYA aid is used to supplement scholarships. At the privately controlled institutions most scholarships are only rebates, in part or in whole, of tuition fees. Where scholarships exist at tax-supported institutions, they are usually only of small sums. In the whole country, the number of scholarships that pay all the essential expenses of a college student is negligible. Without assistance from NYA or other sources, many students would be unable to avail themselves of scholarships.

In many cases, NYA aid is combined with money from home, or another job, or a scholarship, or all three. A brilliant Negro student at the University of Illinois won a small scholarship. He also found a job which gave him his meals. His father, a railroad laborer earning $90 a month, sent him $6 a month. Yet, without aid from still another source, he would not have had enough to pay his expenses. The difference was made up by an NYA job as a laboratory assistant in the Department of Natural History. A student at Vanderbilt University was able to pay for his education by the combination of a scholarship, summer work, $300 in loans from the student loan fund, and an NYA job. These illustrations could be multiplied many times. In most institutions, NYA assistance is under the direction of the same officials who handle other student aid funds, including the parceling out of part-time jobs. In many cases the fitting and joining and penny-by-penny calculation which college personnel officials put into the allocation of aid to needy students would excite the admiration of an efficiency engineer.

Almost one-third of the students receiving NYA college aid are from families with annual incomes of $999 or less. Three-fourths are from families having annual incomes of $1999 or less. About 16 per cent are from families whose incomes are $2000 or more, and for 8.2 per cent the size of the family income is unknown. More than 55 per cent are from families containing five or more persons, and more than 34 per cent are from families of six or more. Three out of five are boys. Negroes and other racial minorities make up 5.8 per cent.

VII

Will There Be
a Revolution?

THIS WAS A QUESTION that weighed heavily on many Americans' minds and hearts in 1931 and 1932. Most people hoped the desperation of Great Depression victims would not trigger a revolution; a relative few hoped the whole social mess would end in revolt. But neither side would have been surprised had there been concerted and national violence to achieve a revolutionary purpose.

Fear of a revolution was very widespread during the last several months of President Hoover's administration, and much of the politics of the period can be understood fully only by viewing political events against the background of anxiety about violent revolt. The vigor with which the army dispersed the Bonus Expeditionary Force from Washington in the summer of 1932, for example, had its roots in revolutionary fear.

Despite extensive and intensive social discontent and despite the general belief in the possibility, even the expectancy, of revolution, there was no serious revolt. At least, there was no revolution if by revolution we mean an armed seizure of power, strife at the barricades, blood in the streets.

The selections here reprinted illustrate the fear of revolution, the kind of thinking that characterized both those who wanted and those who dreaded revolution, some aspects of the class violence that actually developed, and the nature of the post mortem explanations of revolutionary failure.

43 • A SENSITIVE PERSON'S FEAR

That the following poem appeared in the staid, thoroughly respectable Atlantic Monthly *reveals a great deal about American social thought in the winter of 1931-1932. Florence Converse, "Bread Line,"* The Atlantic Monthly, *CXLIX (January, 1932), 55-56. Used by permission of the publishers.*

WHAT'S the meaning of this queue,
Tailing down the avenue,
Full of eyes that will not meet
The other eyes that throng the street,—
The questing eyes, the curious eyes,
Scornful, popping with surprise
To see a living line of men
As long as round the block, and then
As long again? The statisticians
Estimate that these conditions
Have not reached their apogee.
All lines end eventually;
Except of course in theory.
This one has an end somewhere.
End in what?—Pause, there.
What's the meaning in these faces
Modern industry displaces,
Emptying the factory
To set the men so tidily
Along the pavement in a row?
Now and then they take a slow
Shuffling step, straight ahead,
As if a dead march said:
'Beware! I'm not dead.'
Now and then an unaverted
Eye bespells the disconcerted
Passer-by; a profile now
And then will lift a beaten brow,—
Waiting what?—The Comforter?
The Pentecostal Visitor?
If by fasting visions come,
Why not to a hungry bum?
Idle, shamed, and underfed,
Waiting for his dole of bread,
What if he should find his head
A candle of the Holy Ghost?

A dim and starveling spark, at most,
But yet a spark? It needs but one.
A spark can creep, a spark can run;
Suddenly a spark can wink
And send us down destruction's brink.
It needs but one to make a star,
Or light a Russian samovar.
One to start a funeral pyre,
One to cleanse a world by fire.
What if our bread line should be
The long slow-match of destiny?
What if even now the Holy
Ghost should be advancing slowly
Down the line, a kindling flame,
Kissing foreheads bowed with shame?
Creep, my ember! Blaze, my brand!
The end of all things is at hand.
Idlers in the market place,
Make an end to your disgrace!
Here's a fair day's work for you,—
To build a world all over new.
What if our slow-match have caught
Fire from a burning thought?
What if we should be destroyed
By our patient unemployed?
Some of us with much to lose
By conflagration will refuse
To hallow arson in the name
Of Pentecost. We'd rather blame
The Devil, who can always find
For idle hand or empty mind
Work to do at Devil's hire.
The Devil loves to play with fire.
We'd rather blame him,—ah, but this
May be just our prejudice.

44 • THE CITIZEN
SURVEYS THE SCENE

This article by a staff writer of Harper's *reveals anxiety, bewilderment, exasperation, and despair. George R. Leighton, "And If the Revolution Comes . . . ?"* Harper's, *CLXIV (March, 1932), pp. 466-469, 471-474. Published by permission.*

REVOLUTIONS ARE AN OLD STORY to the American citizen. To the Russian they are still a new and startling experience; the American knows the tale of revolution almost by heart. His national existence began with one, many of the most illustrious names in his history books are associated with that celebrated rebellion. Some estimable ladies of the republic have a national organization which commemorates the embattled farmers who refused to take orders from the imperial tax gatherer. The citizen, traveling back in his mind, remembers many a splendid phrase from the revolutionary manifestoes: "All men are created equal. . . . Life, Liberty and the pursuit of Happiness. . . . A Prince whose character is thus marked by every act which may define a Tyrant, is unfit to be the ruler of a free people." A free people! Mountain air in the nostrils of the American! He remembers those who thundered denunciations at the American demagogues. He is not alarmed at the term; he has heard it before. He remembers one such demagogue who was derided as an "Illinois rail-splitter," and because of that derision, the American has cherished the word rail-splitter ever since. He remembers how that rail-splitter in his inaugural address spoke these splendid rebellious words:

The country, with its institutions, belongs to the people who inhabit it. Whenever they shall grow weary of existing government, they can exercise their constitutional right of amending it, or their revolutionary right to dismember and overthrow it.

To the American, revolution is a birthright, an inheritance that no power can take away, a privilege to be guarded most jealously. If he seldom exercises his privilege, he has not forgotten that the right and the responsibility are his.

What is the American with the revolutionary birthright thinking about these days? His own country and the world are now in the midst of a vast economic upheaval. The systems of production and distribution have been badly jammed, and some of the parts will never again be of any use. You and I and the citizen begin to have a feeling that perhaps we shall have to deal with a number of problems that we have never touched before. The word revolution is heard at every hand; we seem to face revolutions of all sorts and kinds. We blink, think of home and children, and then turn to examine the situation. We do this, not as experts or masters of political economy, but as ordinary people, using what intelligence we have, watching the news of the world as our neighbors and the newspapers give it to us. Furthermore, we make this examination not for the fun of it, but to give ourselves some idea of what we are going to do about it. What do we find?

For the most part, the men who now occupy our seats of government were there at the high tide of the boom. They were in office when the crash came and, barring the fatalities of the last elections, they are still there. Mr. Hoover is, of course, the most obvious example. In business the same captains of industry, the same banking authorities, the same investment counselors are holding on to their jobs. It is true that the mortality has been great, but there are a good many fat, prosperous names left. When the storm came, these men, who had so industriously predicted prosperity eternal and who had diagrams and charts to prove it, were helpless. We could have stomached their helplessness with far better grace, perhaps, if the great ones had been willing to admit it. But they were not. We ourselves had been crippled; so had our neighbors. It was impossible for us to conceal the consequences of our idiocy, and there was nothing to do but make the best of it and try to start again. But the captains and the senators and the cabinet members could not admit their folly or their helplessness. They had been omnipotent and omniscient for so long that a stepdown was impossible.

And so we were treated to a most extraordinary spectacle. We saw these men, like a troop of savages, attempt with chantings and loud cries to abate the wrath of the storm. It is needless to rehearse their shibboleths and incantations, their magic words "optimism" and "just around the corner." We know them all by heart and we know they didn't work. But now, as we move into the third year of hard times, we discover that these gentlemen are still positive, still knowing, as farsighted as ever they were. We learn that they had no share of responsibility for the disaster. The eminent banker who declared twelve days before the crash that "the industrial condition of the United States is absolutely sound and our credit system is in no way critical" is still authoritative and serene. Recently he appeared before a Senate committee and testified that the extravagant lending of money to corporations and individuals for speculation "should have been stopped ten years ago." Stopped by whom? He declared that the bankers would never be governed by any code set up by themselves, and, when questioned about the possibilities of government control over unruly finance, was horrified. "We are frankly skeptical," said he, "that the ideal can be attained; freedom for the individual to engage in whatever business he chooses and to develop that business in accordance with his talent and judgment is a privilege which all Americans cherish. It involves freedom to make mistakes."

Freedom to make mistakes! A remarkable statement in the face of an army of bankrupts and an ever-growing horde of unemployed. Is it for this freedom that he and his colleagues plead for public confidence and support while every available means of publicity is invoked to cajole money out of hiding? . . . What can the citizen think as he listens to the pontifical utterances of Senator Watson and Secretary Doak? What of the bland assurance of Mr. Fess and Mr. Smoot? What says the greatest Secretary of the Treasury since Alexander Hamilton? What rugged verities are spoken by Mr. Schwab and Mr. Taylor? It may be summed up in one word: Courage! If we can only hold on courageously, things will come out all right in the end and prosperity will be back again, this time to stay forever. Everything is all right. The only trouble is that we won't believe it. And from all this we can draw but one conclusion: The captains and the cabinet members have learned nothing. . . . Even the Dean of the Harvard Business School is willing to admit that "Capitalism is on trial and on the issue of this trial may depend the whole future of Western civilization."

One does not have to be a profound student of economics to discern some of the embarrassments that confront our present system. The results of a tangle of tariffs and a mountain of agricultural products are two obvious ones. But behind these embarrassments there has gradually grown up a suspicion that the profit system, as we have known it, is its own destruction. Fragments of this idea have appeared in universities; more than one scientist has publicly declared it; occasionally some industrial leader feels uneasy and hazards a vague guess. In a nutshell the suspicion is this: That the combination of the machine and the skill of organization has made it possible to produce more and more goods, more and more raw material, more and more food with less and less labor. Although this meant larger immediate profit for the producer, it meant that in the long run fewer and fewer people were employed and so had less and less money to pay for these goods. While this has been going on, profit has again been put back into more and more highly geared and concentrated production, turning out an ever-increasing stream of goods in exchange for which there are steadily less wages and salaries. There is a contention, it is true, that labor which is thrown out of work by the machine in one industry is able to find employment in another. But some of the bureaus of investigation, for which Americans have such an enduring passion, have discovered that only a fraction of these rejects find employment. And all the while, of course, profit is being turned back, not to provide employment, but to produce more goods. In the end one sees the producers, fewer and fewer in number, engulfed in goods which they can neither sell nor use, swamped in specie which has no value, while opposed to them is a vast army, laborers, white collars, professionals and all, with neither food nor clothing nor the money to pay for them.

Our capitalist system is founded, of course, upon profit; profit has been its life blood. What, indeed, would be the use of going into business if you couldn't make a profit? Many of our fellow-citizens are ruefully pondering on this theme right now. If the various opinions and suspicions which we have just rehearsed should prove true; if profit should disappear not for two years, but for good, what an uncomfortable situation ours would be. Our livelihood, our jobs, our incomes large and small, derive from this system. Trustingly and of necessity we have counted for survival on this system and if it should go back on us, the prospect would be rather disconcerting. . . .

But what if the profit system fails . . . ? The citizen considers the possibility of a collapse. Perhaps it is inevitable, perhaps it isn't; in any case he wishes to be prepared. Certainly he would be a fool if he felt otherwise. He looks about him to see how others are behaving as they face the possibility. What does he discover?

On the right are the conservatives, those who profess themselves to be content, in the main, with the *status quo* and see no reason why, with a little tinkering, profit and individualism should not hold their own throughout eternity. As the citizen hears them talk and reads their counsels of confidence in the press, he marvels that men can be simultaneously so dissatisfied with the present state of the profit system and so satisfied with the system itself; and he wonders whether such an attitude of mind could ever propose or reconcile itself to bold and drastic remedies. He shakes his head. These men are too frightened: frightened at what the present situation might lead to and frightened still more at the thought of trying any different policies than those which have prevailed in the past. The citizen decides to see if there are not other men in whose ideas there is more promise of courageous action.

He determines to investigate the so-called Liberal camp. He subscribes to the various Liberal magazines and reads them assiduously. It is sad business. He begins to wonder if sunlight ever penetrates the offices of these publications. He imagines the editors, like so many Niobes, sitting in desolation, surrounded by their slaughtered children. Roused at last, the citizen goes down to see one of these editors. All is dejection. The editor groans in agony at the memory of Sacco and Vanzetti, he denounces boodlers, thieves, and shysters, he writhes at the spectacle of Liberty in chains.

"But, good God," says the citizen, "if these things be true, what shall we do?"

"Reform," says the Liberal.

"Why are you so downcast then? Is there no hope for reform?"

"Very little."

"But why, then, bother about it?" demands the citizen.

"What else can I do?" replies the editor, who at once sets to work writing an editorial asking why Secretary Adams doesn't resign since he can't support Mr. Hoover's disarmament plan with more zeal.

Baffled, the citizen goes away. How about the Socialists, he wonders. At least Debs had nerve. He investigates, but here again finds little to repay him. The moths have been busy with Mr. Debs's organization, and the citizen finds only a little group left, mild and inoffensive, led by a wealthy lawyer and a former clergyman. The Socialists are Liberals too, the citizen discovers; they are earnest in wanting to patch things up, but of coherent plan or program with which to face a vast economic upheaval, there is no sign. In disgust, the citizen takes himself off. What's the use, he thinks. These dolorous editorials come from a leisure class, they are the offspring of income. I might have written them myself. That's all very good, but if by chance, profit and income lie down and die, where will these gentlemen be? They are as timorous as the conservatives; they will go no farther than argument on paper. To the Liberal there is no more terrible word than "action." At the mere sound they scatter like frightened sheep. To grasp quickly and with dispatch is impossible for the Liberals, since to them action still has but one meaning: a bombshell or a hand grenade. The citizen is looking for someone who has an idea and is prepared to act upon it—not talk. Forthwith, he cancels his subscriptions and prepares to have a try with the Radicals. At least, he thinks, we'll have some action there. The downtrodden know what they want.

The first thing that strikes his eye is an article in the *New Masses* by Mr. Michael Gold. Mr. Gold has been examining the Liberal plans and program and in his article describes their schemes with some malice. "The corporations will be merged into a few great national trusts," says Mr. Gold. "A dividend of eight per cent will be guaranteed the former shareholders; a planning board made up of Stuart Chase and his friends will run the industries; Utopia will arrive by stealth, like a god in the night. They quarrel with the Communists as to means. But what are their own proposed means for bringing in this eight per cent Utopia? We are not told; I am afraid we shall never be told, for if there is anything the American Liberal lacks, it is a sense of economic or political reality and a sense of organization."

There, thinks the citizen, is a man who seems to be awake. If the system die, what use will there be in reforming a corpse? Surely this man and his friends are on the right track. The citizen hears that a Communist mass meeting is to be held that night, and, after a frugal supper (for times are getting harder), he sallies out in search of light and truth. With great expectation he attends the meeting. Three speakers thunder denunciations against the bloodthirsty tyrants and are roundly cheered. This is all very well, thinks the citizen, but what are they going to do about it? Uneasy, he feels that if he substituted "Jeffersonian principles" for "dictatorship of the proletariat" and "Republican boodlers" for "bloated capitalists," the meeting would resemble a Tammany rally. He asks for details concerning action and what they are going to do. "Demonstrate!" replies his neighbor. "Protest!" says the man on the other side. "Yes," says the citizen, "but what I want to know is, what are you going to do to get power and what are you going to do when you get it—right here in America?" "Mass! Demonstrate!" is the reply.

A pretty girl in the crowd asks the citizen to subscribe to the *Daily Worker*. He does so, hoping that he will find help there. The next afternoon the first copy arrives. "On with the Struggle Against the Fascist Dictatorship in Bulgaria" screams a headline. "Hands Off China! Stop munitions shipments to the Chinese militarists!" cries another. All very well, thinks the citizen, but how will you go about it? And what are you going to do about America? You Communist gentlemen present yourselves as the most far-sighted group in America. If that is so, you should be the ones most ready to take charge if profit dies. What, then, are you and Mr. Gold and the others prepared to do? When the new day comes arithmetic, the laws of chemistry, and rates of speed will still be doing business at the old stand. The consumer will still be hungry three times a day, he will need shoes and pants just as he did before. You will have the problem of distribution on your hands, just as much as capitalism ever did. What's your scheme?

Your master, Lenin, in his days of exile, was wont to say that experience would teach the worker how to plan and execute and govern. . . .

He examines carefully the text, "What Is To Be Done," which a Communist acquaintance studies so assiduously. This may have been of use in 1902, he thinks, as an argument and plan of operation for a newspaper run by exiles, but now! One would as soon consult a 1902 Burlington time table for a good train out of Chicago. Vainly the citizen asks: Where are your engineers, statisticians, managers, executives, teachers, and planners? If you haven't them in full flower, where are you developing them? And to all these questions there comes to the citizen but one cry: Mass! Demonstrate! Protest! Words, mass meetings, hunger marches, more masses, more protests, more demonstrations. His ears roaring, the citizen sits down on a curbstone and wonders what in God's name he is going to do; and we may perhaps sit down on the curbstone beside him and wonder too.

Through the citizen's mind run many things. He sees an army of bankrupts, victims of ever-returning depressions; he remembers a miner's time sheet, showing monthly wages due $31.88, minus $22.00 for "transfers." Support a family on this for a month! He remembers the advice given to salesgirls working long hours for $9.00 a week: "If that isn't enough to live on, get yourself a boy friend." He remembers the farmers of Arkansas who, having exhausted all credit through years of selling grain for less than it cost to raise it, sacked the grocery stores of the county seat. He remembers skilled workmen who have been out of work, not since the depression began, but through the boom. The citizen can only ask himself: What will this army do if the barriers give way? Will they not demand retribution? All these things have happened under the system by which I live. I have not myself been responsible, but that will avail me nothing if the system goes to pieces; I shall have to face those demands for retribution. How shall I be prepared to deal with the problems of a collapse, what shall I do if all the pent-up wrath breaks out? What if, after a long succession of catastrophes, I should awake some morning and learn that the great banks of the country had gone down, that the Federal Reserve had succumbed; what if, day after day, the newspapers brought word of further disasters: the stalling of utilities, the stoppage of trains, the crippling of communication, until at last the Federal government suspended the writ of *habeas corpus,* proclaimed martial law throughout the land, and established a dictatorship? And what if, despite all this, the function of government was powerless? What then? What should I do? To which questions the answer is: We don't know.

45 • "HUNGER RIOTS"

These news stories from The New York Times, *January 21 and February 26, 1931, are typical of several that appeared in the nation's press sporadically during the early depression. The evidence suggests that most such riots were organized rather than spontaneous, but that to organize a "hunger riot," given the circumstances, was not a particularly difficult task.*

OKLAHOMA CITY, Jan. 20 (AP).—A crowd of men and women, shouting that they were hungry and jobless, raided a grocery story near the City Hall today. Twenty-six of the men were arrested. Scores loitered near the city jail following the arrests, but kept well out of range of fire hose made ready for use in case of another disturbance.

The police tonight broke up a second meeting of about one hundred unemployed men and arrested Francis Owens, alleged head of the "Oklahoma City Unemployed Council," who was accused of instigating the raid.

Before the grocery was entered, a delegation of unemployed, led by Owens, had demanded of City Manager E. M. Fry that the authorities furnish immediate relief. Owens rejected a request by Mr. Fry for the names and addresses of the "Unemployed Council," said to number 2,500 men and women, both whites and Negroes.

The raiders disregarded efforts of H. A. Shaw, the store manager, to quiet them.

"It is too late to bargain with us," the leaders shouted, as they stripped the shelves.

The police hastily assembled emergency squads and dispersed the crowd numbering 500, with tear gas. Only those who were trapped in the wrecked store were arrested. Five women among them were released. The windows of the store were smashed as the raiders attempted to flee.

John Simmons was held on a charge of assault after he had leaped on the back of Lee Mullenix, a policeman, when the officer attempted to enter the crowded store.

Floyd Phillips was charged with inciting a riot. The police said he was one of the speakers who harangued the crowd at the City Hall before they began a parade that ended at the store.

MINNEAPOLIS, Feb. 25 (AP).—Several hundred men and women in an unemployed demonstration late today stormed a grocery and meat market in the Gateway district, smashed plate glass windows and helped themselves to bacon and ham, fruit and canned goods.

One of the store owners suffered a broken arm when he was attacked as he drew a revolver and attempted to keep out the first to enter.

One hundred policemen were sent to the district and seven persons were arrested as the leaders.

ST. PAUL, MINN., Feb. 25 (AP).—A crowd, after attending a meeting to protest against unemployment, forced its way late today into a small store owned by George Baglio, near the downtown section, and took more than $50 worth of merchandise, mostly cigars, cigarettes, candy and apples. Police arrested three men and held them without charge.

46 • AN AGRARIAN RADICAL
DISCUSSES THE COMMUNISTS

This selection is excerpted from the newsletter Congressman Thomas Amlie of Wisconsin, a LaFollette Progressive, sent to his constituents. The Elkhorn (*Wisconsin*) Independent, *December 15, 1932.*

ON THE OPENING DAY OF CONGRESS there arrived in Washington about 3,000 hunger marchers. They came principally from the large industrial centers where economic conditions have become highly acute. Upon their arrival in the city they were congregated on New York Ave., which was shut off from traffic and which was surrounded by capital police on all sides. The marchers were kept there for approximately three days, and compelled to sleep in the open.

This group was led by communists and at least half of the members were communists. I spent three hours talking to them on the last night that they were here in town. They were extremely bitter because of the treatment that they had been accorded in Washington. When I was out at this camp, I saw a great many things done on the part of the police to provoke these people. The treatment that they received did more to make communists of these hunger marchers than all the talking that was ever done by communist agitators. Some of the leaders of this march were complaining to me very bitterly about the rough treatment that the members had received from the police. I asked them if this was not precisely what the leaders had hoped for when they got these people to come on the march. They only smiled. . . .

During the latter part of last week we had approximately 250 farmers here from the various agricultural states in the union. These farmers were demanding legislation even more radical than that demanded by the hunger marchers.

On the whole, 90 per cent of these 250 men were real dirt farmers. Most of them were men in the twenties or early thirties. . . . There was almost as much bitterness on the part of these farmers against the government and constituted authority as there was on the part of the hunger marchers from the industrial sections. . . . A number of these farmers announced that in several midwestern states there would be no further evictions through mortgage foreclosures.

47 • AN ANGRY RANCHER'S REVOLUTIONARY IDEAS

As Congressman Amlie noted, the nation's farmers, certainly not Communist or even Marxist, were in a belligerently ugly mood. This testimony is by Oscar Ameringer, whose comments on agricultural waste while people went hungry were reprinted in selection 13. Unemployment in the United States, Hearings *before a Subcommittee of the Committee on Labor, House of Representatives, 72nd Cong., 1 sess., on H.R. 206, H.R. 6011, H.R. 8088 (Washington: Government Printing Office, 1932), pp. 100-101.*

SOME TIME AGO A COWMAN came into my office in Oklahoma City. He was one of these double-fisted gentlemen, with the gallon hat and all. He

said, "You do not know me from Adam's ox." I said. "No, I do not believe I know you." . . . He said, "I came to this country without a cent,
but, knowing my onions, and by tending strictly to business, I finally
accumulated two sections of land and a fine herd of white-faced Hereford
cattle. I was independent." I remarked that anybody could do that if he
worked hard and did not gamble and used good management. He said,
"After the war cattle began to drop, and I was feeding them corn, and by
the time I got them to Chicago the price of cattle, considering the price of
corn I had fed them, was not enough to even pay my expenses. I could not
pay anything."

Continuing, he said, "I mortgaged my two sections of land, and to-day
I am cleaned out; by God, I am not going to stand for it." I asked him
what he was going to do about it, and he said, "We have got to have a
revolution here like they had in Russia and clean them up." I finally asked
him, "Who is going to make the revolution?" He said, "I just want to tell
you that I am going to be one of them, and I am going to do my share in
it." I asked what his share was and he said, "I will capture a certain fort.
I know I can get in with 20 of my boys," meaning his cowboys, "because
I know the inside and outside of it, and I capture that with my men." I
rejoined, "Then what?" He said, "We will have 400 machine guns, so
many batteries of artillery, tractors, and munitions and rifles, and everything else needed to supply a pretty good army." Then I asked, "What
then?" He said, "If there are enough fellows with guts in this country to
do like us, we will march eastward and we will cut the East off. We will
cut the East off from the West. We have got the granaries; we have the
hogs, the cattle, the corn, and East has nothing but mortgages on our
places. We will show them what we can do."

That man may be very foolish, and I think he is, but he is in dead
earnest, he is a hard-shelled Baptist and a hard-shelled Democrat, not a
Socialist or a Communist, but just a plain American cattleman whose
ancestors went from Carolina to Tennessee, then to Arkansas, and then
to Oklahoma. I have heard much of this talk from serious-minded prosperous men of other days.

As you know, talk is always a mental preparation for action. Nothing
is done until people talk and talk and talk it, and they finally get the
notion that they will do it.

I do not say we are going to have a revolution on hand within the next
year or two, perhaps never. I hope we may not have such; but the danger
is here. That is the feeling of our people—as reflected in the letters I have
read. I have met these people virtually every day all over the country.
There is a feeling among the masses generally that something is radically
wrong. They are despairing of political action. They say the only thing
you do in Washington is to take money from the pockets of the poor and
put it into the pockets of the rich. They say that this Government is a con-

spiracy against the common people to enrich the already rich. I hear such remarks every day.

I never pass a hitch hiker without inviting him in and talking to him. Bankers even are talking about that. They are talking in irrational tones. You have more Bolshevism among the bankers to-day than the hod carriers, I think. It is a terrible situation, and I think something should be done and done immediately.

48 · THE REBELLION OF THE PRAIRIE FARMERS

The most serious display of class violence in the early depression came from the farmers of the Upper Midwest rather than from the unemployed industrial workers. This article describes the activities and ideas of farmers in the National Farm Holiday Association, which in the summer of 1932 tried to raise farm prices by stopping the shipment of food into cities until prices went up. Mary Heaton Vorse, "Rebellion in the Cornbelt: American Farmers Beat Their Plowshares into Swords," Harper's, CLXVI (December, 1932), pp. 3-7. Used by permission of the author.

SUDDENLY THE PAPERS were filled with accounts of highway picketing by farmers around Sioux City. A Farmers' Holiday Association had been organized by one Milo Reno, and the farmers were to refuse to bring food to market for thirty days or "until the cost of production had been obtained."

"We have issued an ultimatum to the other groups of society," they proclaimed. "If you continue to confiscate our property and demand that we feed your stomachs and clothe your bodies we will refuse to function. We don't ask people to make implements, cloth, or houses at the price of degradation, bankruptcy, dissolution, and despair."

Reno, their first leader, was crying to them, "Agriculture as we know it has come to the parting of the ways. We will soon have no individually owned and operated farms. We have come to the place where you must practice what every other group does—strike! Or else you are not going to possess your homes."

This is literally true. In no group of farmers can you find anyone who is secure, and this is what has brought the farmers out to the roads and into action. They are not interested in a back-to-the-land movement. What they are interested in is a keep-on-the-land movement. They discovered at once that this had brought them more notice from press and legislature than all their desperate years of peaceful organization.

The strike around Sioux City soon ceased to be a local matter. It jumped the Missouri River and crossed the Big Sioux. Roads were picketed in South Dakota and Nebraska as well as in Iowa. Soon Minnesota followed suit, and her farmers picketed her roads. North Dakota organized. Down in Georgia farmers dumped milk on the highway. For a few days the milk supply of New York City was menaced. Farmers in Bucks County, Pennsylvania, organized, and potato farmers in Long Island raised the price of potatoes by a "holiday." This banding together of farmers for mutual protection is going on everywhere, but the center of this disturbance is still Iowa and the neighboring States.

The Milk Producers' Association joined forces with the Farmers' Holiday. All the roads leading to Sioux City were picketed. Trucks by hundreds were turned back. Farmers by hundreds lined the roads. They blockaded the roads with spiked telegraph poles and logs. They took away a sheriff's badge and his gun and threw them in a cornfield. Gallons of milk ran down roadway ditches. Gallons of confiscated milk were distributed free on the streets of Sioux City.

Omaha, Council Bluffs, and Des Moines were blockaded as well as Sioux City. In all these cities numerous deputies were sworn in to help the respective sheriffs. The Governor of Iowa ordered the roads cleared. Trucks attempted to rush through the lines of picketing farmers. A few trucks were escorted through the farmers' lines by armed deputies.

The armed deputies at James, ten miles out of Sioux City, started to convoy a fleet of thirty trucks through the lines. Guns were pointed. The farmers stood fast. Before an audience of bystanders the trucks were turned back. No shots were fired.

On another highway, farmers bared their breasts, daring the armed deputies to shoot. The deputies did not take the dare.

At Council Bluffs there were sixty arrests. A thousand farmers marched on the jail. The prisoners were hastily released on nominal bail.

In the East there were rumors that the pickets were not bona fide farmers, but a disorderly element from the cities and groups of unemployed or "reds." One of the local papers took a canvass of the men in the Woodbury county jail in Sioux City, where ninety pickets were confined, with this result: five were farm owners; twenty had owned farms and were now renters; twenty-five had always been renters; fifteen were farm boys, living with their parents; seventeen were farm laborers long living in the community, and there were eight packing house employees and workers in other industries living in Sioux City.

Yet in spite of this inquiry, city officials in Sioux City and prominent business men gave interviews to the effect that the picketers were paid by the Democratic party or "instigated by Milo Reno." Naturally this blockading the roads was unpopular with the business men. High city officials went to the Governor to ask for State troops. Sheriff Davenport of Sioux City made a similar request of the Governor. But Governor Dan Turner had brought the troops out during the so-called "cow-serum war" last year with disastrous political effects.

Leaders of the movement ran round to the picket lines and begged the farmers to stop picketing. There was an organization meeting of the executive committees of the Farmers' Holiday Association of ten States. What threat of troops, or jailings, or arrests could not do, the Executive Committee did. By the twenty-first of September the roads around Sioux City were cleared for the first time in six weeks.

But the farmers had learned the lesson that direct action pays.

The picketing had not been stopped when we arrived in Sioux City. . . .

Highway No. 20, leading to Sioux City, has been the scene of some of the sharpest clashes between deputies and farmers. It has won itself the proud name of "Bunker Hill 20." On the night we visited No. 20 a score of men were sitting round a campfire. A boy was sprawled out on an automobile cushion asleep. Everyone was in overalls. Their sunburned faces shone red in the firelight.

A lamp in a smaller tent glowed in the darkness. A trestle table stood near at hand. The Ladies' Aid bring substantial meals to the picketers. The irregular circle round the fire, the high moonlit poplar trees, the lighted tent were like a stage set for a play. There was an air of immense earnestness about the farmers. They had been swung completely out of their usual orbit, but they are absolutely sure of the righteousness of their cause. An old man with white mustache said:

"They say blockading the highway's illegal. I says, 'Seems to me there was a Tea-party in Boston that was illegal too. What about destroying property in Boston Harbor when our country was started?' " He sets the note of the evening.

"If we farmers go down bankrupt," says one of the younger men, "everything in this country goes down. If we get enough to live on, everybody's going to go to work again."

"When we can't buy," says another, "there can't be any prosperity. We ain't been buying nothing, not for four years."

"My binder's fallen apart so, don't know how I'm going to get through this year." The conversation moves slowly from one man to another with quiet deliberation. There is a cry:

"Truck!"

They hurry out in the roadway. All of them carry heavy stakes, some made from axe handles. None of them is armed, though a young fellow pointed to a little mound of quarter bricks.

"Plenty of Irish confetti," he said cheerily. Beside the road, handy to use, are heavy spiked logs and planks bristling with spikes to throw in front of trucks. This truck is empty. There is a short conference. The truck passes on its way.

"Good-night, boys," calls the driver. "Good luck!" He is one of them, part of the movement that is just beginning to realize its power. We go back to the fire.

"There are not so many picketers on the roads as there were," we suggest.

"There don't need to be," says the man next to me. He is an older man with heavy grooves in his face. His big hands rest on his club. Next him sits Davidson, a "committee man." He is a young giant towering over the others. He wears a clean shirt with a knitted sweater over it, and he has had a fresh haircut. Davidson takes up the tale.

"We've got so organized," he says quietly, "the farmers ain't coming over No. 20 any more. The Holiday Association bought some time on the radio—KSCJ—and we radioed the farmers to stay home, and they're doing it."

"We don't need but a few fellows now," said Ben Grey, another committee man. He is a young fellow with a felt hat on the back of his head, a little shorter than Davidson, in blue shirt and overalls and high boots.

"We know an hour before a truck is on the road," explained the old farmer. "One of our folks will see it way off and telephone down to us. The telephone operators are all with us. We can get a hundred farmers here in a few minutes if we need 'em. So we don't need to have so many picketers on the roads now we're organized."

"I heard about how there was a fellow bootlegging milk through here. Heard about how he was laughing at us on No. 20. Said we was a lot of scabs, didn't know what we was doing."

"Say, if he comes through, we ought to learn him something." This from the older farmer with the white mustache. "We certainly should turn him back on a dirt road and learn him a lesson."

Again there is a cry of, "Truck!"

The farmers run forward, the sleeping boy awakes. This time it is the bootlegging milk truck. A long intricate dialogue follows. Everyone takes his turn. The milk bootlegger is a plausible fellow with a high whining voice.

"Now, friends," he entreats, "you wouldn't want to put me out of business, would you, like them big fellows would like to put out of business all of us little fellows?"

"We wouldn't want no hardship visited on him that we wouldn't want visited on ourselves," says one.

They put it to the vote. The specious bootlegger has won them over, to the disgust of the committee men.

The next evening the farmers had a meeting at the Golden Slipper dance hall on Highway 141 to vote whether road picketing should continue. Long before the time for the meeting, farmers' cars choked the roadways.

There are a thousand people in the hall—double that outside. Newcomers could only wriggle eelwise through the crowds. Farmers in store clothes, farmers in overalls, farmers in old hats and caps, dirt farmers of Iowa coming to vote about picketing. They have come from South Dakota and Nebraska as well as from miles back in Iowa. They have come from Cherokee, and there are pickets from Council Bluffs and Clinton.

The dance hall has pseudo-modernistic decorations, silver triangles against green and black. Black silhouettes decorate the hall—an odd "arty" decoration for this page of history to be played against.

There is a shout of, "Everybody outside!"

The hall is cleared, a double file of men stands at the door. Each picket passes through the gauntlet of two lines of men. He must be recognized and accredited in order to vote. Only pickets can vote.

"Anybody know this fellow? John, have you seen him?"

"He says he's been at 141."

"Yes, I know him. He's been there." The man passes through.

"Seventy-seven. Who's on 77? This fellow says he comes from 77." No one on 77 knows him. The man is turned back. The hall begins to fill. No one is allowed to go out again for fear that he might return and vote again.

Outside, on a cattle truck, speeches are being made, one of them by a communist. Any mention of a debt moratorium is sure to be welcomed with applause. Inside the hall the ballot has been taken.

They vote two to one to close the roads.

As we went from picket line to picket line the talk harked back continually to 1776 when other farmers blockaded the highways. Up in James they had a "battle" with deputies last Wednesday. They liken it to a revolutionary battle. Over in Stevens in South Dakota, across the Missouri to Nebraska, we find similar groups of farmers who talk of "revolution." These farmers feel that they have a historic mission. The word "revolution" occurs often among them, but what they mean is a farmers' revolt. They do not understand revolution in the communist sense. They think of themselves as fighting the banking interests of the East or the "international bankers" about whom they are perpetually talking.

They have sat still for years and seen prices of food and animals which they raised slide down the hill to ruin. The bread lines in the cities grew, and the number of unemployed swelled to millions while their fruit rotted on the ground because there was no market for it. Now they are out to do something about it.

To them the solution of this evil situation seems simplicity and sense itself. In the slow shift of their talk there are no threats, there is no braggadocio.

These farmers who sat around campfires picketing highways, who came miles to meetings, have the serenity of faith. They feel the certainty and power of a young, vital movement, American and militant.

49 · A REVOLUTIONARY POST MORTEM

*Radicals of all persuasions were critical of Franklin D. Roo-
sevelt's policies, especially during the first several months of his
New Deal. They had reason to be: FDR's actions had clearly de-
flated the likelihood of revolution. The writer of this selection
saw two main reasons why there was no revolution: American
traditions; and blunders of the Left. Lillian Symes, "Blunder
on the Left: The Revolution and the American Scene," Harper's,
CLXVIII (December, 1933), pp. 90-91, 93-94.*

IF THIS ARTICLE were being written in the month of October, 1932, instead of in the same month of 1933, it would be unnecessary to begin with
the explanation that the "Revolution" referred to in the sub-title is the
Social Revolution hailed these many years by the followers of Karl Marx,
and not the more recent phenomenon so frequently termed "the Roosevelt Revolution." To a large number of persons no doubt any serious
consideration of the former in these still optimistic days of the latter is
altogether irrelevant and immaterial. Just recently I met on the street an
elderly conservative of my acquaintance who, a year ago, voted for Mr.
Hoover in a desperate but none too hopeful effort to hold quite intact the
capitalistic system. "Well, anyway," he announced briskly, "this fellow
Roosevelt may not be sound, but he has certainly taken the wind out of the
radicals' sails." The Red Menace, in his opinion, had petered out. Good
old Capitalism, in the tradition of the British Empire, had muddled
through.

If this were the whole truth, any examination of the radical scene in the
United States would indeed be irrelevant, except perhaps as an autopsical
report. But though business is codified, prices have risen, and three million
out of our former twelve million unemployed have returned to jobs, only
the economic ignoramus is ready to retire into that state of blissful indiffer-
ence to such matters as characterized the 1920s. As I write, one of the
larger newspaper syndicates is featuring a series of interviews with financiers and business leaders entitled *Can Capitalism Survive?* The question
is answered, naturally, in the affirmative, but the question itself implies
that there still exists a remnant of doubt, a vague suspicion that perhaps
something more than a "shot in the arm" may possibly be needed to turn
the trick. In spite of this doubt, however, there is in general a comforting
conviction that the Revolution as personified in our various revolutionary
parties was scotched at the last election. Strikes may be blazing on a dozen

fronts, but solid citizens, who in 1932 were stocking their country homes with canned goods and even, so I am told, mounting machine guns behind their cornices, are inclined to agree with one of their number who stated soon after the election that "there is something wrong with the Reds in this country if that's the best they can do in a depression like this."

Strangely enough, the sentiment has been frequently echoed during the past year among the assorted radicals themselves—and American radicalism is not given to undue soul-searching. Nor is it unaccustomed to disappointments and hopes deferred. Like the more apprehensive reactionaries, it has hailed the Revolution before. As recently as 1920, after Russia and Hungary had turned red, and Italy was flirting with sovietism, and the whole international horizon was taking on a bright red glow, to the D.A.R., the Mitchell Palmers, and the new American Communists alike, the Revolution was just round the corner. All of them were mistaken. . . .

By the end of 1930 "the System" was proving to the hilt every charge the intransigent radicals had ever made against it, and the objective conditions favorable to the rapid growth of a revolutionary climate of opinion were at hand. Radical organizations do not, as a rule, increase their membership during periods of depression; but such periods, if prolonged, breed disillusion, unrest, resentment—fertile soil for the radical seed. The revolutionist had only to point his finger at the spectacle of breadlines and bursting granaries and cry "Look!" A child could see that capitalism had failed to "work." Torn by its own inherent contradictions, it seemed to be setting in motion a whirlwind which any radical group might ride, and left-wing hopes . . . burgeoned again as breadlines lengthened and financiers jumped from twentieth-story windows. This might well be the final crash.

That mood of profound disillusionment and unrest which the radicals anticipated actually generated late in 1931 and reached its crest in the summer of 1932, but not, strangely enough, where they had every right to expect it—among the dispossessed proletariat standing in endless breadlines, drooping on park benches, huddled in cheerless rooms. . . .

It was Mr. Roosevelt who rode the whirlwind and having sufficient discernment to realize that his tremendous majority was a mandate to do something—no matter what—and do it quickly, he has so far continued to ride it. The NRA was his principal answer to that mandate; and though there is a growing suspicion that it is an inadequate one, the average American with no program of his own has been ready to support anything that seemed to offer relief. The country's most "radical" gesture since the Civil War, a gesture toward state capitalism, goes forward under the pressure of the middle classes and the respectable auspices of the party of State's rights.

In the meanwhile, what of the Revolution? Does the failure of the radicals to capitalize to any extent the country's unquestioned unrest during a period of such extreme provocation to radicalism prove, as so many patriots love to believe, that there is something inimical to radicalism in the American tradition and temperament, or does it merely indicate that there is something unrealistic—so far as the American scene is concerned —in the methods of the revolutionaries?

It would be manifestly unfair to lay the entire responsibility for the weakness of the social revolutionary movement in America upon the various groups that have been functioning in its behalf. A number of objective factors, quite beyond their control, have accounted in part, at least, for the backwardness of their movement and of political radicalism in general in the United States. We have, it is true, a radical, even a violently radical tradition. But it is a tradition of individualistic, not collectivistic radicalism. The individual buccaneer, not the leader of unpopular causes, has been the American hero. Anarchism is undoubtedly the philosophy most native to our temperament, as it is the most futile in a complicated industrial world. The country attracted the restless individualist. The tradition of the frontier, remaining long after the frontier itself had disappeared, defeated for many years the inexorable collectivist logic of the machine process. From Bacon's Rebellion in 1676 down to our latest disturbances in the Corn Belt, Americans have flared out violently against specific injustices. Our most frequent rebels have been, however, our hard-pressed agrarians with a stake in the soil.

But the Great American Illusion has been in process of disintegration for nearly three decades. As early as 1903 John Mitchell, the conservative leader of the United Mine Workers, declared: "The average wage-earner has made up his mind that he must remain a wage-earner." The statement was a little premature perhaps, but the objective conditions of American life, except for a very brief period in the mid-twenties, have become increasingly friendly to what the Communists call "the radicalization of the masses" while the revolutionary movement itself has made very little progress. The depression was made to order for its purposes. But what happened? Revolutionary propaganda, aimed ostensibly at the unemployed and underfed, the partly employed and underpaid, at a rank and file that came nearer than at any time in its history to having "nothing to lose but its chains," missed its target and hit instead a large covey of poets, painters, novelists, and dialecticians. These have their place, and a valuable one, in any mass movement. But the trouble with the American social revolution has been that it has never achieved the status of a mass movement. And this is where the radical soul-searching must begin. Its difficulties are no longer mainly objective. Its own propaganda and tactics must now bear the responsibility for its isolation from the American masses. In Europe the various revolutionary parties, whatever their shortcomings, have been rooted in the needs and aspirations of labor. The labor movement and the radical movement have been practically synonymous. In the United States the latter has never lost its dilettante character. Except for a brief decade after 1900, when men as dissimilar in temperament and as intellectually unsophisticated as Eugene Debs and William Haywood were sensing the spirit and talking the language of the American rank and file, it has approached its task in the spirit of a captious foreign schoolmaster with a preconceived curriculum and a heavy Germanic or Slavic accent, ignoring the historical background and the prevailing psychology of its pupils.

50 • THE REVOLUTION: A SOPHISTICATED DISSENT

This article by a distinguished economic historian appeared in August 1932, just after the rout of the Bonus Army, while the farm strikes were in progress, when many people thought revolution imminent. Yet the article has something of the post mortem about it, like the previous selection. Few people at the time thought as freshly or as clearly as this author; they only feared or hoped. George Soule, "Are We Going To Have a Revolution?" Harper's, CLXV (August, 1932), pp. 277-280, 284-286. From The Coming American Revolution, *copyright, 1934 by George Soule and reprinted by permission of* The Macmillan Company.

IF YOU WANT TO HEAR discussions of the future revolution in the United States, do not go to the breadlines and the mill towns, but to Park Avenue and Wall Street, or to the gatherings of young literary men. Well-fed people will anxiously inquire when you think the revolution is coming. They will admit in a large way that profits must be abolished and that some form of Communism might be desirable. In the next breath they may express doubt whether the Democrats can muster enough votes to defeat Mr. Hoover for reelection, or they may oppose moderate reforms like unemployment insurance, or may support the sales tax, which transfers burdens from the rich to the poor. Nevertheless, they vaguely expect profound changes. But you will find that searching for actual flesh-and-blood revolutionary proletarians is a thankless task. Most of those who really suffer from the depression are, according to the best-informed reports, simply stricken dumb by it. Like the Republican administration, they are awaiting nothing more drastic than the return of prosperity.

The strange inertia of those who would benefit most by a revolution and, therefore, it is supposed, will create it, is a subject for frequent remark. When an economist heard that the son of a prominent banker had become a Communist he replied that he would be more impressed if the son of a prominent workman had become a Communist. As a matter of fact, if one can believe the reports of the party membership drives in the *Daily Worker*, converts are numbered by dozens or at most hundreds rather than by thousands or hundreds of thousands. There are a few strikes and riots, to be sure, but why are there not more? The unemployed number between eight and ten million.

A man in close touch with workers' movements of all sorts received a telephone call not long ago from the chairman of a committee engaged in raising money for unemployment relief. "Our funds are running low," said this gentleman, "and we are having difficulty in collecting more. I think it would help if a good scare were thrown into our contributors. They don't realize how desperate the situation is. Can't we have a bread riot?"

"Well, I'll see what I can do by consulting my Communist friends."

"Oh, that won't do at all," was the reply. "Everybody expects the Communists to riot, with or without cause. What we need is an unmistakable expression of resentment and desperation, a real mass movement."

"In that case, I'm afraid I can't help you. The masses are in a desperate condition all right, but unfortunately there is no sign that they feel the slightest resentment. They just sit at home and blame prohibition."

This distressing lack of authentic bread riots may shortly be supplied when relief funds run out, as it is almost certain that they will. But bread riots do not necessarily mean revolution. People may smash windows because they are hungry without wanting a governmental overturn or knowing how to bring it about. . . .

The most solid recent gains of the revolutionary faith have taken place among the intellectuals. So marked has been the drift of writers toward the left that it has been discussed at length in the critical reviews. These persons, who are, with few exceptions, of middle-class origin and training, have identified themselves emotionally with the worker. Not, however, with the American worker as he actually is and thinks, in the great average, but as he ought to be and ought to think, according to revolutionary theory. The worker, in this sense, is not a concrete or representative person, but an abstraction, a Platonic ideal. The workers may not be conscious of the class struggle, but that makes no difference to these intellectuals; the class struggle is there just the same, and the workers are unconscious of it only because their minds have been poisoned by bourgeois ideology. Given the right leadership and education, they will respond. . . .

It would be easy . . . to dismiss the whole subject with a superior smirk, to join the humorous writers of the respectable press in kidding the parlor-pinks. But that is not, I think, either a just or a sound conclusion from these observations. The revolt of the intellectuals has a more valid meaning than it would have if one accepted all their phrases and assumptions at face value. Of course they are not proletarians, and cannot become proletarians. The revolution to which they look forward probably is not imminent. The class struggle does not at this moment threaten to split the American people and lead to a triumph of the down-trodden workers. But the mistake may not lie in the intellectuals' sense of the needs of modern society or its main drift. The mistake may reside in their beliefs as to the exact course which revolution is to take, and in their timing of the process. I believe that, in one sense of the word, we are veritably in the midst of a great social revolution. But a hard-boiled look at the facts indicates that the prevalent popular beliefs about what a revolution is and how it comes about are naïve and unscientific.

These popular beliefs—held, apparently, both by the literary radicals and by the Park Avenue conservatives—may be briefly summarized as follows:

1. Capitalism may soon come to an end by a final collapse.
2. A revolution is a violent overturn of political government.
3. Nothing is essentially changed, or can be changed, before this overturn; after it a brand new order is suddenly set up.
4. The revolution is brought about by rioting mobs who overrun the capital and loot and massacre; there are barricades in the streets, and the air is noisy with gunfire.
5. The riots and mobs result from the discontent of an oppressed class, whose misery is so profound that it is driven to revolt. Actual starvation is the usual motive for revolution.

Every one of these beliefs is almost completely unfounded. A mental picture of revolution based only on these assumptions is sure to be misleading.

First let us examine the collapse of capitalism. This is a vague term. Precisely what is meant by it? The closing of banks? The inability to get money with which to buy goods? Wholesale bankruptcies and defaults? Vanishing of capital values through the shrinking of trade and the disappearance of profits? Widespread unemployment? Starvation? There is not one of these phenomena which has not occurred in previous depressions. In 1907 all banks were closed for days and nobody could get a check cashed. We have had numerous financial panics in which, for a time, no new money at all was invested, and the rates for even collateral loans rose to prohibitive heights. Failures, shrinkage of trade, unemployment—these are the common marks of hard times. Our unsystematic system always fails to work when we have a crisis. Perhaps the difference is one of degree. The system may not be in danger when the curve of economic activity sinks 20 per cent or 30 per cent. But perhaps at, say, a decline of 47 per cent it will pitch over into the abyss. In order to make the argument conclusive, let us imagine that the drop of the curve will be 100 per cent. All businesses shut down, all railroads stop running, all banks are closed. All stocks and bonds, all deeds to real estate become worthless. Everybody is unemployed, nobody has a cent of income. What would happen?

What would happen would depend, not on exterior conditions, but upon what was in people's minds. If they were still imbued with habits of trading, of individualistic competition, of accumulation, they would immediately start to rebuild capitalism. . . .

Capitalism is not going to collapse. It *did* collapse in the fall of 1929. It has collapsed many times before—1921, 1893, 1873, for instance. The point is that a collapse of capitalism does not necessarily lead to a revolutionary change. The revolution depends on what is in men's minds and habits. Capitalism fails, in some degree, every time we have a depression. It is rebuilt every time we come out of one. The whole building does not crash down in dust and splinters, to be sure, but parts of the roof give way, walls sag and crumble, foundations rot. Whether we replace them or abandon the old structure and erect a new building depends on something more profound than the chronic unworkability of individualism in production and distribution. Kreugers may commit suicide, railroad companies may go into receivership, banks may close. But that does not mean that new Kreugers, new railroad companies, and new banks may not eventually take their places, and carry on in essentially the same way.

Nor is it true that a revolution is a sudden, violent overturn of political government. That is, the kind of revolution the intellectuals really are talking about is not that. Governments are overturned by violence every few years, and all over the world, without bringing any change in the way people make their living, or in the relationship of classes, or in the ideals of rulers. . . .

The progress of a typical revolution may . . . be crudely divided into the following steps. These steps are not strictly successive; some go on simultaneously with others.

The development of wide disparities of wealth and power;

Blind, sporadic, and unsuccessful protests from the oppressed classes;

Stern and efficient repression of discontent;

A long process of widespread disillusionment;

A long process of criticism, ridicule, and reformulation of ideas by intellectuals;

Loss of faith in themselves and their institutions by many in the ruling classes;

Rise in welfare and power of the oppressed classes;

Reforms from above;

Accession to power of moderate revolutionaries;

Last of all, what is usually called revolution—violence and dictatorship by an extremist minority—perhaps to be followed by temporary reactions.

The final developments do not always occur. They did not occur, for instance, in the American Revolution: the moderates remained in power and established a stable government. Minor revolutionary changes in English government have been made without any violent revolt by the extremists. A revolution need not reach the final stages if the moderates are sufficiently capable and resolute to make the necessary changes and to defeat the inevitable opposition from the reactionaries. But if they allow confusion to go on, and if the success of the revolution is endangered, the aroused activists among the people will almost inevitably support a radical dictatorship by the hundred per-centers.

If there is truth in this analysis, it is not strange that while the masses in the United States now appear to be inert and non-revolutionary, there are revolutionary fears in high places, and the chief vocal opposition to the existing regime comes from a few writers and technical experts. This is precisely what we should expect. Ideas of revolutionary implication are bound to arise first among the best educated and those near to power, not among those who are in the depths of penury and hopelessness.

Acknowledging that prediction in this field can have no pretension to scientific assurance, and that the unexpected may always occur, let us fancifully lay out—on the basis of what has usually happened in the past —the probable course of any future overturn of capitalism in this country. It will presumably take some such form as this.

First, there will in the course of time be many riots, strikes, and demonstrations, not for the most part revolutionary in purpose, but prompted by immediate conditions. These will be firmly suppressed by groups who have supreme faith in the traditional forms of "Americanism." They will not produce a revolution.

Meanwhile those who deal in ideas will increasingly express dislike of the existing culture and will expose and ridicule its outstanding figures. They will build up new conceptions of the right way to conduct affairs. Not all intellectuals will do this, but those who do will gain a larger and larger following. This process will be, as it has been in the past, spasmodic. It will grow rapidly at some times and will falter at others. But, over a long period, it will make headway. It will eventually provide a body of new ideas, sanctioned not solely or even mainly by insecure proletarians, but by a large body of cultivated, comparatively well-to-do Americans. The most efficient advocates of the new order will not be unwashed day laborers from the steel mills but white-collared citizens of Main Street. There will be general acknowledgment, except among a few capitalists, corporation presidents, politicians, members of patriotic societies, and the more densely ignorant strata, that a society governed by competition, unchecked private acquisition of wealth, and lack of intelligent foresight and planning, is injurious, ridiculous, and outmoded.

Reforms will be made which will increase the power and wealth of the potential governors of a new society and of the classes with which they are allied. The importance of the business executive (divorced from ownership and profits), of the technician, of the management engineer, of the practical social scientist will be greatly enhanced in industry, finance, and politics. Organized farmers and organized labor will achieve greater recognition than in the past, and in co-operation with active management will force the adoption of measures of planning and control which will improve their status. Their leaders will become really influential.

The result of these reforms will be, not to satisfy the rising classes and leaders, but to make them more radical and active. We had a taste of this development just after the War, when organized labor and the organized farmers had become more powerful than ever before, when unemployment had virtually disappeared, and the farmers were really making money, and when movements for government ownership of railways and other economic and political changes made real though temporary headway. The vigorous agitation for the Plumb Plan in 1919 was a result, not of the desperate condition of railway labor, but of its growing power.

Corruption and incompetence among the traditional powers of government and finance will become more prevalent and injurious than ever. These powers will be sustained less than at present by faith in their legitimacy and necessity, and more by cynical clutching for immediate advantage, stupid assertion of outworn dogma, and ineffectual efforts at repression of the rising forces. Their elements of strength and intelligence will be drained away by the new movements.

Abuses and confusion will finally produce a crisis which will lead the newly powerful classes and leaders to move actively for more thoroughgoing changes than have previously been made. Almost nobody will believe that the old regime can or will do what is necessary. A shift in the governing powers will take place—probably by constitutional means. Then, and only then, will begin the critical period when the capacity of the more moderate reformers who have gained power will be tested, and when it will be decided whether the irreconcilable revolutionaries will gain the ascendancy.

On the basis of this prediction, it looks as if we had begun to float on a revolutionary tide but were still far from its flood. Prophecy of this sort, as I have already said, is extremely uncertain. Nobody can tell how rapidly the current may flow around the next headland. All one can do is to chart the course which it has generally followed in the past. But of one thing I am sure. As long as people wait for the downtrodden and the hopeless to produce a revolution, the revolution is far away. Revolutions are made, not by the weak, the unsuccessful, or the ignorant, but by the strong and the informed. They are processes, not merely of decay and destruction, but of advance and building. An old order does not disappear until a new order is ready to take its place.

VIII

Some Case Histories

ONE OF THE INADEQUACIES of historical writing is that too little is written of the activities, social ideas, and aspirations of ordinary people who were not prominent in any way. A large part of the reason that historians, as a rule, have neglected this basic aspect of the past is that most "common men" are not very articulate and do not leave an extensive written record. Nor do librarians usually make an aggressive effort to gather what sources do exist for this kind of historical writing.

During the 1930's, however, a few social scientists studied the impact of the Great Depression on ordinary people. They left us a scattering of case histories. These records provide us with some family biographies, which, to at least some degree, reveal what the economic calamity meant in human terms and how the affected families viewed the situation. We are enabled through these case histories to see the Great Depression through the eyes of some of its victims.

The selections in this chapter are based upon interviews with depression families and upon records of municipal relief offices. Four of the selections are from an extensive study the WPA Division of Research conducted in Dubuque, Iowa, 1937-1939. The others are from a study by Professor Eli Ginzberg of Columbia University and his assistants, in which the interviewing was done in 1940. Only the names of the people in the case histories have been changed.

51 • FROM FARM TO SHOP TO RELIEF:
THE BEUSCHERS

This large family, like many others, especially in the smaller cities, tended to judge the Great Depression by rural values although they were industrial workers. This selection is from the Dubuque Study. Jessie A. Bloodworth and Elizabeth J. Greenwood, under the supervision of John N. Webb, The Personal Side (*Washington: WPA Division of Research, 1939*), *pp. 90-91, 94-105. This was a mimeographed publication.*

At home

Mr. Beuscher	62
Mrs. Beuscher	60
Paul	13
Katherine	17
Jeannette	19
Bob	21

Married and away from home

Charles	23
Celia	25
Butch	26
Eileen	28
Helen	30
Caroline	32

Interviewing completed
December 13, 1937

Mr. Beuscher, 62 years old, had been working for 29 years for the Dubuque railroad shops when they closed in 1931. He was recalled to work at the shops after he had been unemployed for 4 years. Tall, gangling, weather-beaten, he stoops forward when he talks so that he may follow the conversation with greater ease, for he is more than a little deaf. He expresses opinions decisively and vigorously, his black eyes gleaming from under bushy black brows.

Mrs. Beuscher is 2 years younger than her husband. She is the mother of 11 children, but has found time to make dresses and coats and suits, not only for her own family, but also for customers outside the home. A genial, mild-mannered woman, she is earnest in her speech, but always ready to laugh at her own and other people's foibles. Her eyes, merry but tired, are protected with spectacles that slide down on the bridge of her nose when she bends over reading or sewing and that are pushed up on her forehead when she raises her head to talk or to listen to an especially amusing radio program.

Four children remain at home: Bob, 21, a high school graduate, has had only short-time employment and is now out of work; Jeannette, who completed a high school commercial course last spring, is now clerking in a 5-and-10-cent store on Saturdays; Katherine, a high school junior who goes out occasionally with her "boy friend," cleans the house on Saturday mornings; Paul, attending junior high school, is privileged as one of the "Knothole Gang" to see the local ball games at 10¢ a game and contributes his proceeds from the sale of magazines, sometimes as much as "a whole 15¢," to his mother's purse.

One daughter died several years ago. The other children are married and now have their own households. But during the early years of the depression Charles, then unmarried, was at home; and Celia and Butch, who had had their own homes, came with their families to the Beuscher home when they could no longer pay rent.

Mr. Beuscher was educated haphazardly in country schools in Wisconsin during the seasons when work was not too pressing on his father's farm and his "old man" didn't "make him saw wood" in preference to sending him to school. He worked as a "hand" on his father's and neighboring farms until he came to Dubuque, with his wife and two children, in 1902. He was employed at the boat works for a few weeks before being taken on as a boilermaker's helper in the railroad shops. Promoted to a job as boilermaker in 1910, he continued at the same job, except for brief interruptions because of illness, a disagreement with his foreman, and, again, a general railroad strike, until the closing of the shops in 1931. . . .

The Beuschers never had a savings account—they thought it more practical to pay as much as possible on the house, especially as the rate of interest on the mortgage exceeded that on savings accounts—but they did invest in insurance policies for all members of the family. As the 10-payment life insurance policies carried for the older children had matured, they had been cashed in, but premiums on policies carried for Mr. and Mrs. Beuscher and the four youngest children were kept paid up to date until the spring of 1931, when the Beuschers found themselves with a mortgaged home, five children still largely dependent on the parents, and no regular income.

As they "look back on it," Mr. and Mrs. Beuscher scarcely know how they did manage to get along during the time that he had no regular work. The irregular income from Mrs. Beuscher's sewing continued, though she was forced to lower prices until earnings averaged no more than $3 or $4 a week. Instead of buying any new clothing, Mrs. Beuscher made over the old dresses and coats which, though discarded, had been packed away in the attic trunks. Insurance policies were cashed in one by one. Mrs. Beuscher's 20-payment life insurance policy, with face value of $500, netted her $137; cash surrender values of the four policies carried on the younger children averaged about $35. Though they were able to keep Mr. Beuscher's policy, $200 was borrowed against the face value of $1,000. Premiums have now been paid to date, but interest on the loan has been deducted from the value, now no more than $600.

For a year after Mr. Beuscher lost his job, the family's only cash income was the four hundred seventy-odd dollars obtained from the insurance policies and Mrs. Beuscher's irregular earnings, as contrasted with the pre-depression regular income of about $130 a month, Mr. Beuscher's full-time earnings. In spite of all the Beuschers could do to reduce expenses and to raise cash, not all of the bills could be met: payments due on the principal of the mortgage and the property taxes had to be disregarded, and Mr. and Mrs. Beuscher were harassed with worry over the $68 grocery bill, for they had never before asked for credit, except from week to week. Expenditures for replacements of household equipment were eliminated from the budget. By the time Mr. Beuscher returned to work, the family had almost no bedding; this was the first special item purchased when the family again had a regular income from private employment.

Although they had heard about other families, some of them in their own neighborhood, who had applied for relief grants, the Beuschers had never thought of requesting relief for themselves until one day, in the fall of 1933, Mr. Beuscher came home from a neighbor's to say to his wife, "Do you know what Jim said? He said we ought to try to get relief." Mrs. Beuscher was so "shocked" that she gasps, even 4 years later, when she recalls her emotion. But after talking things over, Mr. and Mrs. Beuscher agreed that application for relief was a virtual necessity. Mr. Beuscher remembers going down to the courthouse for the first time as the hardest thing he ever had to do in his life; his hand was "on the door-knob five times" before he turned it. The investigation, which the Beuschers recognized as necessary and inevitable, was so prolonged that Mrs. Beuscher "really didn't think" that the family would ever get relief. But finally, after about 2 months, a grocery order of $4.50 was granted. Mrs. Beuscher had long before learned to "manage" excellently on little, and though the order was meager, the family "got along" and "always had enough to eat." Mrs. Beuscher believes that the investigators "did the best they could"; she re-sents only their insistence on the disconnection of the telephone, on which she depended for keeping in touch with her customers.

Soon Mr. Beuscher was assigned as a laborer to county relief work, for which he was paid, always in grocery orders, $7.20 a week; this increased amount gave the family a little more leeway. Yet they were still without much cash. Payments even of interest on the mortgage had had to cease. Because they anticipated foreclosure of the mortgage, the Beuschers applied for a Home Owners loan, which was refused, since there seemed to be little chance of Mr. Beuscher's getting back to work. "Things looked pretty bad then," and Mr. Beuscher was considered a "bad risk" because of his age. Though Mr. and Mrs. Beuscher were "terribly disappointed at the time," they are glad now that they are not burdened with such a debt.

Mrs. Beuscher cannot guess how the family could have managed during the depression without the home, but Mr. Beuscher found home ownership more of a handicap than a help, for relief grants made no allowance for taxes or interest payments, while "bums" who had never tried to save or look to the future had their rent paid "regularly."

While the relief grants continued, a married daughter whose husband, as a collection agent, found his commissions going lower and lower, and a married son, who "hadn't a sign of a job," moved in with the parents. There were then 13 living in the 7 room house. Of course, the children had come home only after a general discussion in which it was agreed that this was the best plan, and everyone had thought of the arrangement as quite "temporary"; actually Celia and Butch and their families remained in the household for about a year. For a time, Eliot, the son-in-law, was able to contribute $5 a week, which probably covered any additional expenditures for himself and his wife and their two children, although there was no attempt to keep separate household accounts. But soon he could make no collections at all, and payments to the Beuschers ceased.

Eliot and Butch found that they could not obtain relief grants for their families while they remained with the Beuschers, nor could the grant for the entire household be increased. They did all they could to help the family: worked with Mr. Beuscher for the gas company to pay the gas bills, and for the coal company to pay the coal bills; they worked in the garden and helped to saw wood for the family's use.

For a time Charles was able to contribute a little to the family income by playing ball on professional teams in various towns; almost every week end during the baseball season he accumulated $7 or $8 in this way. But since he could find no regular work in Dubuque, he soon went to Detroit, where he stayed with a married sister. Though it was not absolutely necessary for him to leave home, in his absence there was "one less mouth to feed," and he was in a better position to seek work. He has since paid his back board bills to his sister, and is now married and working in a neighboring Iowa town.

The family's garden, for which the city furnished some of the seeds and the plot of ground on the city island, added fresh vegetables to the list of staples which alone could be purchased on the grocery orders; there were even some vegetables to be sold from house to house, and Mrs. Beuscher canned a little almost every day, just as the vegetables were ready for use. One summer she put up 500 quarts of vegetables. The family had never had a garden before 1932, both because there was little space and because they had "never thought of it," but Mr. Beuscher has continued to garden even now that he is back at work. Since the island garden plot could be reached only by boat, transportation was something of a problem, solved when Mr. Beuscher and three of his neighbors chipped in $2 apiece for the materials from which they built a jointly-owned boat. Only infrequently did two or more families set out to work in their gardens at the same time; so they were forever having to halloo across the water to ask that the boat be brought back to the town side to pick up more gardeners.

Grocery orders were supplemented with surplus commodities. The only other outside assistance which the family received was a sack of seed potatoes for Mr. Beuscher's garden planting in the spring of 1932 and several tons of coal during the winter of 1933-34 from a private charitable organization to which the Beuschers had in previous years contributed with the thought that they were "giving something away"; now they consider these contributions the "best investment they ever made"; they have been "repaid a hundred-fold."

Although the Beuschers never felt comfortable about receiving relief, it came to be more or less an accepted thing. "You know, you went down to City Hall, and had to wait in line, and you saw all your friends; it was funny in a way, though it was pitiful, too. . . . People went down to the relief office, and talked about going, just the way they might have gone anywhere else."

The family received food orders for only a few months, as Mr. Beuscher was soon assigned to the CWA Eagle Point Park project as a laborer, earning 40¢ an hour. Later he worked on the lock and dam project at 50¢ an hour. Mr. Beuscher cannot understand why there was so great a difference between the wage rates of laborers on work projects and those of skilled carpenters. Although he was glad to be assigned to projects, there was little essential difference in his feelings about direct relief and about "work relief"; he worked hard for his pay, but still felt that he was being "given something." He has heard many times that persons on relief do not want work and will not accept jobs in private industry, but he knows from project employees whose reactions were similar to his that such is not the case, except perhaps in a very few instances. Nothing makes him "more mad" than this criticism of project workers.

Mrs. Beuscher believes that relief, as such, has not fostered dependency. "Of course, there have always been some people who have wanted something for nothing," but "the right kind of people—the people we know, except maybe a very few—" have invariably tried to remain independent, applied for relief only as a last resort, and made every effort to go back to private employment. It may be true that some persons have become so discouraged and disheartened that they have ceased to look for jobs, but any such discouragement Mrs. Beuscher considers "purely temporary." Men will go back to private employment as soon as there are jobs to be had "without standing in line day after day waiting" on the chance that someone may be hired from among the men at the factory gates.

On principle, Mr. Beuscher decidedly favors work projects as against direct relief. "Men should be made to work for what they get," and the "majority of them—at least 70 per cent—" prefer to work. In any event, however, Mr. Beuscher believes that some direct relief will always be necessary as there are a "few people who aren't eligible for pensions and can't work."

Some time before the time that Mr. Beuscher was called back to work at the railroad shops, Eliot and Butch had reestablished a household for their two families. They received relief for a time, but finally both found work in local factories, and Butch moved to a home of his own. Now, they are independent, as are the Beuschers, senior.

Bob tried at various times to be assigned to a CCC camp. The family does not fully understand the many delays, though they believe that boys from smaller family groups were sent in preference to Bob because other families were more demanding and insistent than the Beuschers. But Bob's turn finally came in the fall of 1935. He liked the woods work, except when the temperature was well below zero. During a prolonged cold spell he asked for and was granted a transfer to kitchen duty. He was chagrined when the temperature dropped still lower, and the woods workers were permitted to loaf indoors while he labored in the kitchen where the thermometer stood at 5 above zero. Again he requested a transfer, which was arranged just as the weather warmed up enough for the woods workers to be sent out every day. On the whole, he considers it quite a joke that he managed always to choose "the wrong thing." He was enjoying the work most "just when he came home," after a 10-month stay, to take a job as a saw-operator, paying 30¢ an hour, with the Mississippi Milling Company. Several increases had brought his hourly rate up to 37¢ when he was laid off because of a general reduction in the force in August 1936. During the winter months the plant "took on every kid they could find"; then when the warehouse was overstocked the younger workers were laid off in great numbers.

Although Mr. and Mrs. Beuscher "don't say the depression is over," times have been better for them since the late fall of 1935, when Mr. Beuscher was called back to his old work at the shops at the old rate of pay. Mr. Beuscher considers this "regular work," and, as such, far superior to relief work, especially as he now "feels more independent." Still, it is not as it was in the old days when 1,500 men were employed rebuilding damaged and out-worn cars. Of the 130 men taken back at the shop, only 25 remain at work, which now consists of wrecking instead of reclamation, and no one of the 25 men knows how long his work will last. Mr. Beuscher was one of those to be recalled and to remain at work because of his "seniority right."

While he was out of work, Mr. Beuscher had regularly made the rounds of the local factories looking for jobs and had kept active his registration with the State employment office. Though he frequently grew discouraged with looking for work, Mrs. Beuscher thinks that he "enjoyed it in a way." He and his neighbors used to get together in the evenings, air their many disappointments, and decide not to bother going out again to look for jobs. But invariably the following morning found them "off again." When Mr. Beuscher learned that a few men were to be rehired, he went to the shops to explain that he was available. Soon, he was called back. Since his return to work, the Beuschers have paid up all back bills, including interest on the mortgage, property taxes, and street assessments which totaled about $500. Within the past month, the Beuschers have been able to claim the deed to their home, as the principal of the mortgage has been reduced to $1,500. The interest rate from now on will be only 5½ instead of 7 per cent.

Mrs. Beuscher thinks that perhaps young people have had the most discouraging experiences in the search for work. After Bob was laid off at the mill, he made every effort to find other employment. He reported regularly at the State employment office, which referred him to only one job, a job as chronometer reader for a battery factory. Bob thought that he could do the work, as he had had some practice in chronometer reading in his high school machine shop work, but when he reported at the factory he was told that only a man of 35 years and 200 pounds could be employed. "The local factories will not file applications" and usually offer jobs only to those men who are waiting at the plants when openings occur. Thus, when the word goes around that some factory is "hiring"—which may mean only that one man, perhaps "a relative" of another employee, has been taken on the day before—the men all go to the factory to wait for jobs. Bob has spent many hours and days "waiting" at the gates of factories in Dubuque and in Illinois towns to which he has either hitchhiked or traveled on the family's railroad pass.

Bob has thought of going to Detroit, where he would live with one of his sisters while hunting work, but Mrs. Beuscher tells him, "If you don't have a job, your place is at home, not with your brothers-in-law, who have a hard enough time taking care of their own families." One of the brothers-in-law has recently had his hours at the factory cut in half.

Finally, Bob heard that an insulating company was expanding and taking on more men. Next morning he went to the plant at 7 o'clock; he stayed all day. Of the 30 men waiting, only 1 was hired. On the second day Bob was given a job weighing and carting raw materials. He had worked a full 8-hour day and about 2 hours of the second working day when some of the machinery broke down and the plant was closed for repairs.

Jeannette, like Bob, has kept a registration active at the State employment office. She is now clerking on Saturdays in a 5-and-10-cent store and hopes to have several days' work just before Christmas. Although she would prefer stenographic work, she says that she has been willing to take what she can get. She talks to the other kids and knows that none of her friends has a regular full-time clerical job.

Mrs. Beuscher believes that "the depression has changed people's outlook." In a way she is more "comfortable" now than when both she and Mr. Beuscher worried about bills and tried to plan for the future. Now, they "just live from day to day," with the feeling that since they "lived through the depression" they can face anything to come. Of course, it was fun to plan and look ahead, "and that's one way we've lost." This resignation and acceptance of what the future may bring, Mrs. Beuscher accounts a "sign of age" as well as a result of the depression. Another "sign of age" is Mr. and Mrs. Beuscher's being content to spend leisure time at home; lack of money "was the start of it," and when they were once again reasonably secure, they had "lost the ambition to go." . . .

Mr. Beuscher is intensely interested in discussions of the causes of extensive unemployment. As a reader of 5¢ weeklies he cannot agree with "editorial writers" that there is no serious "technological unemployment." From his own experience, Mr. Beuscher knows the work of many men has been taken over by machinery. When he first worked as a helper, it was a good 10-hour job for 3 men to hammer by hand 300 rivets; after the introduction of pneumatic drills, 1,200 rivets could be placed in the same length of time with about the same effort. Once a freight train crew of 5 men handled about 20 cars; now a crew may be responsible for 5 times as many cars, "and not the old 40-ton cars, either, but 60-, 80-, or 100-ton cars." And so it goes, in railroad shops, on the trains, and in other industries as well. Though it has been claimed that displaced workers are absorbed by new industries, Mr. Beuscher believes that the proper balance has not been maintained, as the new machinery wears longer than the old and need not be produced in such great quantity.

Mr. Beuscher has only one suggested solution for the problem of unemployment: persons of "wealth" should be persuaded to invest their money in industries that might increase or create new employment. He believes also that there should be a better "distribution" of the money paid for commodities. But Mr. Beuscher does not hold "radical" ideas. At one time there was quite a group of Socialists in Dubuque; now the movement has "died out." Mr. Beuscher expresses his feeling about the group by telling gleefully an old story. A friend of Mr. Beuscher's approached one of these Socialists, who had a remarkably fine garden, and asked, "John, you believe in distribution, don't you?" "Yes." "Then I want you to give me your carrots and cabbages."

Mr. and Mrs. Beuscher are agreed that they would not in any event be willing to give up property which they might have struggled to accumulate. However, they would not want great wealth, as they would scarcely know how to spend or handle it. Mr. Beuscher is nearing his 63d birthday; at 65 he will be eligible for a Railroad Retirement pension of $62 or $63 a month, the precise amount depending on the extent of his earnings during the intervening period. His greatest present hope is that he can work steadily until he reaches the age of 65; his greatest fear, that the work will peter out between one day and the next. When he leaves the shop, Mr. Beuscher would like to be able to buy a small plot of ground, but this is only a wish, not an expectation. He would not want to go back to farming as a renter or laborer, but he would like to farm if he could own his land, just enough to work comfortably with his efforts alone.

Though the Beuschers are reasonably well satisfied with remaining in Dubuque, they consider it "the cheapest town there is," so far as wages go. The local factories have "never paid what they should, but then rents are low here, too." Mr. Beuscher thinks that he would not be "telling anything" by explaining the reason for the low wage scale, for "everybody knows that a few factories control the town." Mrs. Beuscher says with some dismay that she has read recently that "even office workers in Dubuque get less than in any other city in the United States." Then she rises to the defense of the town, which has "good schools" and a comparatively new radio station; it numbers among its famous people a movie star, the wife of a movie star, and a great football player. On the whole, "it's not a bad place to live"; and anyhow, the family "can't leave now because you even have to pay to get across the toll bridges" into the adjacent states of Wisconsin and Illinois.

52 • EX-BUSINESSMAN:
THE DONNERS

Mr. Donner, an owner of a small, independent business who became a WPA worker, provides a good example of the kind of "descent from the middle class" that concerned the author of selection 35. From the Dubuque Study, pp. 283-290.

Mr. Donner	53
Mrs. Donner	48
Louise	14
Dick	12

Interviewing completed
March 15, 1938

In good years, while Mr. Donner had his own printing business in Chicago, it "was nothing" for him to take the children downtown on Saturday afternoons and spend $2 or $3 on trivialities for each of them, and Dick and Louise "never thought of going into a drug store" without having sundaes or sodas. When, in the early thirties, the business started downhill, both Mr. and Mrs. Donner were even more concerned about the children than about the business. Though they tried not to let Louise and Dick know how worried they themselves were, they did explain that now there was less money to spend because "business was bad." As it happened, the children surprised their parents by their casual acceptance of deprivations. They used to tell their father not to buy the things they especially wanted unless "business was good." They did, though, expect Christmas toys in 1933, for they still believed in Santa Claus.

Mr. Donner has had no private employment since the spring of 1934, when he finally gave up the printing business which he had owned and operated for 15 years. Then he and Mrs. Donner and the two children came to Dubuque to Mrs. Donner's parents. Since the fall of 1934 he has been employed most of the time on emergency work projects. He is now a WPA timekeeper.

He looks the part of the business man that he has been. He is broad and well-built, well-dressed, and well-groomed. Both Mr. and Mrs. Donner are cordial and gracious and talk rather freely about their depression experiences.

When Mr. Donner was 13 years old his family moved from Dubuque to Chicago. After completing a 2-year business college course in 1907, he began work in the office of a Chicago insurance firm. He was soon promoted to salesman; he continued at this job until 1918, when he took over a Chicago printing establishment. His mother had inherited the business from her uncle, and Mr. Donner purchased it from his mother. He continued to make payments to his mother until 1931; the business was paid for only "just before it was lost." Through the twenties the business had prospered. Mr. Donner employed from 12 to 30 men; "at a conservative estimate" the business was worth $15,000 in 1929, and Mr. Donner's income averaged about $300 a month.

Awareness of the depression came early to the Donners, who had savings in one of the first banks to fail after the 1929 stock market crash. The Chicago bank that went under early in November, 1929 paid only 30 per cent of the total deposits. Through 1930 and 1931 Mr. Donner's business was fairly good; he considered himself rather fortunate, for many of his friends had already begun to suffer heavy losses.

Mr. Donner continued to hope to meet "prosperity just around the corner" as long as he dared, but the time came when he could no longer wait for prosperity. He thinks now that he held on too long, but he had no way of knowing that the depression would last so long, and that in the end he would save nothing from his business. He hated to discharge his employees, so kept as many as possible as long as possible. He also hated to see his huge presses standing idle. All of the family's assets were converted into cash to be put into the business, and besides, Mr. Donner borrowed from relatives money which he has only recently succeeded in repaying. The Donners gave up the large home which they had been renting but had hoped to buy as soon as the business was paid for, put their furniture in storage, and moved into furnished rooms. The furniture has now been reclaimed, but it "just missed" being sold for storage.

Finally, Mr. Donner had fired all of his employees, sold some of his presses, and rented a part of the floor space. But he still couldn't give up altogether. He was gathering up what orders were to be had even when he did the printing, the delivering, and the bookkeeping all alone. He was worrying so continually and so excessively that he lost 35 pounds in a few months and couldn't sleep at night.

Mrs. Donner had lived in Dubuque until her marriage. Her parents still have their Dubuque home, a huge but somewhat ramshackle place in a good residential neighborhood. Mrs. Donner and her parents had been urging Mr. Donner to give up his business and move to Dubuque over a period of some 6 or 7 months before he finally consented to do so. He had been thinking that if he couldn't support his family in Chicago, what chance would he have in Dubuque? But there were at last only two alternatives; either the Donners would go on relief in Chicago or they would come to Dubuque to Mrs. Donner's parents. Neither possibility was a very happy one, but above all things Mr. Donner was anxious to remain off relief rolls; so he came to Dubuque in the spring of 1934.

Mrs. Donner's family had the second floor of their home made into an apartment for the Donners, who have their own entrance. The apartment is roomy and airy and attractively furnished. For about 5 months after coming to Dubuque, Mr. Donner was unemployed, though he managed to keep busy—he was so anxious to have "something to do"—by painting the doors and window frames and sashes of the family's home. He had kept in touch with the employment office, as well as with "every factory in Dubuque." His first job came when he was assigned as a common laborer, on a nonrelief basis, to the Dubuque lock and dam project. His work consisted largely of gathering up lumber and carrying it to, or away from the scene of operations.

Although Mrs. Donner was glad enough for her husband to be working at anything, it hurt her to see him put on overalls for the first time in his life. "He had never had a pair of overalls, not even when he was a little boy." Mrs. Donner managed not to say anything until he was out of the house, but as soon as he had gone she ran into the bedroom and began to cry; she thought she "just couldn't stand it." When her brother insisted on knowing what was the matter, and she told him, he laughed at her for worrying about Mr. Donner; his putting on the overalls and going out on a job like that just "showed the stuff he had in him." Mrs. Donner thinks that only the "strong-minded" have lived through the depression without becoming either too bitter or too resigned.

Mr. Donner continued to work on the locks until he got a brief-lived job with a tanning company, then hiring many extra persons to handle Government orders for leather mittens and jackets to be distributed among the relief clients. Mr. Donner understands that most of the employees were assigned on a relief basis, but the company had the privilege of hiring a certain proportion of nonrelief employees. For his work as packer and, later, as cutter Mr. Donner was paid 40¢ an hour. This work, too, was quite different from anything he had ever done in the past; he had scarcely even seen factory machines in operation. The first day he operated a ripping machine, he pushed one hide a little too near the needle, which ripped off a finger nail. After having worked for several months for the tanning company, Mr. Donner was laid off, along with many other workers, when the special orders were filled.

His next job was as timekeeper on a WPA project; he was assigned on a nonrelief basis through the employment office. Mr. Donner attributes his assignment to one of the better jobs to his "good education" and to his experience as bookkeeper when he had his own business. For the past 2 years he has been working as timekeeper on WPA projects.

Mr. Donner feels that the depression really hit hardest the families like his, who had been used to a relatively "high standard of living." For 25 years Mr. Donner's earnings had averaged not less than $300 a month. Since he now earns only about $90 a month, he thinks that his income has been reduced, proportionately, more than that of the average WPA worker. He is nevertheless sympathetic with relief clients and especially with the WPA workers who earn "a few dollars a month" less than he.

These past several years, the Donners have heard a great deal about the unemployed men who don't want to work and won't look for jobs and about the "shovel-leaners" on WPA jobs. "Of course," Mr. Donner says, "there are a few loafers on WPA projects; but there are also a few loafers on jobs in private industry." But on the whole, as Mr. Donner knows from having seen hundreds of WPA workers come and go, they are most eager to have employment and to do what is expected of them, or even "more than is expected." "Besides," Mr. Donner explains, "several factors should be taken into account before any of the WPA workers can be criticized for not doing a first-rate job: many of the men working as common laborers haven't been accustomed to hard physical labor; a good proportion of them have large families to support on their earnings of $12 a week and are always undernourished. And the men really shouldn't be expected to do $25 worth of work for $12."

Mrs. Donner, too, has noted how eager the men are to have work. It was she who now recalled that some of Mr. Donner's former employees, unable to find work elsewhere, came again and again to his shop asking to be put to work at anything and at any wages. Unfortunately, he had nothing to offer them; he supposes that some of them are still unemployed. When men were first put to work in the Dubuque County stone quarries, it made Mrs. Donner "feel good" just to see so many men with jobs once again. "Of course, it was too bad that they had to work in the stone quarries," but there it was—and it was good that they had something to do. Even when they began work at 8 A.M. Mrs. Donner could see them coming to work in the quarry just across from the family's home 20 or 25 minutes before starting time. "And talk about men not wanting to work —why, one day last month when the weather was very cold, and the streets were coated with ice, and one of the trucks which carried the WPA workers to their jobs refused to start, one man walked 2 miles to the project on the frozen-over Mississippi River." Mr. Donner believes that some men have applied for relief before it was absolutely necessary to do so; on the other hand, many have waited to apply until there was no alternative.

Mr. Donner says that he doesn't "know what the country would have done without the WPA." One thing is fairly certain: "there would have been a revolution." The WPA projects have been advantageous in many ways; not only have men been given work but also cities have had, at only a small proportion of the total cost, improvements which they might otherwise not have had for years. Dubuque, for example, now has a municipal swimming pool, built as a WPA project, a recreation pavilion, and "the largest man-made rock garden in the world, a good advertisement for Dubuque," in Eagle Point Park. Mr. Donner puts no stock in the criticism, which he has frequently heard, that expenditures for materials used on PWA and WPA projects have been excessive. The rock used for the building of the recreation pavilion cost only 10¢ a ton, a bid of 12½¢ a ton having been turned down as "too high."

"Even though most of the WPA workers," Mr. Donner believes, "feel deep down in their hearts that they have been given work which doesn't absolutely have to be done, they can still feel that the work is worth-while." Some of it would perhaps have been necessary later on, if not just now; other projects, if not strictly essential, have added new community resources to those previously available. The chief deficiency of the WPA program, according to Mr. Donner, is that the money poured into WPA has not served to improve business conditions or to create new jobs in private industry, perhaps partly because WPA earnings have been too low; most WPA workers can buy only the barest necessities. Still, higher wage-scales might have validated the criticism that "government is competing with private industry" and encouraged men to remain on WPA rolls.

Mr. Donner does not see any immediate prospect of his leaving the WPA rolls. Business today is little better than when Mr. Donner returned to Dubuque more than 3 years ago, and "numbers on WPA rolls in the county are increasing." From his correspondence with friends in Chicago and other cities Mr. Donner gathers that conditions elsewhere are much the same as in Dubuque. In his opinion, the recession [of 1937-1938] has been the result of "spite work" on the part of certain industrialists; he does not anticipate that it will last very long. "The depression of the early thirties" he thinks, "was bound to come sooner or later when there was so much overspeculation, and overcapitalization, and an excess labor supply" resulting from long years of unrestricted or little-restricted immigration and the "displacement of men by machines." He thinks that perhaps unemployment could be minimized by limitation of the amounts of stock issued by corporations and payment of dividends only on actual investments.

For many years, Mr. Donner has been interested in social legislation; he approves of the Social Security Act in general, though he is dubious about the need for so large a reserve for the old-age benefits fund. As one having some knowledge of insurance, he believes that such a reserve is greater than necessary to meet all demands that would be made on the fund over any given period of time, and would "take too much money out of circulation."

What Mr. Donner would really like is to return to Chicago and go into the printing business again. If business is again "as good as it was last summer when most of the Dubuque factories were working 24 hours a day," there may be some possibility of his returning to Chicago; in the meantime, there is none. He has done everything he can to find a job other than on WPA projects: he has taken four civil service examinations, and has kept applications on file with the State employment office and with all of the local factories. There is nothing more to be done. He is not particularly hopeful of finding work; neither is he particularly discouraged. There is no bitterness or resentment evident in his expression of attitudes and opinion.

53 • "IT COULD HAVE BEEN WORSE": THE RENICKS

This family considered itself fortunate because it was barely able to stay off relief. The Dubuque Study, pp. 215-221.

Mr. Renick	42
Mrs. Renick	40
Peggy	12
John	10
Rose	8
Anna	6
Jackie	3

Interviewing completed
February 9, 1938

The Renicks, with their five children, occupy their own four-room bungalow at the very end of a residential street in the north part of town. The bungalow is well-kept and quite attractive, though much too small for the growing family. The seven of them fill the small living room where the big stove is located. Four of the children, 12, 10, 8, and 6, attend school. The youngest is a lively towheaded boy of 3.

Joseph Renick, 42 years old, tall and muscular, makes an excellent appearance. Though his formal education did not extend beyond the eighth grade, he is well informed and highly intelligent; well poised and gracious; and exceedingly forthright in manner. He had worked for the Stevenson Phonograph and Radio Company for 2 years and then for the Key City Lumber Company from 1924 until thrown out of work by the depression in 1934. Though he had no work in private industry for nearly 2 years, he was employed most of the time on emergency work projects on a non-relief basis. Two and a half years ago he was called back to the Key City Lumber Company where he is still employed.

Monica Renick, 40 years old is short and round. Jolly and friendly, she talks freely of the family's difficulties in making ends meet on a limited budget. She makes all of the children's clothes, does her own baking, and cans from 400 to 500 quarts of garden produce every summer. Last summer she found time to paint the exterior of the house; and she shocked some of her conservative neighbors as she climbed about on the ladder in overalls. Mr. and Mrs. Renick did most of the work on the house when it was built 8 years ago. Mr. Renick dug the foundation and helped with the carpentry. Mrs. Renick did all of the inside painting and varnishing. The home was purchased through a building and loan company for $3,000, monthly payments amounting to $24. The Renicks owned the lot which has a 420-foot front and a depth of 1,400 feet, providing ample garden space.

As a youngster Mr. Renick had, for 3 years, walked 2½ miles from his mother's farm to school in Dubuque. After completing the eighth grade, he worked on the farm until drafted for service in the army in 1918. He had been in training camp only 5 months when the Armistice was signed. After returning home he worked on a farm and ranch in South Dakota for 3 years. The first year he was paid $100 a month. At that time corn was selling for $1.10 a bushel in South Dakota and cattle brought an equally high price. As prices dropped Mr. Renick's wages were reduced accordingly; he received only $80 the third year he worked on this ranch.

From 1922 to 1924 Mr. Renick worked at the Stevenson plant, the last 2 years in the finishing department. He finished phonographs by hand and was paid 80¢ an hour. The work, however, was not steady; from September to Christmas this department was very busy, but the rest of the time the work was somewhat uncertain, depending on orders. Though he enjoyed work at Stevenson's, he was anxious to find a steady job, after his marriage in 1924. During a slack season at Stevenson's in 1925, he was employed by the Key City Lumber Company where he continued to work until January 1934. This company handles all kinds of building materials, and in the winter, coal and coke. Mr. Renick was the last man hired, and, in consequence, the first to be let out when this company found it necessary to reduce its force. For 6 years Mr. Renick was paid at the rate of 40¢ an hour for a 60-hour week. During the last 2 years, however, he received a weekly rate of $28, and there was almost no limit to the number of hours and no pay for overtime.

Almost immediately after Mr. Renick's layoff from this job, he was placed on the lock and dam project at common labor by the public employment office. He worked on this project for 13 months, receiving 50¢ an hour for a 30-hour week. He had been unemployed only a month after his lay off from the project when the employment office placed him on a paving job which lasted 4 months. When this work was completed, Mr. Renick was unemployed for 2 months. There had been considerable illness in the family: Mrs. Renick had had an operation and had also given birth to a child; one of the children had had a tonsilectomy. Medical bills amounted to more than $200. The family also owed a grocery bill of $50, and payments to the building and loan company were several months in arrears. Fifty dollars had been borrowed on an insurance policy to apply on hospital bills. The Renicks decided they would have to ask for relief, as much as they disliked the idea. Mr. Renick had exactly 45¢ left the day he went to the relief office to make application. He was given a blank to fill out and bring back to the relief office the following day. While he and Mrs. Renick were "laboring" over this blank, Mr. Renick was called to a neighbor's telephone to be told that he should come to work at the Key City Lumber Company the next morning. After the telephone conversation, he joyfully announced to his wife, "We don't have to fill out that blank; I go back to work tomorrow." The Renicks feel that fate was unusually kind to them, as they both had felt so depressed over having to ask for help.

After his return to the Key City Lumber Company, Mr. Renick was paid 50¢ an hour until the recent strike, when the rate was increased to 55¢. He now averages $26.40, as the hours have been reduced to 48. Most of the time he drives a truck, but at present he is working in the yard. The work of continuously loading trucks is very heavy. He prefers driving a truck because he is then responsible for unloading only his own truck. The work is very dirty, especially when he handles coal. Mrs. Renick has to wash his work clothes three or four times before they are reasonably clean.

Since Mr. Renick's return to work the family has caught up with some of its bills, though $100 is still owed on the medical bill. Mr. Renick's veterans' bonus of $127 was used to make small payments to different creditors. Now two of the children need tonsilectomies, and Mrs. Renick needs to have her teeth pulled as she is suffering from rheumatism. She is trying to save the cost of the plates this winter but has not been very successful. Mr. Renick recently strained his back and was unable to work for a week; this set them back again. The building and loan company has been very considerate, allowing them to pay only the interest of $10 while Mr. Renick was out of work. Now they are paying $15 though they should pay $24. Mrs. Renick estimates that food costs approximately $50 a month as all of the children eat heartily. Mrs. Renick uses 100 pounds of flour a month for baking. School clothing for the children is a problem, but she makes garments over many times. By dyeing two old dresses she recently made the 12-year-old daughter a very "good-looking" snow suit. She put in 2 days on this suit but "it looked as good as any in the stores when it was finished." School tuition for the four children amounts to $1.70 a month. The Sisters don't expect payment from unemployed families, but Mr. Renick has always been very conscientious about paying the tuition if at all possible, for he knows the school needs it.

Mr. Renick blames the Chamber of Commerce for low wages in Dubuque. "Once," he says, "while I was employed at Stevenson's, the Chamber of Commerce tried to get the plant superintendent to lower wage rates, but the superintendent told the Chamber of Commerce to jump in the river." The men who sponsored the establishment of a river terminal in Dubuque were "directly responsible for the railroad shops moving out of Dubuque." This terminal has never employed many men. Mr. Renick also blames the Chamber of Commerce and "a handful of employers" for the fight against unions. Some of the older men in the manufacturing plants "will never join the union." Mrs. Renick's father, now 75 years old, began work at the Mississippi Milling Company when he was 16 years old and is still employed there. He sides with the employers and would never consider joining the union. Mr. Renick has belonged to the truck drivers' local since October. At one time the teamsters had a good union in Dubuque, but "the treasurer absconded with the funds" and embittered many workers against organization. The present truck drivers' union is run in a "strictly businesslike fashion," and the treasurer is bonded. Mr. Renick believes that the unbusinesslike nature of many of the early "wildcat" unions in Dubuque has been responsible for some of the prejudice on the part of workers against labor organization. Mr. Renick "would hate to see the CIO come to Dubuque," as he believes it is "too radical." This radicalism is caused, he believes, by "the large proportion of foreigners in the CIO."

Mr. Renick sees little difference in the present business recession and the depression of 1930, except that banks are not closing now. "The capitalists," in Mr. Renick's opinion, "are responsible for the present recession, just as they were responsible for the 1930 depression. Big business tried to run the country but made a mess of it; President Roosevelt tries to straighten out the mess and they are bucking him." Much of the recent legislation has been "fine for the working man, but the industrialists won't stand for some of the laws that cost too much; the depression will continue until the industrialists are pulled into line."

Mr. Renick believes that the Federal Government has done more than its share in respect to unemployment relief and the States should now assume more responsibility. The administration of relief, in his opinion, is particularly difficult because of the tendency of some people to misrepresent their needs. "It is very bad for people to stay on relief too long, as it is apt to make them lazy and dependent. For that matter, though, idleness makes a man develop habits of laziness."

While Mr. Renick was unemployed, he read current magazines at the public library and borrowed books to read at home. Since he has been working, however, he gets home late during the winter and never has time to go to the library; in the summer he spends all of his spare time in the garden. The Renicks are very proud of a cabinet radio, given to them recently by a relative. Mrs. Renick and the children listen to the music and stories, but Mr. Renick enjoys most the discussion of current events. . . . The Renicks seldom go to movies except when Shirley Temple is at the 16¢ neighborhood theater. . . . The Renicks are anxious to send the children through high school, if possible, and believe they can manage it unless Mr. Renick should again become unemployed.

54 • URBAN IRISH IMMIGRANTS: THE COREYS

For an immigrant without industrial skills the Great Depression was long and hard indeed. Eli Ginzberg, et al, The Unemployed (New York: Harper and Brothers, 1943), pp. 203-207. Used by permission of the author.

COREY FAMILY

Status Home Relief   *Religion* Catholic
    Man: born 1904 Ireland to U.S.A. 1927 Citizen No
    Wife: born 1909 Ireland to U.S.A. 1929 Citizen No
Education
    Man: Graduate, Catholic High School—Ireland
    Wife: Elementary school—Ireland.
Medical Status
    Man: Negative.
    Wife: Very thin, looks undernourished.
Woman's Work History Domestic from age of 14 in Ireland. In U.S.A., department store packer, factory worker until marriage.
Married June, 1930, N.Y.C.
Number of Children in the Home Seven   *Ages*—5 months to 8 years.
Basic Occupation Before Relief Billposter.
Average Income before Relief $35 to $40.
Private Employment Terminated March, 1937.
First Accepted for Relief May, 1937.

SUMMARY

Home Relief   From May, 1937, *to date.*

ABSTRACT OF HOME RELIEF RECORD

OCT.,
1933   *First Application:* (Social Service Exchange—No record.) Man is a billposter, employed by an outdoor advertising company since 1928. Since September, 1932, he has had only two or three days work a week at $5 a day and, during the past three months, only a few days all told. Last week he worked only one day, and the week before only six hours. Friends have helped with food. The couple and their two children live in two furnished rooms at $6 a week. They have moved four times in the last year. The children were described as robust and healthy and, according to the investigator, "home very untidy and ill-kept. Furniture old and battered. Evidence of poverty but no suffering."

Case Rejected because part-time earnings exceeded the deficit that would have permitted Home Relief supplementation.

MAY 12,
1937   *Reapplied.* Billposters have been on strike for the past six weeks and the family has had no income during that time. They are destitute. The woman is pregnant. The family saved $60 for confinement expenses but were forced to use it for food. The investigator described the Coreys as pleasant and willing to co-operate. Their rental at this time was $30. The investigator communicated with the advertising company and learned that Mr. Corey had an excellent record. So far as the company is concerned, they did not recognize the strike and stated that in their opinion Mr. Corey had quit his job and their responsibility was at an end. They said that there was no strike, that the places of those who left had been filled by other employees. The man to whom the investigator spoke made no prediction about re-employment.

The family had bought furniture on the installment plan and now the company was threatening to repossess it. Investigator wrote the furniture company, asking them to wait.

MAY 19,   *Case Accepted.*
1937

JULY,
1937   Investigator "explored re-employment possibilities." The local to which Mr. Corey belongs appears to have split with the international union and the international now refuses to do anything about reinstating members of the local.

AUG.,
1937

Josephine born at home. Berwind Clinic physician and Henry Street Settlement visiting nurse in attendance.

SEPT.,
1937

Man going to employment agencies, looking for work. He asked for WPA employment, but this was denied because he is an alien.

OCT.,
1937

Investigator helped the family reach an agreement with the furniture company permitting them to pay $2 or $3 a month out of their Home Relief budget instead of the required $5 a week.

JAN.,
1938

Family received court summons about the furniture. Investigator wrote the company asking for leniency.

FEB.,
1938

Employees of the furniture company arrived with a marshal's notice and removed all the furniture, with the exception of two mattresses. Mr. Corey was told by a representative of the furniture company that he was unjustified in leaving a $40 a week job to go out on strike. Investigator referred the family to the St. Vincent de Paul Society for furniture.

Investigator called St. Vincent de Paul and asked that the family be given furniture.

Investigator called the Department of Public Welfare housing unit about the possibility of a furnished apartment for the family.

Family moved to a ground-floor apartment, five rooms, rental $30.

APRIL,
1938

Budget revised to deduct Unemployment Insurance Benefits at $15 a week, but the man did not receive them and much hardship resulted while this matter was investigated. The Unemployment Insurance Benefits were to have been received automatically, ten days after the "notice of rights," but this did not happen.

MAY,
1938

Full food allowance was granted, but no rent was given until the matter of Unemployment Insurance Benefits could be clarified.

JUNE,
1938

Man reported that he is receiving Unemployment Insurance Benefits, $15 each check. It was decided that since the family had been deprived of their Home Relief income during recent weeks, the first four checks were not to be deducted from the budget, but were to be used for the rent arrears of $60. The man is to make further application for the four additional checks to which he is entitled.

JAN.,
1939

Investigator discovered a new floor lamp in the apartment and questioned the family about it. Investigator knew that such floor lamps were being sold in a "bargain package" by Edison Company. This "bargain package" included a radio, an electric iron, a toaster and a floor lamp, all for $24.50. The family denied this until the investigator confronted them with proof. She had checked with the Edison Company and learned that Mrs. Corey had made the purchase. Finally Mrs. Corey admitted that she had bought this package, but had sold the radio to a friend for $10. She used $2.50 of this $10 to make the necessary deposit and planned to use the rest of it for the monthly payments of $2 each until the amount is exhausted, after which she will take the payments out of her food budget. Investigator also visited the woman who was said to have bought the radio to check on this statement and found it to be true.

APRIL,
1939

Man goes out daily looking for work. He goes to markets, etc., any place which might need someone who is strong and able to do manual labor. He stated that he is willing to do anything. He reports at the New York State Employment Service office regularly.

MAY,
1939

Family took $5 from their food budget to buy a communion outfit for their daughter. Investigator questioned the family closely about the possibility of outside income.

JUNE,
1939

Last Entry: Woman five months pregnant. She hadn't told investigator about it earlier because she "didn't think it was important enough."

The social worker who had abstracted the Home Relief record talked with the investigator and unit supervisor. In the investigator's opinion—he feels he knows the family quite well—the Coreys are a good, simple couple, who worry about their large family but continue to have children because they are deeply religious and feel that they must obey all the dictates of the church. He thinks that there is an excellent marital relationship. He knows that Mr. Corey helps his wife with all the work in the home and that he is more than willing to do anything in the way of a job. He is without skills, other than billposting, and there is little chance of his getting back into this work because the local of which he was a member has been ousted by another local which now has a strong contract with the advertising company. Investigator believes that there will have to be a really widespread upswing in business before an unskilled person such as Mr. Corey could be placed. He knows that there is real need in this family, believes that they are deserving people, and helps them as much as he can with clothing allowances whenever he has them to give. (This investigator is not the one who made an issue of the purchase of the floor lamp—he considered that episode unfortunate and needlessly painful.) The investigator thinks that it would be good for Mr. Corey to be given a WPA job because the man needs works in order to maintain his self-respect. He thinks that Mr. Corey should be helped to achieve citizenship since this would make him eligible for WPA. In his opinion and that of the supervisor, private agencies should help these people become citizens. In this instance they think that the Catholic Charities should assume that responsibility.

55 • URBAN JEWISH IMMIGRANTS: THE BERGERS

It is interesting to note in this case history how firmly the family held to the values acquired when the father was a small business man. The family paid the rent regularly, even when it meant cheapening their diet to the point that welfare personnel thought such a diet impossible and cut off their relief for suspected fraud.

BERGER FAMILY

Status   WPA   Home Relief Supplementation   *Religion*   Jewish
  Man: born 1893   Poland   to U.S.A.   1913   Citizen   1934
  Wife: born 1895   Poland   to U.S.A.   1920   Citizen   1939
Education
  Man: Very little formal education. Attended Hebrew school Poland.
  Wife: No formal education.
Medical Status
  Man: Negative.
  Wife: Negative.
Woman's Work History   Never worked outside of home.
Married   1912, Poland.
Number of Children in the Home   Two   *Ages*—14 and 17 years.
Basic Occupation before Relief   Grocery clerk. Previously small businessman.
Average Income before Relief $20 to $30 weekly.

Private Employment Terminated   October, 1936.
First Accepted for Relief   November, 1936.

SUMMARY

Home Relief   From November 2, 1936, to November 23, 1936. Closed
    to WPA.
WPA   November, 1936, *to date* with the exception of:
    Home Relief for two weeks in August, 1939, following WPA layoff
    because of 18-month ruling.
    Reinstated on *WPA September, 1939.*
    Applied for and received *Home Relief Supplementation of WPA*
    wages, *March, 1940, to date.* Earlier applications rejected.
    Few reclassifications or shifts while on WPA—was a laborer; at pres-
    ent—*watchman, $52.80 a month.*

ABSTRACT OF HOME RELIEF RECORD

OCT.,
1936
First Application: (Social Service Exchange—No record.)
Family is living in four rooms at a rental of $28 and has
lived here since 1934. Their rent is paid to October 31st.
The man was a grocery clerk from 1929 to October, 1936,
when he was laid off because the owner's brother-in-law was
in need of a job. Mr. Berger earned $20 a week and on this
the family managed fairly well. Their rent had been $25 a
month until last year, when it was raised to $28. Mr. and
Mrs. Berger are said to have been panic-stricken at the
thought of public assistance. They are especially concerned
about their rent, which they have always paid in advance.
The man stated that they had always managed adequately,
but had not been able to save any money because of their low
income. Therefore, they had no resources and it was necessary for them to come to Home Relief only two weeks after
Mr. Berger lost his job. The man said that he is "too proud
to stay on Home Relief long."

NOV. 2,
1936
Investigator visited Mr. Berger's former employer, the
grocer, who said that Mr. Berger is a "most honest, diligent,
conscientious worker" and that he was sorry to let him go.
He said that his wife's brother was unemployed and that she
had prevailed upon him to give this brother the job.

NOV. 2,
1936
Case Accepted.

NOV. 17,
1936
Man assigned to WPA as a laborer at $60.50 monthly.

NOV. 23,   *Case Closed to WPA.*
1936

NOV. 9,   *Applied for Home Relief supplementation.* There is an esti-
1937   mated budget deficit of $4.05 semimonthly. Family is still
living in the same apartment; their rental is now $31. It was
raised recently and it is for this reason that Mr. Berger is asking for help. He says that he applied for supplementary
assistance at Borough Hall, when first assigned to WPA,
and was told that a family with only two children was not
eligible for supplementation. The investigator questioned
the family's management to date. Both Mr. and Mrs. Berger
said that they managed somehow by doing without meat,
fruit, etc., by purchasing no new clothing, and by saving in
every possible way. Mrs. Berger cried as she talked about
their difficulties. She explained that she watches every penny;
that her husband takes his lunch with him and that her boy
walks to school because they do not have the carfare to give
him.

NOV. 16,   Investigator visited the grocer to whom the Bergers owe
1937   a debt of $25. The grocer says that he extended credit to
them because they are the type of family who try their best.
He knows that they would not apply for assistance unless
their need was great.

DEC.,   *Case Rejected* "because it does not seem possible for this
1937   family to have managed without some other kind of assistance."

JAN. 4,   *Reapplied for Supplementation:* Mr. Berger says that the last
1938   time he applied for supplementation he was ashamed to say
that he had borrowed money in order to manage. He says
that he borrowed from a friend, $10 or $15 at a time as he
needed it for rent, and then paid it back when he got his
check. He now owes two friends $15 each. He pays a little
on these debts and then borrows again when the need for
rent or utility bills becomes acute. Mrs. Berger showed investigator the contents of the kitchen cupboard. There
seemed to be little more than potatoes. Mr. Berger showed
investigator his old, torn coat. Investigator reports that "during the interview, Mr. and Mrs. Berger were not resentful at
any time. Mr. Berger was resigned to the interview and
slightly disgusted." He did not see the reason for such an
intensive investigation. "Investigator still not able to understand the family's ability to manage on about $5 a week for
food." The woman was told to keep a daily record of food

expenses for the next few days. Man says that he has talked with other men on the job who have families the size of his. They are two or three months in arrears with their rent. He says that he could not stand this; that he has to feel that his rent is paid no matter what else happens.

JAN. 25, 1938   Mr. Berger presented a diet list kept by his wife. The family seems to have been living on a diet which excludes milk, meat, or fish. They use potatoes, evaporated milk, canned fish, etc., as indicated by the list for a week.

FEB. 8, 1938   Man at the District Office. Still no decision by Home Relief. According to investigator, "visitor stated that the list of foods composed by his wife seemed to create some doubt in our minds of the ability of the family to manage over a period of a year on such a diet without there being some apparent decline in health." The decision on the case is left up to the nutritionist. Man states that the family's need is great; that otherwise he would not have applied. He says that the $3 increase in rent brought about the present emergency. He says that they also hope to be able to get some clothing if they are accepted for supplementation.

FEB. 15, 1938   The nutritionist stated that in her opinion "the family could not have lived on this budget for any length of time without seriously impairing their health."

FEB. 15, 1938   *Case Rejected.* "It seems apparent that the family has not explained management freely."

AUG. 16, 1939   *Reapplied for Full Home Relief.* Man was dismissed from WPA, August 10, 1939, because of the 18 month ruling. Questioned again about how the family has been able to manage, they replied they have managed somehow so far. Their rent was increased to $33. They have a roomer who pays $10 a month and Isaac, who was graduated from high school this June, received $3.80 a month from NYA while at school. Mrs. Berger is unable to say how much she needs for living expenses, repeating what she has frequently said in the past, that she managed with what she had on hand. The home is described as crowded, with a boy and girl sleeping in the living room so that the roomer may have a room of his own. Man is anxious for work. Goes to stores and markets but is unable to obtain work. He says that he wants to return to WPA rather than stay on Home Relief.

AUG. 31,   *Case Accepted.*
1939

SEPT. 12,   *Reassigned to WPA* as a laborer at $52.80.
1939

SEPT. 14,   *Case Closed to WPA.*
1939

FEB.,   *Reapplied for Home Relief Supplementation.* When asked
1940   why they had not applied sooner they said Isaac had received
             $15 a month from NYA while at City College, which he en-
             tered last fall, and that he had given it all to his mother to
             use for the household expenses. She gave him carfare and he
             took his lunches from home so that he used little of the $15
             himself. He was dropped from the NYA rolls this semester
             because his average fell below C.
                 The rent was raised two months ago and is now $34. They
             were able to make ends meet until this month with the help
             of the $10 from the roomer and Isaac's $15 income. Their
             rent is paid to date but they still owe $15 to the grocer. He
             has been lenient because they pay something regularly, but
             recently they have failed to keep the bill down and were told
             that the grocer must have something on account before ex-
             tending further credit.

MAR.,   *Case Accepted for Home Relief supplementation.*
1940

MAY,   *Last Entry*—Clothing check for $5 granted.
1940

56 • THE PHYSICALLY HANDICAPPED:
THE DIMARCOS

*This case history of a totally deaf couple has a special qual-
ity since much of it is in the DiMarcos' own words, which they
had to write to communicate with their interviewers. The Dubuque Study, pp. 361-374.*

Mr. DiMarco	37
Mrs. DiMarco	33
Shirley	3

Interviewing completed
January 4, 1938

Mr. and Mrs. DiMarco are both stone-deaf. Bernard DiMarco, having been deaf since he was 2 years old, does not speak at all. Mrs. DiMarco, who had learned to talk before she gradually lost her hearing as the result of an injury when she was 8 years old, speaks a little now, in a harsh toneless voice, but for the most part she depends on talking with her hands.

Since neither of the DiMarcos can read lips, conversation with those who cannot talk with their hands must be written. Mrs. DiMarco is very articulate, she responds quickly and readily, and writes with facility and clarity; her spelling and punctuation are somewhat erratic, but her vocabulary is varied enough, and her phrasings are sometimes picturesque. She is friendly, eager, intelligent, quick to catch the meaning of gestures and facial expressions, which she watches intently. She is slight and pale; one leg is slightly twisted; her chin is pimply, and her eyelids red and raw behind her eyeglasses.

Mr. DiMarco is exceedingly dark, with a mop of black hair and a black stubbled chin. He does not write so fluently as does Mrs. DiMarco, and, being less articulate and less aggressive, prefers to let Mrs. DiMarco, who "knows better" than he what to say, do the talking for the family. He writes answers to questions about his employment only painfully, with many pauses for erasing, scratching his head, and asking Mrs. DiMarco what to say or how to spell certain words. He, too, is slight and not very husky, and he must find his glasses and put them on before he can read or write at all.

Mr. and Mrs. DiMarco have a strong feeling of identification with the deaf; they distinctly feel that they belong to a group set apart, and they do not comprehend general problems except in relation to the deaf. Unemployment to them does not imply a problem faced by millions of the hearing; it is the special problem of the deaf. Their own problems have of course been intensified by their physical handicap, and the DiMarcos do not dissociate any of their difficulties from the deafness which has been always with them. What recreation they have is, naturally enough, shared only with other deaf persons. When they have sought jobs, they have hunted out plants where other deaf persons were already employed, not only because the manager who had hired one deaf person would be most likely to hire another but also because they wanted to associate with other deaf people. When they consider leaving Dubuque to look for work elsewhere, they think in terms of the numbers of deaf persons living in various other towns, once again not simply because there may be more jobs open to the deaf where the deaf have congregated but also because they want to join the already established clubs for the deaf.

The DiMarcos are intensely conscious of prejudice against the deaf.

Neighbors, landladies, employers, relief workers, persons to whom they have gone in the vain search for jobs have often, the DiMarcos feel, been unfriendly and unsympathetic, or at least indifferent, because they "do not care for the deaf."

The DiMarcos are now living in a moderately well-furnished three-room apartment, the second floor of a brick house in a semiresidential district of the downtown area. When the Stevenson plant closed late in 1931, Mr. DiMarco lost the job of disc sanding which he had held for almost 10 years, except for occasional layoffs. During the past 6 years, he has had no regular work; for such odd jobs as he has done he has usually not been paid in cash. Steady work on WPA projects during the past 2 years is as near as he has come to regular employment. Job-seeking is complicated by his deafness, and he sees little chance of finding any regular full-time work, aside from WPA, in Dubuque.

The DiMarcos have a 3-year-old daughter, a blue-eyed, tow-headed youngster, bright and well-trained. They are exceedingly fond of Shirley, but they try not to spoil her. Already, they are planning for her future, and hoping to be able to send her to business school. They are anxious always to learn from those who can hear Shirley's prattle whether she "talks good" and are delighted when her remarks are quoted to them. Mrs. DiMarco tries to talk to Shirley so that she can learn to pronounce words plainly; and she also asks the neighbors to talk to her.

Bernard DiMarco was born in Italy in 1900. He writes spontaneously, near the end of an interview, "I am naturalized. I came to U.S.A. in 1902 been in U.S. for 35 years." His father, according to Mrs. DiMarco, "ran away from the Italian frontier. He didn't like the army and guard life so came here and took out naturalization papers—then after he earned enough sent for Bernard and his mother and sister." On the boat, crossing from Italy, the 2-year-old Bernard contracted spinal meningitis, which presumably caused his deafness. On reaching New York, he and his mother and sister had to remain in quarantine for 3 months before they could join his father, a coal miner in southern Illinois. The family managed well for a time, and Bernard was sent to a school for the deaf in Jacksonville, Ill. But in 1910 the father was killed in a mine accident.

Bernard remained in school, working part-time in the shoe shop, until he was 17, when he left to help support his mother and three younger brothers, two of whom were deaf.

After he left school, and before he came to Dubuque, Mr. DiMarco had a succession of jobs, none of them lasting longer than 1 year, and none very well paid or involving much skill or responsibility. He summarizes his employment history thus: "In Spring Valley, Ill. I worked at the Overall factory for about 1 year, 1918-1919—pick overalls after the girls sewed and tie bundles then carry & sort & bale them & weigh and address them. I quit because the girls often went on strike so I got a job at the Roofing Co at Ottawa, Ill—do the work at the tile yard. They shut down after about 1 year so I came back to Spring Valley where my Home is, worked at the Overall factory for some 6 months. Then they shut down. I got a job at Wright store & do the cleaning & Polishing stoves. After about 6 months they laid me off so I got a job at Ottawa again stayed for 3 months so I quit in 1922 & came to Dubuque. I forgot to tell you—I worked at trunk factory in Spring Valley, Ill., for 8 months nailed the boxes & trimmed & painted them (wardrobes). When Harding was President I was out of work for 1 year."

Mrs. DiMarco states that Bernard came to Dubuque in the hope of getting work with the Stevenson Radio and Phonograph Company. "He heard of a lot of deaf working there and was lonesome alone down home so came to see if he could get on too and he did." In Mr. DiMarco's words, "When I was working at Ottawa, Ill., I read in Chicago paper about it Stevenson's so I wrote to my friend who worked there and asked him if I could work —He wrote and told me to come right away so I quit & came to Dubuque & met him & led me to a house to board. The next morning he took me to Stevensons & told me to see Mr. Smith, who was hiring men & women so I asked him about work. Smith is a good man & hired all deaf men to work. There were about more than 20 deaf men before I came. There were about 85 deaf people in Dubuque while working there. Now there are about 18 people here. Some of them Dead. At first I asked Smith if I could paint or Varnish. He said Filled so he put me in where I disc Sanded."

Mrs. DiMarco is proud of Mr. DiMarco's being "the best Disc Sander they had. . . . They could not get the men to work on it so asked him to work or try it and he got so adept at it they couldn't go without him." Before coming to Stevenson's, Mr. DiMarco had never done any wood work. He preferred this job to any of the earlier ones, and found it much the best paid. When he put in overtime, he sometimes earned as much as $85 within a 2-week-pay period, but "Most of times over $50—2 weeks."

"They often put him on other jobs," Mrs. DiMarco writes, "when he got ahead on his Sanding Job and he knows quite a few jobs in the Radio Cabinet business, rubbing, hand sanding assembling and lots of other jobs." Work at Stevenson's was still quite regular when the DiMarcos were married in 1929.

Shortly before her marriage Mrs. DiMarco had come to Dubuque to work with Bernard at Stevenson's. She has been crippled since she "was 8 years old, that resulted in my deafness. The lameness first started from what we aren't sure but think I stepped on a rusty nail and blood poison set in. Then for about 5 years I was alternately in Hospital & out—I couldn't walk for 2 years—after about the 2 years I was able to get around & go back to school again." Mrs. DiMarco attended public schools before going to a school for the deaf in Chicago, where she remained for 2 years. "I only went through 8th as my parents were poor and had a large family. They couldn't afford it."

The winter after Mrs. DiMarco had left the school for the deaf, she was asked to return to take the place of the kindergarten teacher, who had resigned in midterm. "Mother was ill when school closed and I stayed at home all summer. Then about the time school reopened no doubt I would of gone back but my left limb began bothering me again. . . . I was in the hospital at Freeport, Ill. for 5 mo. Then they brought me home but it was 2 or 3 years before it healed up. . . . I had to go back to Hospital. Some friends took me to Rockford, Ill. to a (I think it was National Fraternity Society of the Deaf) picnic, it was there I met Mr. DiMarco & he kept at me until he finally got me to come to Dubuque. He got me a job at Stevensons & I worked there one summer [the summer of 1929].

"I was with a group of girls who put stain & stripes on the Radio Case legs & shellacked them. I had to stand up a lot (nearly all day) and it was awfully hard on my left leg. I used to get terribly tired. But it paid well. However when you have to pay board & keep etc., you know how it goes. Money has wings. Some days we would be real busy & earn good wages then others not so good. On the average I'd get 30 to 35 every 2 weeks.

"We were married in 1929 just before the crash." The Stevenson plant closed late in 1931. Earlier, Mr. DiMarco had been laid off twice, each time for a period of several months. The first layoff came just after the DiMarco's marriage. "He had always helped his mother, so didn't have much saved up. We had thought we could manage alright as his job paid well and still help his mother some but we lost out. She went on relief like we did when the factory shut down. We were particularly hard hit as we had bought our furniture on installments and had that to bother us. It was worse to see prices come down on furniture & know ours had cost more. We had to pay & pay but we got it settled at last. Just last year it was finished. The WPA was a godsend to us."

A sewing machine was the first of the DiMarcos' purchases after their marriage. As Mrs. DiMarco "loves to sew," she had told Mr. DiMarco that she couldn't get along without a machine. Besides buying furniture, Mr. DiMarco soon after his marriage had taken out an insurance policy which had no cash surrender value in 1931, and so was allowed to lapse. "Also we had started to save in National Bank but it closed in Jan. [1932]. We lost on that, had $5 left not bad but I wished I had that $5 to pay the gas & rent then." "The plant closed first in 1929. We did not get any help for 6 mo. We went to his mothers then to my mothers trying to find another job but nothing doing. Then the plant reopened & sent for him. It worked until December then shut again for several months." During one of these layoff periods, Mrs. DiMarco is not sure which, "he went home and got a better Job Cement factory but when Stevensons reopened they sent for him. He didn't go back so the boss went down after him. I only wish he hadn't maybe he'd have a job now as Stevensons shut down & the Cement factory didn't but they won't take him back now."

"Then [in December, 1931, the Stevenson plant] shut paramently & we had to go to St. Vincent Depaul Society for aid. Nothing improved & they dropped us. We got no aid from the relief office & were put out of that house so in desperation when the relief refused us I went to Mr. Tabor at the Bakery & begged for a job but he phoned [the county poor relief investigator] and forced her to help us. She never seemed to like us and we didn't get only what she had to give us. Then the C.W.A. started & I went to see [the director of the county emergency relief office] & she gave him a slip entitling him to consideration & they put him on C.W.A. That was the first real relief we had—after that things didn't go so bad with us. When it stopped we seemed to get a little more consideration. Then the W.P.A. has been in effect and it's a lot better than relief I must say. I always hated to go and ask for things."

Mrs. DiMarco does not remember just when the first application for relief was made. "It was after we were put out of the first place after Stevensons shut down anyway. The St. Vincent Depaul Society helped us for 3 or 4 mo. before that anyway. I think it began in 1930 that they first started helping us. Mr. Edwards offered us three small rooms of his. He says the relief did not pay him regularly & they claim they did so after 2 or 3 years they had an argument and they came over and told me to move out of his place so I did. We got these rooms then. Mrs. Baker our landlady here has put us out several times & changed her mind. She tells us we must go this spring but she may change her mind, she says she wants well to do people here not ones like us who if we lost our job couldn't pay. Seems we are kicked around like a foot ball. There was a period just before the W.P.A. started we got behind with the rent but we made it up after W.P.A. started. Before that period they paid the Rent regularly for us, then they made a change of every other mo. Of course with no way to earn it we couldn't pay the other month, that's how we fell behind."

In the meantime, while the family was dependent on the weekly grocery order of a little more than $2, supplemented by occasional grants of surplus commodities, the DiMarcos had been sinking deeper and deeper in debt. Mrs. DiMarco "should say we were in Debt about $350 or So. There is probably about $50 yet unpaid. Some of them let Bernard work some off during his unemployment, or we made exchanges and etc. We kept pegging away & got most of it Cancelled somehow."

Exchanges were "mostly by mutual interests. We'd meet them or Bernard (He is restless and can't stay quiet long) would go out prowling around & meet them & they'd ask him to lend a hand they'd take so much off, etc. I don't remember clearly just what all he did do. This seems like a dark cave or something we'd been walking through. I dont know how we managed yet but we cut down on the electric & water bills & everything & kept them at a minimum. He did any & everything he could think of to earn a little."

Both Mr. and Mrs. DiMarco tried to find work, but in Mrs. DiMarco's words "they don't seem interested in a deaf man won't listen to us. I've been in the Candy Factory & Halls trying to get on also and they won't talk just shake their head as if I were a freak. I wish I could make them understand we have to live like others. I don't work out much I can't seem to find anything I can stand as I'm not overly strong but if I could I'd sure take it. I did sewing for people for awhile to earn a little when we had rent & things to pay every month & were on relief with nothing else on. I sometimes help people clean house, if I can find anyone who will take me. The last two or three years I haven't done anything as I had Shirley to keep."

On the CWA airport project, Mr. DiMarco earned $15 a week "digging." When this work ended, he was given employment of "2 or 3 days a week on a sewer job for the city." A former city manager, in Mrs. DiMarco's opinion, "never liked us deaf. He come upon Bernard working once & spoke to Bernard. Bernard told him he was deaf & he wanted him sent home but the men on the job stood up for Bernard & he remained." On WPA projects Mr. DiMarco has been paid $12 a week. This is Mr. DiMarco's story of his employment during the depression: "At Eagle Point Park—just help the men do the work trucking, wheeling crushed Rock & cement for almost more than 2½ years till last Dec. 17—we transferred to Riverside Park—building fires and raking Brushes. Relief work before W.P.A.—in quarry before Relief work." For the relief work he was paid only in grocery orders.

He prefers WPA to relief work and to direct relief, but does not give his reasons for the preference. He has tried to find employment other than on WPA, but "can't get—lots of men idle here. I make a little money by selling cartons, magazines & papers to buy clothes & groceries & pay cash on meat." The Riverside Park project keeps him busy only 3 days in the week. According to Mrs. DiMarco, "He is always out looking for any odd jobs that will turn up on his off days. Watches for a chance to peddle circulars for the stores or get empty cartons for people shipping things. It don't pay much but every little helps out."

"He likes [the WPA work] pretty well only we'd like private work if we could find it & better wages. The Doctor bills sometimes overcome us & we find them hard to pay. Mr. DiMarco has trouble with boils once or twice a year and generally has to go & get medical treatments. Then this summer after he had a spell of them I found myself in the family way and not long after that a miscarriage & I had to go to Hospital & it seemed such a mess. I still owe him some on that & for medicine. Then we feel we should pay our Old Age pension [the Iowa state tax] & don't find it possible to scrape it together also a few bills (grocery) etc. that we had to run up before we got relief & haven't found the way to pay yet, etc."

Perhaps if Mr. DiMarco had had more education, he might be in a better position to find work now, especially "if he had had a chance to learn a special trade." "But it's awfully hard on us deaf—as they don't seem to care for a deaf person when they can get one who can hear. I would like to see him take a course in barbering or something so he could go into business himself. I'd like to learn power machine operating too maybe it would help me in some clothing factory. Not here in Dubuque as Halls don't care for Deaf but maybe in Davenport or some other town."

Mrs. DiMarco is confident of her husband's ability to do a job well, especially in view of his experience at the Stevenson plant. "I'm sure if someone would only be interested enough to try him out they would find him a good steady worker also. We can't seem to find a person who will give him a trial. Some deaf here haven't such good records. I think that injures the reputation of the rest of us. There are all kinds of deaf just like hearing people." . . .

Mr. DiMarco formerly belonged to a club for deaf men, but "they decided to discontinue it as there isn't enough deaf here any more. There are about 15 deaf people here. We get together as much as we can. They are all unemployed also except for 2 or 3. Two are well off and the other has pull with relatives & they give her a job. I don't have any relatives here to help us so it was harder on us than most." . . .

From time to time, the DiMarcos have thought of leaving Dubuque in the hope of finding work in some more friendly town. "There don't seem much else for us to do but leave sometime no future for us here that I can see. Mr. speaks some of going to Dixon Illinois where some of my people live & try the Cement Co or Milk Co or some of those large places. We would become affiliated with Rockford deaf if we did—Around 80 there now. Davenport might be a place also—I have a sister who moved there —we thought of going down sometime & trying. There are 35 or 40 deaf there. Seems odd when we used to have more than them to have them above us now."

The DiMarcos' preoccupation with the problems of the deaf is evident in their responses to questions relating to general problems, just as in any discussion of Mr. DiMarco's employment, chances of getting work now, experiences during the depression, or recreation. In answer to a question as to whether Mr. DiMarco has thought about what may have caused so much unemployment, or what should be done to reduce unemployment, he writes, "I am thinking about moving out & look for better job Illinois. I get jobs easily but hardly in Iowa. In Iowa they begin not to hire any deaf men to work because of Insurance. In Cedar Rapids, Iowa there were about more than 15 deaf men but now about 5 men left. They wont hire any more." As an elaboration of his comment, Mrs. DiMarco writes, "The Deaf find it difficult to get jobs because factories have insurance & refuse to insure the deaf in their employ."

Mrs. DiMarco's own answer to a question as to whether the DiMarcos have thought about what should be done for the unemployed or to minimize unemployment was as follows: "We read what the deaf think. The National Association for the deaf think the deaf are as good risk in insurance as the hearing and I know they should not be prejudiced against us if only we could make them understand that our other senses are sharper because we can't hear and we are mostly all able to hold our own with the hearing in nearly every job we care to tackle. We don't waste time in talking like the hearing or get interested in something else like they do because we have to use our hands if we do & that would injure the work so we keep doggedly on. Any of Bernard's bosses will tell you he can hold his own." She adds, "I am glad to help you in any way we can & the deaf in General if it will interest anyone in them God knows we need it. Do you suppose we ought to stay on here in Dubuque or try to get away. I don't know whether we'd be any better off somewhere else or not. If only I knew where there was a steady job."

The DiMarcos' hopes for the future are centered in Shirley. Mrs. DiMarco is planning to teach her by the same methods used in kindergarten classes in the Chicago school for the deaf. "I want her to go through High School and if possible some kind of *Business school*. I'm afraid we won't be able to but we are already trying to fix it. We make her put all the pennies anyone gives her in a little bank & bank it. I also insured her—25¢ a week. Hard to pay but if anything should happen—" The DiMarcos now carry no insurance except the small policy for Shirley. "They ask too high premiums on a deaf person & he would pay out double the mortuary sum so we decided against it. There are some Societies for the deaf we'd rather join if we felt we could pay them but I'd hate to join up now unless I was certain I could keep them paid up & we would be taking an awful risk with no permanent job and not being sure of ourselves now."

Mrs. DiMarco takes pride in keeping her home looking neat and attractive. On one occasion she wrote, "I don't think I told you the other times you was here that we have an account for clothing and other necessities. I just got my new curtains, my old ones were in shreds. When this is paid I hope we can get some new rugs." The WPA pay checks have been "a godsend."

SPECTRUM  PAPERBACKS

Other SPECTRUM *Books . . . quality paperbacks that meet the highest standards of scholarship and integrity.*